D0992239

AS THEY SAW FORREST

as they saw FORREST

Some recollections an

No. 3 of a Series
Monographs, Sources and Reprints
in Southern History, Bell Irvin Wiley, Editor

Riders With Old Bedford
WILLIAM WITHERSPOON
JOHN MILTON HUBBARD
JAMES DINKINS
JOHN W. MORTON
GILBERT V. RAMBAUT
EMMET HUGHES

From The Opposing Side
A. C. ROACH
WM. F. SCOTT

Bystanders At A Battle
ORLANDO DAVIS
SAMUEL AGNEW

Contemporary Commentator
GENERAL VISCOUNT
WOLSELEY

In His Own Words
NATHAN BEDFORD FORREST

omments of contemporaries

edited by

ROBERT SELPH HENRY

BROADFOOT PUBLISHING COMPANY
Wilmington, North Carolina
1994

"Fine Books Since 1970."
BROADFOOT PUBLISHING COMPANY
1907 Buena Vista Circle
Wilmington, North Carolina 28405

THIS BOOK IS PRINTED ON ACID-FREE PAPER

Library of Congress
Catalogue Card No. 55-9808
ISBN NO. 0-916107-21-3

Original Copyright 1956
McCOWAT MERCER PRESS, INC.
This Edition Printed 1991, 1994
BROADFOOT PUBLISHING COMPANY
Wilmington, North Carolina

FOREWORD

The author of any good book on a historical subject has to work through a vast amount of material. Owing to limitations of space, he is able to weave into his narrative only a small part of the roughage that he accumulates. Hence he goes to press with a sense of incompleteness, and with considerable regret of his inability to share more fully with his readers the fascinating sources that lie back of his book.

Such was the experience of Robert Selph Henry, eminent historian of the Confederacy, who in 1944, after many years of preparation, completed *"First with the Most" Forrest,* a book which soon won recognition as the best biography of the South's "Wizard of the Saddle." The desire to share the overflow of research was especially strong in the instance of the Forrest study because Forrest was the sort of character who inspired an unusual amount of colorful comment. Out of this situation, and a deep interest in Forrest on the part of Seale Johnson of the McCowat-Mercer Press, originated the present volume in the Monographs, Sources and Reprints Series.

The narratives that make up the book vary greatly in character. Viscount Wolseley's articles are the thoughtful comments of a high ranking British officer who was also a profound student of the art of war and a gifted writer. Wolseley never knew Forrest personally, but his discerning appraisal of the man and his methods did much to establish the Confederate cavalryman's reputation as a genius in combat leadership. William Witherspoon's, John Hubbard's, John Morton's, James

Dinkins', and G. V. Rambaut's narratives are accounts of men who served with Forrest, each of which has a flavor all its own. Hubbard's story, written by a school teacher-private who was an astute observer, a scrupulous reporter and a talented stylist, is the best of the four. Indeed, it deserves a high place among personal narratives by common soldiers in any of the American wars. Reproduction of the accounts of Wolseley and Hubbard would be sufficient justification for the book here published.

Excerpts from A. C. Roach's and W. F. Scott's writing afford a glimpse of the experiences and impressions of those who fought against Forrest, while the comments of Orlando Davis and Samuel Agnew show the impact of war as waged by Forrest and his opponents in North Mississippi on Confederate civilians.

One quality that all the narratives have in common is a reflection of a genuine respect for the courage, boldness, aggressiveness and power over men that characterized Forrest and made him one of the great fighting generals of all time.

It seems especially fitting that this composite of writings about Forrest should be compiled by a Tennessean and published by a firm located in the heart of the country over which Forrest and his men fought some of their hardest campaigns.

BELL IRVIN WILEY

CONTENTS

LIST OF ILLUSTRATIONS

INTRODUCTION

Nathan Bedford Forrest, although he never had under his command at one time more than 15,000 men, was in command at one time or another of approximately 100 organizations designated as regiments, separate battalions or batteries.

Such organizations in the Confederate service usually mustered far less than their authorized strength but with the procession through them of recruits, casualties and replacements it is quite likely that, first and last, as many as 50,000 individual Confederates came under Forrest's command.

The succession of organizations with which he was identified began with the company in which he enlisted in June, 1861—a company which became part of the Seventh Tennessee Cavalry, a regiment which was to come under the command of its former member in January, 1864.

Forrest's first command was the battalion which he organized in October, 1861, and which was enlarged to regimental status in March, 1862. With this regiment he fought at Fort Donelson and Shiloh and about Corinth. In June, 1862, he was transferred to a new field and left the regiment, which became officially the Third Tennessee Cavalry but continued to be better known as "Forrest's Old Regiment."

His second body of troops, and his first brigade, was organized in June, 1862. With it he captured Murfreesboro, disrupted Buell's recently restored railroad communications, and marched with Bragg into Kentucky.

There he was once more transferred away from his command and sent to a new field to organize a new brigade. With this force, formed in Middle Tennessee in the autumn of 1862, Forrest made his first great raid into West Tennessee, pursued and captured the Streight raiders, and fought at Chickamauga. A year's service with him stamped the organization indelibly with his name, as Forrest's "Old Brigade."

But Forrest himself was again transferred and, as a Major General, sent into North Mississippi in October, 1863, with an "army" of less than 300 men.[1] In his new field of operations he proceeded to raise still another force, including what was left of the "Old Regiment" and fragments of fifteen other units. The new force was brought to numerical strength by vigorous recruiting in West Tennessee and the Kentucky "Purchase," as well as in Mississippi and Alabama, and was brought to fighting strength and combat effectiveness by the unique training and leadership of its commander.

---

1. The troops which Forrest was permitted to take with him were his staff and escort, 75 men; Morton's Battery, 67 men; and McDonald's Battalion, 139 men. These organizations came closer than any others to the distinction of having served with Forrest throughout the war. The escort company dated from his first brigade command. McDonald's Battalion had been part of the "Old Regiment" which, after Forrest's departure, was separated into two battalions. One, commanded at first by Major R. L. Balch and later by Major Charles McDonald, was variously known by both these names and also as the Eighteenth Tennessee Cavalry Battalion. It saw service under General Van Dorn in Mississippi and came with him to Middle Tennessee. After his death, it came again under Forrest's command and was selected by him to accompany him to Mississippi. The other battalion, led by the preacher-soldier Lieutenant-Colonel D. C. Kelley, remained in West Tennessee and Mississippi and did not again come under Forrest's command until he returned to that area at the close of 1863.

Morton's Battery dated from the first West Tennessee raid of December, 1862, when it was equipped with two Rodmans captured from Colonel Robert G. Ingersoll's Illinois troops at Lexington and two Parrotts taken when, on August 31, 1862, Colonel T. Alonzo Napier's battalion captured the United States armed transport *W. B. Terry* in the Tennessee River. An account of this precursor of a later and more famous bout between Confederate cavalry and Tennessee River boats is to be found in *Official Records,* Series I, Vol. XVII, Part 1, pp. 52, 53.

With this little army, five times reorganized as units were added to or subtracted from it, or were consolidated as they fell below strength, Forrest fought the rest of the war.

With such kaleidoscopic shifts in command and organization it is not astonishing that only a handful of soldiers served throughout the war with Forrest.[2] But significantly, individuals as well as organizations who served with him even for a season tended ever thereafter to identify themselves with Forrest.

The young men who so identified themselves were not given to the keeping of diaries—partly, perhaps, because of the strenuosities of service under Forrest—and until long after the war were not given to the preparation or publication of recollections or memoirs. This tardiness in writing of their experiences may have been due, in part, to the very promptness with which a general account of Forrest and Forrest's Cavalry was prepared by General Thomas Jordan, who had been Beauregard's chief of staff, and J. P. Pryor, a journalist, commissioned to undertake the task. Their work of 704 pages, completed in 1867, was one of the very earliest of war biographies and is a foundation stone of the Forrest literature.

Neither Mr. Pryor nor General Jordan had served with Forrest, however, and it was not until 1879 that one who had done so published a memoir of his service. In August of that year Brigadier General James R. Chalmers addressed the Southern Historical Society, which published the address in Volume VII of its *Papers*. The relation between Chalmers and

---

2.   One who did was John P. Strange, young Memphis merchant who became sergeant major at the organization of Forrest's first battalion and who, as Major Strange, was his Adjutant General at the surrender. Another who served throughout except for a period of captivity in a Federal prison, was Major Gilbert V. Rambaut, Memphis hotel man who was Forrest's commissary chief. Major Rambaut began to write his recollections of service under Forrest in 1896 but died shortly after undertaking the task. Major Strange died a few years after the war without writing what might well have been an outstanding memoir.

Forrest was, in some respects, unique. At Shiloh, Forrest served under Chalmers; after February, 1864, Chalmers served under Forrest. They had had differences but the differences had been adjusted and they had become friends as well as commander and second-in-command. To the distinguished membership of the Society meeting at the White Sulphur Springs the urbane and scholarly Chalmers brought a new concept of the "unlettered soldier," Forrest.

In the same year in which General Chalmers thus contributed to the revision of the then currently accepted concept of his former commander, another distinguished Confederate, Lieutenant-General Richard Taylor, did likewise in his delightful *Destruction and Reconstruction*. He did more, in fact, for in an account of his first meeting with Forrest after he had come under his command in the closing months of the war, General Taylor put down, probably for the first time in print, Forrest's famous prescription for victory, "Well, *I got there first with the most men!*"[3]

In the next decade, soldiers of lesser rank who had fought with Forrest began to publish recollections of the impressions which he had made upon them. Sergeant Frank T. Reid of Morton's Battery wrote of the unforgettable "electric effect of his presence" on the battlefield or on the march.[4] Private J. P. Young of the Seventh Tennessee Cavalry used a different, yet similar, comparison—"his immediate presence seemed to inspire every one with his terrible energy, more like that of a piece of powerful steam machinery than of a human being."[5]

---

3. Taylor, Richard, *Destruction and Reconstruction: Personal Experiences of the Late War* (New York, 1879), p. 200. The steps by which this statement has been distorted into the form in which it is now commonly quoted are outlined in Henry, Robert S., *"First With the Most"* *Forrest* (Indianapolis, 1944), pp. 18-21.
4. In Lindsley, John Berrien, *The Military Annals of Tennessee: Confederate* (Nashville, 1886), p. 851.
5. Young, J. P., *The Seventh Tennessee Cavalry (Confederate)* (Nashville, 1890), p. 77.

Two other characteristics which seem to have impressed themselves upon his soldiers was the General's willingness to turn his hand to whatever work was to be done, and the way in which he *led* men rather than *sent* them. On a certain dark and rainy night, when vacant storehouses at a river landing were being torn down by hand to build boats with which to ferry the Tennessee, Lieutenant Hanson remembered "the General as busy as anybody."[6] And Forrest's favorite command, as recalled by Sergeant R. R. Hancock of Barteau's Second Tennessee Cavalry, was simply "Come on, boys!"[7]

But it was from across the seas, and from a source no less distinguished than Viscount Wolseley, soon to become commander-in-chief of the British Imperial forces, that the first outstanding "outside" recognition of the genius of Forrest came, in an article "General Forrest," published in two installments in the April and May, 1892, issues of the *United Service Magazine* of London.

Viscount Wolseley visited the Army of Northern Virginia during the war but he had no direct contact with the war in the West. His "Forrest," however, is obviously based on information received from those who had served with Forrest as well as on reading and study. Because of the light thrown on how fighting with Forrest seemed to a British soldier of wide experience and broad views, as well as its importance in directing professional military opinion to Forrest's record, the article is reprinted herein.

Since the publication of the Wolseley article there have been numerous memoirs of personal experience and several more formal biographies. From the former class, five have

6. Hanson, G. A., *Minor Incidents of the Late War* (Bartow, Florida), p. 78.
7. Hancock, R. R., *Hancock's Diary, or a History of the Second Tennessee Cavalry, C. S. A.* (Nashville, 1887), p. 323.

been selected for reproduction in part—the *Notes of a Private* by John Milton Hubbard, Company E, Seventh Tennessee Regiment, Forrest's Cavalry Corps, C.S.A.; the *Reminiscences of a Scout, Spy and Soldier of Forrest's Cavalry* by Private, afterward Lieutenant, William Witherspoon of the same regiment; Captain James Dinkins' *Personal Recollections and Experiences in the Confederate Army;* Major G. V. Rambaut's account of Forrest at Shiloh; and "A Brief Sketch of the Character of Gen. Nathan Bedford Forrest" from *The Artillery of Nathan Bedford Forrest's Cavalry* by Captain John W. Morton, who was Forrest's Chief of Artillery.

As is true of almost all extant material from those who fought with Forrest, these notes and reminiscences were written long after the events of which they tell. The selection is subject to the further infirmity that it includes nothing of the period between June, 1862 and November, 1863, when the General and those who fought with him performed some of their most famous exploits. But this volume is not another life of Forrest. It is rather an effort to gather together in their original form some of the reminiscences through which can be glimpsed something of the overwhelming impact of Forrest upon the men who followed him in their youth.

While these notes lack the high value of contemporaneity, they are not mere afterthoughts written in the reflected light of Forrest's growing fame, for even while the war lasted the soldiers who followed Forrest recognized his qualities. "When I enlisted in his old regiment," wrote Dr. John Allen Wyeth— speaking of a time after the Fourth Alabama Cavalry had passed from Forrest's command—"the men who had served with him never ceased to sing his praise . . ."[8] So it was that

8. Wyeth, John Allan, *With Sabre and Scalpel: The Autobiography of a Soldier and Surgeon* (New York, 1914), p. 393, giving an account of

the interest which these soldiers of Forrest's aroused in young Wyeth, who himself never served with the General, led him to undertake thirty years later the monumental researches which have made his *Life of General Nathan Bedford Forrest* a towering landmark in the literature of the subject.

—ROBERT S. HENRY

---

why and how Dr. Wyeth undertook his famous Life of Forrest, begun in 1895 and published in 1899.

The Life is dedicated to Miss Emma Sanson, the sixteen year old girl who guided Forrest to the hidden ford over Black Creek and so helped in the capture of the Streight raiders. In the spelling of her name, Dr. Wyeth followed the spelling used by General Forrest and by Jordan and Pryor, and since used by four other biographers of Forrest—Mathes, Sheppard, Lytle and Henry. That the spelling is incorrect and should have been "Sansom" is definitely established by the researches of Mr. Monroe Cockrell of Evanston, Illinois, who has checked the spelling in land grants, deeds, legislative enactments and on monuments, and has corresponded with surviving members of the family in Texas, including Mr. Mert M. Johnson of Dallas, son of the heroine. The information collected by Mr. Cockrell has been deposited with the University of Alabama.

Micajah Sansom, father of Emma, removed from Social Circle, Georgia, to Cherokee (now Etowah) County, Alabama, in 1852. There he acquired a total of 280 acres of land, now the site of Alabama City, part of the city of Gadsden. He died in 1859 and was buried in the family plot.

Emma Sansom was born at Social Circle, August 16, 1847. In 1864 she married C. B. Johnson, a private in Company L, Tenth Alabama Infantry. In 1876 they moved to Callaway (now Little Mound), Upshur County, Texas. There the Johnsons reared a family of seven children. (Their first-born, Mattie Forrest Johnson, died in childhood in Alabama and was buried there, in the family plot.) Mr. Johnson died in 1884. His wife survived him by sixteen years and died August 9, 1900. She is buried in the Little Mound Cemetery, back of the Baptist Church of which she was a member, beneath a family monument which also bears this inscription: "E.S.J. Girl heroine who piloted Gen. Forrest across Black Creek and enabled him to capture Col. Strait."

In Acknowledgment

Our sincere thanks to all who have so graciously contributed in the forming of this book:

Mr. Ralph Newman, Chicago; Mrs. E. R. Eikner, Memphis; Col. John M. Virden, Army Times Publishing Co., Washington, D. C.; Col. William H. Zierdt, Jr., Editor, *Armor,* Washington, D. C.; Mrs. Mary Forrest Bradley, Memphis; Mr. Andrew Brown, Arlington, Va.; Mr. Roy Black, Bolivar, Tenn.; Mr. Palmer Bradley, Houston, Texas; Mr. Curtis Bray, Jackson, Tenn.; Mr. Leroy Pope, Jackson, Tenn.; Mr. Walter Chandler, Memphis, Tenn.; Dr. Marshall Wingfield, Memphis; Mr. Ray H. Greene, Editor, *The Gilmer Mirror,* Gilmer, Texas; Editor, *Gadsden Times,* Gadsden, Ala.; Confederate Museum, Richmond, Va.; Memphis Museum, Memphis, Tenn.; University of the South, Sewanee, Tenn.; Mrs. A. L. Puryear, Como, Miss.; Mr. John P. Morrow, Jr., Batesville, Ark.; Mrs. John P. Morrow, Sr., Batesville, Ark.; Mr. Monroe F. Cockrell, Evanston, Ill.; Mr. John Rebel Peacock, High Point, N. C.; Mr. Lee Meriwether, St. Louis, Mo.; Mr. L. H. Parks, Newbern, Tenn.; Col. Campbell H. Brown, Nashville; Mr. Enoch Mitchell, Memphis State College, Memphis; Dr. Dan Robison, State Librarian, Nashville; Mr. Robert Quarles, Archivist, Tennessee Historical Collection, Nashville, Tenn.; Harper & Bros., New York City.

RIDERS WITH OLD BEDFORD

COURT-HOUSE SQUARE JACKSON TENN.

A RAIL-ROAD BATTERY

EARTHWORK TO PROTECT THE R.R.

COTTON FORT AT JACKSON TENN.

THE WAR IN THE SOUTHWEST.—Sketched by Mr. A. Simplot.—[See Page 647.]

The Madison County Court House where William Witherspoon was confined as a prisoner charged with being a Confederate spy.

BRIGADIER-GENERAL W. H. JACKSON

Commanding Division of Forrest's Cavalry

COLONEL E. W. RUCKER

Commanding a Brigade of Forrest's Cavalry

BRIGADIER-GENERAL TYREE H. BELL

Commanding "Bell's Brigade" of Forrest's Cavalry

From Dr. Wyeth's Life of General Nathan Bedford Forrest—1899. *Courtesy Harper & Brothers*

Pictured from left to right in their Confederate uniforms are William Witherspoon of Forrest's Cavalry, and his comrade in arms, Milt Hurt. Both of these old soldiers enlisted in Madison County, Tennessee.

Through the kindness of William Witherspoon's daughter, Mrs. E. R. Eikner of Memphis, it is possible to reproduce this photograph, made about 1910 which testifies to another of Mr. Witherspoon's absorbing interests—the game of chess.

DR. J. B. COWAN
Chief Surgeon, Forrest's Cavalry

MAJOR CHARLES W. ANDERSON
Assistant Adjutant and Inspector General, Forrest's Cavalry

MAJOR G. V. RAMBAUT
Chief of Subsistence, Forrest's Cavalry

Wyeth, Courtesy Harper & Brothers

EMMA SANSOM

(From a photograph taken at the age of nineteen, three years after the Black Creek incident)

CAPTAIN JOHN W. MORTON

Chief of Artillery, Forrest's Cavalry

BRIG.-GEN. A. BUFORD

Commanding a Division of Forrest's Cavalry

In Gadsden, Alabama, at the approach of the bridge over the Coosa River, a marble monument bearing Emma Sansom's effigy was erected in 1907 by the Gadsden Chapter of the United Daughters of the Confederacy to commemorate her service to the country.

Courtesy Gadsden Chamber of Commerce

Emma Sansom Johnson's last resting place in Little Mound Cemetery, near Gilmer, Texas.

Emma Sansom's home which was near
Gadsden.

urtesy Ray H. Greene, Editor, The Gilmer Mirror

THE LITTLE CONFEDERATE, CAPT. JAMES DINKINS

"Forrest seemed to know by instinct what was necessary to do. He was pleasant and companionable when he was not disturbed, but no occasion ever arose which he was not master of. He fought to kill but he treated his prisoners with all of the consideration in his power. So he did his own men. But he wanted the latter for service, and not merely to count."

From Captain James Dinkins, Personal Recollections and Experiences in the Confederate Army, 1861 to 1865

CAPTAIN WILLIAM M. FORREST

Aide-de-camp

Wyeth, Courtesy
Harper & Brothers

Capt. Forrest rides into the Gayoso, in search of Gen. Hurlbut.

From A Dual Role, *William Isaac Yopp, Courtesy H. Leroy Pope*

BRIGADIER-GENERAL JAMES R. CHALMERS

COLONEL JAMES W. STARNES
Fourth Tennessee Cavalry—Commanding Brigade

BRIGADIER-GENERAL FRANK C. ARMSTRONG

Wyeth, Courtesy
Harper & Brothers

GENERAL FORREST—A CONFEDERATE.

CAMP SONG—WRITTEN BY GEN. J. R. CHALMERS, 1864

AIR—"*Columbia, the Home of the Brave.*"

The day of our destiny was darkened,
The heart of the Nation stood still,
When Forts Henry and Donelson surrendered.
And Johnston fell back to Nashville.
But the clouds, which then thickened around us,
Served only the plainer to show
The form of that hero arising
To deliver us all from the foe.

CHORUS

Here's to Forrest from the brave Tennessee.
Here's to Forrest from the brave Tennessee.
In our hearts he will triumph forever,
Here's to Forrest from the brave Tennessee.

At Shiloh he charged a division
And covered our army's retreat;
At Murfreesboro won his promotion
When Crittenden acknowledged defeat.
Next Streight went careering before him,
Expecting our rear to assail,
But Forrest, with his fair maiden pilot,
Soon landed the robber in jail.

CHORUS

Chickamauga, Chattanooga, Okolona,
Memphis and Tishomingo Creek,
Union City, Fort Pillow and Paducah,
All, the deeds of our hero bespeak.
Now Athens, Sulphur Springs and Pulaski
Have aroused old Sherman from his lair,
For the boldest of Yankee commanders
Will tremble with Forrest in his rear.

CHORUS—

Next Johnsonville attracted his attention
Where Sherman had collected his stores,
And the gunboats, once terrible to mention,
Floated grandly and proudly at its doors.
But Forrest's artillery battalion,
Morton, Rice, Ed Walton and Thrall,
Soon set fire to his gunboats and transports,
Nor ceased till they had burned them all.

CHORUS

Courtesy
Confederate Muse
Richmond, Va.

COLONEL ROBERT McCULLOCH

Second Missouri Cavalry, Commanding Brigade

MAJOR J. P. STRANGE

Assistant Adjutant-General

BRIG.-GEN. H. B. LYON

Commanding the "Kentucky Brigade" of
Forrest's Cavalry

COLONEL D. C. KELLEY

[Forrest's Old Regiment]

Commanding Brigade, Forrest's Cavalry

AT BRICE'S CROSS ROADS—A painting executed by Frederick Ruple, a native of Switzerland, at the request of Col. V. Y. Cook, Co. H, 7th Kentucky Mounted Infantry.

BRICE'S CROSS ROADS TODAY

Brice's Cross Roads national monument. Notice that somebody didn't know that Forrest had been a Major General for seven months when the battle was fought!

Bridge over Tishomingo Creek in sec. 36, T. 6 S., R. 5 E., looking southeast. Brice's Cross Roads is about ½ mile southeast on top of the hill. The road is essentially where it was in 1864 but the embankment and bridge are of course much later.

Site of the Stubbs Farm "big house" in sec. 36, T. 5 S., R. 4 E., Tippah County, Miss. The house was in or behind the clump of trees. Picture taken from Tippah-Union County line, looking north toward Ripley. The road here follows the ridge between the Tallahatchie River (through Wilhite Creek) drainage to the southwest, and the Hatchie drainage to the north and northwest. T. B. Stubbs owned about 2,000 acres in the present Tippah County and some in the present Union County and the location of the house could be obtained only by putting statements of old citizens together. A company of the 23rd Mississippi was named the "T. B. Stubbs Rifles" for him. He died in 1863 (before the battle) as evidenced by his tombstone in the cemetery just out of the picture to the east (right).

Courtesy Andrew Brown, Arlington, Va.

A CONTEMPORARY ESTIMATE FROM THE OTHER SIDE
GENERAL N. B. FORREST

We give above a portrait of Major-General N. B. Forrest, the great cavalry leader of the Confederates in the West. He has been connected with the war from the first, and the most daring of the Confederate raids have been accomplished by his command. He had a brigade of cavalry at Fort Donelson, and to prevent being captured with the garrison, he cut his way out with a portion of his command. In our advance southward, he has been a most formidable enemy, falling upon our communications, capturing our supply trains, or swooping down upon some feebly-defended town as he did upon Memphis last summer. It was General Forrest, without doubt, that saved General Hood's army from utter destruction, by covering his retreat across the Tennessee. —HARPER'S WEEKLY, February 18, 1865

—*Courtesy Roy Black, Bolivar, Tenn.*

CHAPTER ONE

General Viscount Wolseley on Forrest

Few men of the Nineteenth Century had a wider exper-
ience of war or a better opportunity to know soldiers than
Garnet Wolseley, who started his military career in 1852 as a
Lieutenant and ended it in 1901 as Field Marshal, Viscount
Wolseley, commander-in-chief of Her Majesty's forces. In the
half century of his active military life he participated in
campaigns in Burma, the Crimea, India, China, the Gold Coast,
Natal, the Transvaal, Egypt and the Sudan.

During a good part of the 1860's he was stationed in
Canada. While there he made use of a leave of sixty days in
the autumn of 1862 to make his way through Baltimore and
the "underground" into the Confederate States, where he visited
the army in its camps about Winchester. Colonel Wolseley, as
he was then, wrote in some detail of his observations, both in
Blackwood's of Edinburgh of January, 1863—his first published
military writing—and in his autobiography The Story of a
Soldier's Life, *published at Westminster in 1903, two years*
after his retirement.

At that time, in the twilight of a long life in which he had
seen the great of the world, he wrote that the Army of North-
ern Virginia "interested me beyond any army I ever saw before

or since," and that General Lee "was the ablest general, and
to me seemed the greatest man, I ever conversed with." And,
he wrote, "there is as much instruction, both in strategy and
tactics, to be gleaned from General Lee's but little studied
operations of 1862 as there is to be found in Napoleon's campaign of 1796, which we all read so attentively and recommend
others to master thoroughly, and to inwardly digest."[1]

While in Virginia, Wolseley talked not only with Lee but
also with Jackson, Longstreet and the other professional soldiers who led the Army of Northern Virginia. He noted the
fact that "almost all the best known generals" on both sides
had been educated at the West Point Military Academy, an
institution which he described in his autobiography as "the
best of such schools to be found in any country." He had no
direct contact with the Western forces but from what he heard
afterward, as well as from his study, he came to be among the
earliest of professional soldiers, other than those who had
direct contact with or against him, to recognize the untaught
genius of Forrest.

The first installment of Wolseley's estimate of Forrest
appeared in the April, 1892, issue of the United Service Magazine of London; the second, in the May issue. The closing
paragraphs of the first installment and a major portion of the
second, or May, installment appeared in the New Orleans
Picayune of April 10, 1892.

The Picayune established a reputation for journalistic
enterprise when George W. Kendall's dispatches made it first
with the news from the Mexican War but how it managed to
publish in New Orleans in April extensive extracts from an
article which did not appear in London until May is a minor
mystery of publishing.

---

1. Wolseley, Field-Marshal, Viscount, *The Story of a Soldier's Life*
(Westminster, 1903), 2 vols., pp. 122, 140, 144.

One possible and partial explanation may be found in the circumstance that the third annual reunion of the United Confederate Veterans was in progress in New Orleans at the time of publication. Several references in the Wolseley paper indicate that the author was in correspondence with, or perhaps had conversed with, Confederate leaders, including "an officer who knew Forrest well" and a "distinguished General who is my informant." Could it have been that a proof or an advance manuscript copy of the article was sent to this unnamed informant who carried it to the reunion and while there furnished it to the Picayune?[2]

Partial publication of the Wolseley study in the Picayune, *from which it was reprinted in Volume XX of the* Southern Historical Society Papers, *and extensive quotation from it in Dr. Wyeth's life of Forrest may account for the recurrence of erroneous rumors and reports to the effect that various prominent European soldiers have visited the field of Forrest's operations to study them intensively on the ground.*[3]

---

2. Among Forrest's former officers who were noted in the New Orleans press as being at the 1892 reunion were Generals William H. Jackson of Tennessee and L. S. Ross of Texas, and Captain John W. Morton. Also noted as being there were two of Forrest's former commanders, Generals Joseph Wheeler and Stephen D. Lee, and another war-time associate, General Basil Duke.

3. One such report, published in advertisements in national magazines in the spring of 1948, was that "Hitler sent Rommel to Tennessee in the 'thirties to find the secret of Forrest's success." Mr. Monroe Cockrell of Evanston, Illinois, curious about this report and also about the more widely circulated reports that Marshal Rommel had visited Virginia to study Jackson's operations or had studied the Gettysburg Campaign on the ground, patiently ran down the available evidence on such reports and established that none of them is correct and that, in fact, Marshal Rommel was never in the United States.

In the course of his investigation, he was told that the German officer who studied Forrest's campaigns on the ground was General Adolph von Schell who, as a Captain, attended the United States Infantry School at Fort Benning, Georgia, in 1930-1931. Correspondence with General von Schell developed, however, that he had never been in Tennessee and had made no such study as was reported.

Mr. Cockrell has deposited the original papers of his investigations of these reports with the Library of Congress.

The Wolseley article is here reproduced in full as it appeared in London, including such minor misprints as the spelling of "Stewart" for Stuart, "Kelly" for Lt. Col. D. C. Kelley, "Atalanta" for Atlanta, and "Murfreasboro" for Murfreesboro, and also the reference in connection with the Streight raid to the "great arsenal and workshops of Selina," for Selma, Alabama, obviously confused with Rome, Georgia.

1

It is a remarkable fact that, in the Secession War of 1861-65, almost all the best known Generals of both contending armies had been educated at the West Point Military Academy. Those who desire to emphasise the necessity of close military study for all ambitious soldiers, often point to this fact in support of their contention. During the progress of that prolonged war a few civilians however, were given high military rank. Some obtained it through personal influence, but still more through party interest, and a few by the gallantry and natural military ability they had displayed in battle. But none of these political generals are known to fame; and though one lawyer-general from the North became for the time notorious, the names of very few amongst them will be remembered in history. Of that few, one of the most remarkable was General Forrest, a great organiser and leader of what used to be known in Europe as Dragoons, but now called Mounted Rifles or Mounted Infantry, though still spoken of and written about as Cavalry in the United States of America. When any English writer refers to General Sheridan's men as "Mounted Infantry," a host of gallant American Cavalry officers spring up to defend the title by which his command was, and still is, universally known in America. They seem to regard the designation of "Mounted Infantry" as derogatory, and as doing some injustice to the gallant soldiers who followed that able Infantry soldier, General Sheridan.

In all epochs, the Horse have very naturally thought themselves superior to the Foot. A name has often much to do with the fighting value of soldiers; and if a man is proud of the official designation given to his arm of the service, no one but an idiot who had to get hard work out of that arm, would use any other, no matter how technically wrong such a title might be. You cannot make the Cavalry soldier or the mounted soldier, whatever may be his functions in war, think too highly of himself. His training teaches him that he belongs, as it were, to the aristocracy of the army, and that his work, always in the front, is the most important, and places him in a position far above that of, what the Indian sowar terms, the "Peidal Wallah." This feeling was given full vent to in a cavalry song of the period when Forrest, Fitzhugh Lee, Morgan, Sheridan, Stewart, and other leaders of mounted troops were justly the popular heroes of the day. I can only remember the refrain, which ran thus—

"If you want to smell hell, just jine the Cavalry—
jine the Cavalry!"

In deference to this prejudice on the part of many gallant American soldiers, for whose deeds and valour I entertain the greatest admiration, I shall, in the course of the following article, usually refer to their mounted troops as Cavalry. But it is essential that others should understand it was in reality what we now term Mounted Infantry, and what was in the seventeenth century, and early in the eighteenth, known as Dragoons. In those far-off days, all regular armies were officially divided into and officially described as consisting of Horse, Foot, and Dragoons. The latter were armed as Infantry, with long muskets and bayonets, the former carried in a sort of Namaqua bucket like that now used by our Mounted Infantry.

Dr. Johnson did somewhat to discredit the Dragoon by describing him, as "a kind of soldier that serves indifferently, either on foot or horseback," and by degrees, he has, it may be said, either improved or degenerated—the reader must select his own verb—into the pure Cavalry soldier.

With our Mounted Infantry of to-day, one of the dangers to be still guarded against, as was of yore the case with Dragoons, is the very natural desire of the rifleman on horseback to puff himself out into the more showy and more highly-esteemed cavalry soldier. "In the beginning Dragoons were only Mounted Infantry," says Marshal Marmont; who adds, "They should have always preserved that character."

I have no wish to enter here upon any discussion of the species or the amount of cavalry training given to the mounted troops on both sides during the War of Secession. I content myself with saying that in all the great armies of Europe it is a generally accepted axiom that two years are required to convert the ordinary civilian into a cavalry soldier. According to our notions of what a cavalry soldier should be and of what he should know, it would have been therefore impossible, in the time at the disposal of the leaders on both sides, to have converted their recruits into regular cavalry soldiers.

A general officer, who "rode with Forrest" for the last year and a half of the war, gives us the following information upon this point. Referring to his leader's career, he writes: many of his victories "were achieved with men who had never been drilled one hour together."

These Southern troopers, accustomed to ride from childhood, were doubtless good horsemen; but nevertheless it is surely a misapplication of terms to describe them as "Cavalry."

May I also venture to remind those who write upon this war, that the great leader of mounted troops in the Northern Army was General Sheridan, who had never served in the cavalry at all?

But even supposing there had been time and opportunity to convert the mounted soldiers on both sides into Regular Cavalry, it cannot be too often repeated, that the nature of the theatre of war, precluded the employment of men fighting on horseback like Regular Cavalry. The country was as impossible for the use of large bodies of Regular Cavalry as are the counties of Kent and Essex, in both of which a travelling menagerie would be of about as much use in war as a Cavalry Division, whose troopers were restricted to the purely cavalry duty of fighting on horseback. With the exception of a very small district of prairie country, cavalry in masses could not have manœuvred even at a trot, over the country where any of the great belligerent armies operated. It was compelled to move by the roads. It must of necessity have fought dismounted, though here and there a squadron might charge down a road in "fours," or over some small clearance not yet fenced in, as, in fact, often occurred. A few squadrons might have done good work in patrol or reconnaissance work along the roads, but I very much doubt if it would have been as well done by any Regular Cavalry in the world as it was done in both armies by the carefully selected men who composed the "scouts" attached to the headquarters of each Army Corps, and in some cases of each Division. Be that as it may, however, the military student must not forget that the contending armies in this war moved along roads over a country where the shock of Regular Cavalry was, and still is, a physical impossibility, and where the employment of any large body of Regular Cavalry, as cavalry, was out of the question. But it was a theatre of war where the

Dragoon or Mounted Rifleman, such as those who served under the great leaders I have already named, could be most usefully employed, and they were the first generals who in modern days have taught us what Turenne and Montecuculli knew so well, namely, the use of the true Dragoon, the rifleman on horseback, but who from being mounted, has all the mobility of the horse soldier. To the foreigner who knows no other sort of country than those hedgeless, fenceless, open plains which have been the cockpit of European cavalry from time immemorial, Regular Cavalry has a different importance from what it has for the General who has to plan campaigns, or to fight in the non-prairie States of America, or in close confined countries like Italy or the United Kingdom. India and South Africa are, on the other hand, essentially cavalry regions, where the proportion of Horse to Foot is only to be regulated by the question of forage.

The Generals in the Secession War have taught us that although a country may be entirely unsuited for purely cavalry operations, and where the shock of charging masses of horsemen is a physical impossibility, still, mounted troops are more valuable than ever; but they must be men taught as the mounted troops of both North and South were—that their great mission is to fight on foot. In a letter written a few years after the end of this war, the Cavalry General, S. D. Lee, says: . . . . "Nearly all the cavalry used by the Confederate States, and in fact by both sides, was nothing more than mounted riflemen. The sabre was done away with by the Confederate States cavalry pretty well, and rarely used in action by either party." And again: "In every instance under my observation the revolvers replaced the sabre, etc., etc."* One of the most distinguished cavalry leaders in that war, Major-General T. L. Rosser, in a letter of

---

*Colonel Denison's "Modern Cavalry," pages 363, 364, and 366.

about the same date, writes: "Neither the Yankees nor Confederates employed cavalry in the late war, it was all *mounted rifles*."† Another Southern General who served under Forrest says of his troops, they "were not properly called cavalry, they more nearly resembled the Dragoons of the sixteenth century, who are described as 'mounted foot soldiers.' Jackson's corps were called 'web-footed cavalry,' and Forrest's troopers might well be called 'winged infantry.'" General Maury writes:— "I do not remember to have known a surgeon who of late years has had to treat sabre or bayonet wounds."

After these expressions of opinion from well-known American cavalry leaders I hope I may be forgiven if I say that in neither of the contending armies was there ever a Brigade or Division that would have been regarded as Regular Cavalry in Europe. The cavalry made use of by both belligerents did splendid service, and had a *role* of its own, but that was not the *role* of Regular Cavalry.

A general officer, who was Forrest's second in command, when speaking of his peculiar mode of fighting, said: "His quick dismounting of his men to fight, showing that he regarded horses mainly as a rapid means of transportation for his troops." If we wish to know what large bodies of mounted riflemen can do, we must study the operations of Forrest and of Stewart, and learn it from what Sheridan accomplished with the splendid force under his command in Virginia. Those leaders were the masters of an old but long disused fighting art, and it is from their operations we must learn it now.

This is not the place to discuss the advisability or the possibility of making our splendid Cavalry learn to be as efficient as Foot soldiers as they are now as Cavalry. I for one don't believe in the military jack-of-all-arms, and I feel the result

---

†*Ibid.*

would be a failure; the man would have the efficiency of neither arm. We persuade our Foot soldiers that they are more than a match for the finest man on the finest horse, and we teach our Cavalry that if they will but ride home, no Infantry can stand against them. But what is to be the faith we are to instil into this hybrid soldier? He will have no confidence in himself on foot or on horseback, and the soldier without an implicit faith in his own arm is a poor creature. I strongly recommend those who wish to pursue this subject to read "Modern Cavalry," by my old and esteemed comrade, Colonel G. Denison.

I have thought it necessary to say this as a sort of preface to my brief memoir of a General who must always be regarded as one of the most distinguished leaders of American cavalry in their Secession War.

General Forrest was born in 1821 of very humble parents. He was therefore just forty when he first donned the soldier's garb as a private in "The Tennessee Mounted Rifles." In the wild borderland of civilisation, where he was reared, he had, however, been accustomed to the use of arms from earliest boyhood. There life was held cheap, and even the peace-loving citizen went about his ordinary avocations duly armed with pistol and bowie-knife. Many were the wounds Forrest received, and many his hairbreadth escapes in the personal encounters he engaged in as a young man. "Lynch-law" was often resorted to by the community in which he lived, and in the rude and reckless society of his early surroundings, the first lesson he learnt was, that self-preservation and personal defense of one's own property with steel and bullet, was the first great and most important law of nature.

His father died when the future General was a boy of only sixteen. The eldest son of eleven children, upon him then devolved the care and maintenance of his mother and his many brothers and sisters. They lived on a little rented farm, lately cleared from the wilderness, and it was only by the hardest manual labour he was at first able to provide with food, those who were dependent upon him. The locality was unhealthy, and fever carried off several of the family, and very nearly killed him also. But his naturally robust constitution enabled him to pull through, though it was many months before he fully regained his wonted strength.

His education was most meagre, and what he learnt as a boy, was picked up at odd times from casual schoolmasters. He could just read and write, and do some very simple sums in arithmetic. Indeed, it may be assumed that during all his career as a General, his orders and despatches were written for him by the educated men he collected round him as staff officers. They put into good clear English the views or orders he dictated, but he was, however, very exacting that his letters and his addresses to the men, and all other papers he signed, should contain his own ideas, and not those of the staff officer who happened to be his amanuensis. But though his book learning was extremely scanty, he was brought up in what Napoleon termed, the best of military schools—that of poverty. His early years were little more than a continued struggle for daily existence in the lawless home of his childhood. There he learnt the invaluable qualities of endurance, self-reliance, quickness of decision, and dauntless courage, which are so necessary for the Western pioneer. But if these qualities are essential to the man who has to wrest the backwoods from Indian savagery, they are still more so for him who aspires to lead a mounted force, such as his was during this war. Fond of riding and all sorts of hunting from childhood, he was a finished and a daring horseman when he reached the age of manhood.

I shall pass over this interesting period of his life, where hard work and years of incessant toil were only now and then relieved by an occasional day's sport with his gun, or in riding matches against his neighbour's horses. If fortune endowed him poorly with gold, she gave him what was far more valuable —a business-like and thrifty turn of mind, unflagging application, and a determination to win. He paid that same close attention to the details and minutiæ of all his commercial arrangements and speculations, which enabled him subsequently to clothe, arm, and subsist his troops in the field, without help from the Confederate Government. The result was, that by the time he had reached twenty-one, he had placed his immediate belongings beyond all fear of want.

Many stories are told of his prowess with rifle, revolver, and bowie-knife when quite a youth. A bullying neighbour had a bullock which frequently broke through Forrest's fences to feed upon his growing corn. The owner's attention was repeatedly called to this, but without effect, for he thought he could easily browbeat his hobbledehoy complainant. Roused at last by the bullock's depredations, Forrest warned him he would shoot the animal the next time he found him on his farm. This threat he carried out. Whilst Forrest was reloading, his bullying neighbour appeared upon the scene, fully armed in Western fashion, and at once proceeded to climb over the fence which separated them. Forrest took in the position in a moment; one or other must die or run for it; he would not be that one. Now or never, thought he; so taking steady aim, he sent a ball through the bully's clothes. This shave for his life staggered the would-be assailant, and he fell from the fence to run back home as fast as he could. He never again attempted any trick upon his cool young neighbour, whose reputation for courage and determination to hold his own against all hectoring bluster was thenceforward generally recognised. Without such a reputation, life then on the Arkansas frontier would have been intolerable.

Successful as a farmer, he afterwards took to horse-dealing. An excellent judge of that noble animal, he was very fortunate at this business. By thrifty management of his gains, he was soon able to embark in the still more remunerative but most detestable occupation of slave-dealing. Even amongst the planters who used the services of those who bought and sold their fellow man, those engaged in this nefarious traffic were held in very general contempt. By all who then knew Forrest, however, he was regarded as a humane man, who never in his slave-dealings separated the members of the families which he bought and sold. At this disgusting and degrading business he realised a considerable fortune, and soon became himself a planter on a large scale.

His many adventures with pistol and bowie-knife on shore, and of boiler explosions on the Mississippi River, would alone form an interesting magazine article. But I must hurry on to his military career, which began at the opening of the Secession War in the summer of 1861.

He was then already a man of mark and influence in his own district, and, like nearly every Southerner, held very strong opinions as to the right of each State to regulate its own destiny. In June, 1861, he joined the "Tennessee Mounted Rifles," the cavalry company then being raised in Memphis. He was in the prime of life and vigour, erect in figure, and over six feet in height, with broad chest and shoulders; he required good horses to carry him, for he already weighed over thirteen stone. Like many of the American officers of that time he allowed his dark straight hair to grow long, and wore it combed back from his forehead; but whilst he shaved his cheeks, no razor ever touched his lips or chin. Several prominent Confederate officers affected the style and bearing of their Cavalier forefathers, and seemed especially to despise the Roundhead "crop" of the Regular Army. Their broad-brimmed wide-awake hats, often adorned with a long, graceful ostrich feather, lent additional colouring to the resemblance.

Early in July the Governor of Tennessee sent for Forrest, and gave him a commission to raise a Regiment of Volunteer Cavalry. The general officer commanding in the district was Bishop Polk, who, relinquishing the crozier for the sabre, fought gallantly throughout the War until he was killed in June, 1864, during the Atalanta campaign. In England we have had many soldiers who became bishops, and several bishops who took the field when circumstances required them to do so; but General Polk is the last English-speaking Bishop who was killed in action.

Cut off from all the workshops of the North, it was no easy matter for Forrest to find arms for his newly raised regiment. After some difficulty he succeeded however, not only in buying five hundred Colt's Navy revolvers in Louisville, but in carrying them off from under the very noses of the United States Authorities in that city.

Before many months had passed, a whole battalion of eight companies of mounted men had been enlisted, equipped, and duly armed, and they elected Forrest to be their Lieut.-Colonel. For the first eighteen months of the war the officers in all the Confederate regiments were elected by the men, a system which led to such extremely bad results, it had to be altered to one of selection by the Secretary for War, upon the recommendation of the general officers commanding in the field.

The first station of this newly-raised regiment was Fort Donalson, from which place companies were sent to watch the movements of the Federal gunboats on the Cumberland and Tennessee Rivers, and one squadron was sent even to the Ohio. In their frequent encounters with these gunboats and their attacks upon armed steamers laden with supplies of all kinds for the Northern troops in the field, Forrest not only gained great experience himself, but taught his men the duties of the "Moss-Trooper" of old, the mounted Raider of the present age. Many of his men were first-rate shots, and he now taught the others to become so. As soon as a gunboat opened her ports and came into action, so heavy was the musketry fire poured into them from parties of Forrest's men concealed on the river's banks, that very often the sailors would not stand to their guns, and the Naval commander upon several occasions was only too glad to up-anchor and drop down stream out of fire. By degrees he taught his men to have confidence in themselves, in the power of their rifles, and to be accustomed to the heavy shell fire which these gunboats poured upon them whenever possible. They soon learnt to realise that this sort of fire was more terrifying and appalling in sound than killing in its effects. It frightened and demoralised far more men than it wounded.

He trained his men to make war after his own fashion, but he drilled them very little, especially at first, because he knew nothing of drill himself. He applied his own common sense to carry out the war instinct that was in him. His mind was not narrowed by military apothegms learnt by rote, and his actions were unhampered by military regulations of any sort. He knew what he wanted to accomplish, and he went for that object with all the cunning of an Indian, all the common sense of a business man. One evening in the Crimea, when the siege of Sebastopol was dragging out its very slow and weary course; when nothing looked bright for us, no go, no initiative on the part of our old-fashioned pipeclay generals; when we sought for inspiration as to our next move, not as Forrest would have done from a fertile and really military brain, but from old cut-and-dry rules made by Vauban and Coehorn in a past century and for a past condition of things; when it was evident to the meanest capacity amongst a group of young, ardent, and educated Engineer officers assembled in my tent, that all the military ability was in Todleben's camp, not in ours; I remember well one of the ablest men present horrifying us by enunciating the idea that, if the English Government had any worldly wisdom, the Prime Minister would enter into a contract for the capture of the place with some great firm of contractors who knew nothing of Vauban or of how sieges had been conducted in the Peninsula. He boldly asserted that such a firm, bringing great business-like capacity and common sense to bear upon the problem before us, would make short work of the Redans and Bastions we were besieging with such formality. The novelty of the idea struck me and others who heard it thus propounded, and the germ of truth it contained impressed me all through life when I have seen Generals in command racking their brains for precedents in war, or for rules from Jomini upon which to shape their course of action.

General Forrest did in the field, what my able Engineer comrade felt an active-minded, business man like Mr. Brassey would have done for us at Sebastopol; that is, he went at any job he undertook in a sound, business-like fashion, and by the shortest line, prompted by the common-sense reasoning that was natural to him. Expedients came to him without mental effort, and were adapted to meet each particular difficulty as it arose, just as the American engineer of resource drives a road or a railway through a howling wilderness of woods and rocks and mountains, hundreds of miles away from all complicated contrivances, and often entirely unassisted by modern machinery.

Forrest, the backwoodsman, the farmer, and the slave-dealer, knew nothing of "grand strategy," but he was at once a shrewd, able man of business, and at the same time thoroughly acquainted with the common-sense tactics of the hunter and the Western pioneer. But if his operations be carefully examined by the most pedantic military critic, they will seem as if designed by a military professor, so thoroughly are the principles of tactics, when broadly interpreted by a liberal understanding, in accordance with common sense and business principles. The *art* of war was an instinct in him; its objects must necessarily be evident to most men, but the ways and methods by which those objects could and should be secured came of themselves into the untaught brain of this fearless soldier, this general by intuition. His favourite maxim was, "War means fighting, and fighting means killing." Hence it was, his track was usually marked with blood, and the dead bodies of his enemies were the records he left of fierce charges down roads, and of Federal camps or bivouacs taken by surprise. It may be asserted without contradiction, that no man on either side killed so many adversaries with his own hand as he did during that long war. Forrest's first real fight did not come off until the last week of 1861. Up to that time he had practised his men in long marches, and accustomed them to life in the open air during cold and very trying weather. He thus tempered and hardened his young volunteers to the hardships and rough life of a soldier in the field, and he had time to shake down himself into the, to him, novel position of commanding officer. On the 28th December, 1861, Forrest had marched his regiment, then 300 strong, about twenty miles over execrable roads either deep with mud or rendered barely passable from frost.

In the neighbourhood of Rumsey, Kentucky, he came upon a
fresh trail of the enemy, whom he learnt from the inhabitants
were about 450 in number. A gallop of ten miles brought him
into contact with the Federal rear guard near the village of
Sacramento. Not more than half of his men had been able to
keep pace with him, but with them he charged down the road
and drove in the rear guard upon the main body. He ordered
his men to fall back, in the hope of drawing the enemy after
him, and in this way of bringing them nearer to the remainder
of his regiment, the men of which kept dropping in by fives and
sixes. In this he succeeded. Dismounting about half his men, he
directed them to fall upon the enemy's flanks, whilst, with the
remainder on horseback, he bore down along the road upon his
centre. The rifle fire in flank from these dismounted detachments was too much for the Federal cavalry, who, in spite of
their officers' gallant efforts to make them stand, broke and
bolted to the rear. Many were the hand-to-hand encounters and
hair-breadth escapes of the Southern leader that day, but his
loss was small, whilst the Federals suffered very severely. It
was not so much the defeat of the enemy he rejoiced at, as the
confidence this insignificant success gave his men in their own
strength and prowess. His second in command, Colonel Kelly,
who before the war had been a clergyman—or, in Southern
language, "a preacher"—was as gallant a soldier under fire as
ever smelt powder in any war. In a note written soon after this
action, Kelly refers to his leader in the following terms:—"It
was the first time I had ever seen the colonel in the face of the
enemy, and when he rode up to me in the thick of the action,
I could scarcely believe him to be the man I had known for
several months. His face flushed till it bore a striking resemblance to a painted Indian warrior's, and his eyes, usually mild
in their expression, were blazing with the intense glare of a

panther's springing upon its prey. In fact, he looked as little like the Forrest of our mess-table as the storm of December resembles the quiet of June."

Although I cannot pretend to follow this great leader of mounted troops through his many hard-fought battles, I have dwelt upon this, his first engagement, because it fairly illustrates his mode of fighting upon all occasions. The features peculiar to it were, the invariable hardihood and recklessness with which he dashed upon the enemy with his mounted men whenever and wherever he could do so, generally leading the mounted attack himself whilst his dismounted companies pressed the enemy's flanks, and plied them with a storm of rifle bullets. His personal contempt of danger was remarkable, and it was his practice to be always in front of those he led. With his acute judgment and power of perception he was thus generally able to find out for himself the enemy's weak point, and, having ascertained it, he forthwith went for it with a dashing determination very difficult to resist. No man ever exposed himself more in action than he invariably did, and no man ever impressed those he led and amongst whom he lived, with a more universally felt and acknowledged sense of leadership. The following incident, which occurred quite at the end of the war, shows the value his followers set upon his life:—

When Selma, the great Confederate arsenal on the Alabama River, was captured by the Federal troops, Forrest, in his retreat, crossed the road by night along which his enemy had advanced. When doing so he heard a woman's cry for help, and rushing into the house from whence it came, he there found four "bummers," as the stragglers from the Northern armies in the South were then generally called. Owing to the atrocities committed at times by these wretches, the feeling throughout the South was very strong against them. The Southern men were in the army, and their defenceless women, left at home, were often subjected to the most cruel outrage by these fiends— I will not call them soldiers. In this instance, these four devils having rifled the house of all jewelry and other valuables, had proceeded to attack the women residents. Caught in the act, they met with summary punishment. The scene in that house so fired the blood and roused a craving for revenge amongst the men of Forrest's escort that, before he could stop it, many other "bummers" met that night laden with plunder, fell to rise no more. A Federal piquet was captured, from whom it was learnt that the camp of their squadron—about fifty strong—was close by. Forrest at once determined to surprise it. By this time he had taken so many prisoners that, after providing for their guard, he had not more than about thirty men left for this undertaking. Upon reaching within what he considered was striking distance of the camp, the officer commanding his escort brought him a message from the Rank-and-File to say they would not attack unless their general stayed behind. A night attack under then existing circumstances was too hazardous an operation, they said, for him to risk his valuable life in. In accordance with their flattering request he stayed behind, and in a few minutes the camp of their sleeping enemy was taken, and all those in it either killed, wounded, or captured, with a loss of only one man wounded to the assailants.

The officer of regular troops entrusted with the duty of quickly raising levies for immediate war service is often too prone to think that his one great endeavour should be to "set them up" and so instruct them in drill as to make them look as much like Regulars as possible. As a matter of fact, he almost invariably fails to accomplish this aim, and in his well-meant efforts, too often robs them of their only good quality—in a military point of view, I mean—the fearless dash and go so often possessed by undisciplined fighting men. As with the well-meaning missionary who in persuading the heathen to believe no longer in their idols, robs them of their only spiritual faith, without being able to induce them to accept Christianity in its place the result is usually disastrous. The troops, especially the Horse raised by Monmouth during his rebellion, is a very good illustration of what I mean. But Forrest never fell into any such error. He had no knowledge of military science or of military history to teach him how he should act, what objective he should aim at, and what plans he should make to secure it. He was entirely ignorant of what other generals in previous wars had done under very similar circumstances. This was certainly a great misfortune for him, and a serious drawback to his public usefulness. But what he lacked in book-lore was, to a large extent, compensated for by the soundness of his judgment upon all occasions, and by his power of thinking and reasoning with great rapidity under fire and under all circumstances of surrounding peril or of great mental or bodily fatigue. Panic found no resting-place in that calm brain of his, and no dangers, no risks appalled that dauntless spirit. Inspired with true military instincts, he was, most verily, nature's soldier.

His force was largely composed of wild and reckless men; who all looked to him as their master, their leader, and over whom he had obtained the most complete control. He possessed that rare tact—unlearnable from books—which enabled him not only to effectively control these fiery, turbulent spirits, but to attach them to him personally "with hooks of steel." In him they recognised not only the daring, able, and successful leader, but also the commanding officer who would not hesitate to punish with severity when he deemed punishment necessary.

He thoroughly understood the nature and disposition of those he had to deal with, their strong and their weak points, what they could and could not accomplish. He never ventured to hamper their freedom of action by any sort of stiff barrack-yard drill, or to embarrass it by any preconceived notions of what a soldier should look like. They were essentially Irregulars by nature, and he never attempted to rob them of that character. They possessed as an inheritance all the best and most valuable fighting qualities of the Irregulars, accustomed as they were from boyhood to horses and the use of arms, and brought up with all the devil-may-care, lawless notions of the frontiersman. But the most volcanic spirit amongst them felt he must bow before the superior iron will of the determined man who led them. There was a something about the dark-grey eye of Forrest which warned his subordinates he was not to be trifled with, and would stand no nonsense from either friend or foe. He was essentially a practical man of action, with a dauntless, fiery soul and a heart that knew no fear.

2

To take my readers through General Forrest's military career would be to rewrite to a great extent the history of most of the war in the Southern States of the Confederacy. He was present at the eventful Battle of Shiloh, a brilliant Secessionist victory one day, a defeat the day after. When General Beauregard's line of battle halted on the evening of Sunday the 6th of April in the midst of the Federal camps which had been taken, his troops were thoroughly exhausted, and thought only of obtaining food from the captured supply wagons. Forrest on his own initiative pushed forward his scouts to watch the enemy's doings, and soon discovered that large Federal reinforcements were being ferried over the Tennessee River. He at once perceived the gravity of the position, and did all he could to communicate this to his Army headquarters, but no one knew where they were. In his search to find them, he fell in with the officer commanding an Infantry Brigade, to whom he said, in his own rough colloquial vernacular, "If the enemy come on us in the morning, we shall be whipped like hell." His prophecy was not far wrong, and by Monday night General Beauregard's army was in full retreat. General Sherman pressed the retiring Confederates very hard all Tuesday, the 8th of April; upon one occasion during the day, Forrest with about 350 men keenly watched his opportunity for an offensive return from behind a ridge which afforded his soldiers good protection. The Federal Advanced Guard of two battalions of Cavalry and a regiment of Foot, upon reaching the ridge, at once proceeded to attack it with great spirit, but, in crossing a little intervening ravine and stream, fell into some confusion. Forrest, with his usual quick military perception of such an opening, at once told his bugler to sound the "charge!" and, pistol in hand, dashed in amongst the astonished Federals. The effect was instantaneous. The enemy's horsemen fled back panic-stricken through the woods, scattering their own Infantry, who quickly doubled after them. A scene of the greatest confusion ensued; and Forrest, pursuing for some distance, killed many, and took some seventy prisoners. With his usual hardihood, pushing on well ahead of his men, he soon found himself face to face with the enemy's main body, and under a galling fire from all sides. A ball struck him above the hips, and hurting his spine, at once benumbed his right leg. His horse, though mortally wounded, still enabled him to bolt for his life through a crowd of the enemy, who shouted—"Kill him!" "Shoot him!" etc., etc. An unerring shot with his revolver, he soon cleared a path for himself, and found once more at least temporary safety amongst his own men.

It was many weeks before he was again able to take an

active part in the war. The following description of this affair by General Sherman will, I think, interest my military readers: —"The enemy's cavalry came down boldly at a charge led by General Forrest in person, breaking through our lines of skirmishers, when the Infantry, without cause, threw away their muskets and fled. The ground was admirably adapted to a defence of infantry against cavalry, being miry and covered with fallen timber. As the regiment of Infantry broke, Dickey's Cavalry began to discharge their carbines, and fell into disorder."

A couple of months after the battle of Shiloh, Forrest was sent to command a Cavalry Brigade at Chattanooga, and bidding good-bye to his old regiment, set out in June, 1862, for this new sphere of action. Within a month of entering upon this new command he had taken Murfreasboro in Tennessee. It was one of the most remarkable achievements of his life. His force consisted of not more than about 2,000 badly armed men on horseback. A five days' march brought him before that place at early dawn—the enemy being in entire ignorance of his presence. Surprised in their camp, and charged in the streets of the town, the place was soon taken. It was Forrest's birthday, and the evening before, when he told his men this, he begged they would celebrate it by their courage. His appeal was not in vain; for they never fought better or against greater odds.

After the town had fallen, there remained two camps outside, in which the Federals still showed fight. Before setting out to attack them, many who did not know Forrest regarded this enterprise as rash and doomed to failure; and now several of his officers urged the propriety of being content with what he had already achieved, and begged him to fall back at once with the stores and prisoners he had taken before his retreat

could be interfered with. They little realised the fiery temper
or the military genius of their new commander, upon whom
they pressed this advice. This was the first time his new force,
demoralised by previous failures, had seen him in action. They
were not yet infected with the fire which burned within him,
and he had not yet had time or opportunity to catch hold of
their imagination or their spirit. They had no enthusiasm for
this stranger, nor any great confidence in his ability as a general.
He was, however, determined they should believe in him before
the day was out, as his own regiment had long done. His further operations that day showed a rare mixture of military skill
and of what is known by our American cousins as "bluff," and
led to the surrender of the camps attacked. The General in
command and 1,700 Infantry were made prisoners, a vast
amount of stores were burnt, and four field guns, 600 horses,
many wagons, and a large quantity of arms, ammunition, clothing, and food were taken. It was a brilliant success, and as it
was his first great foray, it at once established his reputation as
a partisan and as a daring Cavalry leader to be dreaded by all
commanders of Federal posts and stations within his sphere
of action.

His raids upon the enemy's lines of communication were
frequent and most successful. No rivers stopped him; and any
detailed accounts of the railways and valuable military stores
he destroyed, and the fortified posts he captured, would alone
fill a volume. His pursuit of Colonel Streight's Cavalry column
for four days and nights in 1863 reads like an exciting novel. It
ended in his saving the great arsenal and workshops of Selina,
and in the capture of Streight and 1,700 of his men by the
600 troopers he then had with him.

He took part in General Bragg's retreat from Tennessee,
and one day, being with the tail of the Rear Guard, an excited

old lady rushed from her house, and upbraiding him, urged him to turn round and fight. As he took no notice of her entreaties, she shook her fist at him and cried out—"Oh, you big, cowardly rascal, I only wish old Forrest was here; he'd make you fight!" Such was then the public estimation in which he was held.

But, as we sometimes find in all armies, his commander-in-chief did not agree with this popular opinion of his merits and ability as a soldier; for, later in the autumn, he was superseded by a very inferior man as a Cavalry leader. He forthwith resigned his commission; but, instead of accepting his resignation, the Central Government promoted him to the rank of Major-General, and assigned him the command of North Mississippi and West Tennessee.

There he had to raise, organise, arm, and equip an entirely new force. With it he did great things in 1864, against large numbers of well-armed and splendidly equipped Federal Cavalry. That Cavalry force, of about 7,000 men under General Sooy Smith and belonging to Sherman's Army, he completely defeated in a fairly open and prairie country suited for the action of Regular Cavalry, had either side possessed any. General Sherman officially described Smith's Division as composed of "the best and most experienced troops in the service." This part of the campaign had been expressly designed by that General with a view to the capture or destruction of Forrest's Force. But Smith was no match for his opponent who out-generalled him, and the result was the reverse of what Sherman had intended and anticipated. Forrest's force during these operations numbered about 3,000 men, one-half of whom were raw and badly-armed recruits. General Grant says: "Smith's command was nearly double that of Forrest, but not equal man to man, for lack of a successful experience such as Forrest's men had had." And yet they were, as soldiers went in this war, well drilled, and commanded by a regular officer; whereas Forrest's men knew little more of drill than their General, who, his friends alleged, could not at any time have drilled a company.

A small brigade of about 700 Kentucky Infantry was now handed over to him; but having found horses for these foot soldiers, they were thenceforward reckoned as "Cavalry." His little army now consisted of two weak divisions, with which, in 1864, he took Union City, attacked Paducah, had a most successful engagement at Bolivar, and finally captured Fort Pillow. In these operations he inflicted great loss in men, arms, horses, and stores upon his enemy, largely reinforced his own command, and refitted it with the captured equipments. Repeated efforts were subsequently made by General Sherman to capture or destroy Forrest's apparently ubiquitous force. He several times drew a great cordon of Brigades and Divisions round him—but all to no purpose: he defeated some and escaped from the others. His hairbreadth escapes from capture, when thus closely surrounded by numerous bodies of troops, each larger in itself than his whole command, read more like the pages of romance than the history of military events. All through his operations, one great secret of his success was his intimate knowledge of the enemy's movements and intentions. His campaigns were made in districts where the inhabitants were heart and soul with him, and it was therefore much easier for him than for the Federal Generals to obtain useful information. His system of reconnaissance was admirable, and, for the reason just given, he could venture to push his scouts out in twos and threes to very great distances from headquarters.

A prominent Northern General said: "We never know where Forrest is, or what he is going to do, but he always knows where we are, and what we propose to do."

He loved the game of "poker," and applied not only its phrases but even its system and practice to his military operations. When he came upon the enemy in force, he would say, "I'll give him a daar anyhow," and would push his command in amongst them until he found, as he would say, "We can't make it and must pull out." Then he would attack upon some unexpected point, and "make it."

One Federal General was removed from his command at Memphis for having failed to do anything against this now redoubtable commander. Shortly afterwards Forrest himself marched into Memphis, and took possession of the newly-appointed Federal General's uniform, which was found in his room. The disgraced General, in vindication of his own conduct, wittily said: "They removed me because I couldn't keep Forrest out of West Tennessee, but my successor couldn't keep him out of his bedroom."*

It is not my intention to enter here into the much vexed question of Forrest's dealing with the garrison of Fort Pillow. The story was told at the time in the *Northern Press*, with a skilful seasoning of horrors which only those can equal who are accustomed to prepare these sort of repasts for the public, or who have some party object to accomplish. He reached that place at nine a.m., the 15th of April, 1864, after a ride of about seventy-two miles since six p.m. the previous evening, and having surrounded the place, he duly summoned the commandant to surrender with his garrison as prisoners of war. Negotiations followed, which occupied some time, but led to no result. The signal for assault, being then given, the place was quickly taken. There was a heavy loss on both sides, but all things considered, including the intense ill-feeling then existing between the men of Tennessee who fought on one side and

---

*Forrest sent this uniform back to its owner, who, in his turn, sent Forrest some grey cloth and gold lace to make into a Confederate uniform.

on the other, I do not think the fact that about one-half the small garrison of a place taken by assault, was either killed or wounded, evinced any very unusual bloodthirstiness on the part of the assailants. The unexpectedness of this blow, and the heavy loss in killed and wounded it entailed, served much to increase Forrest's reputation as a daring Cavalry leader, and to intensify the dread in which his name was held far and near amongst his enemies.

An officer who knew Forrest well gives me the following description of the force under his command about this time:— The two friends had breakfasted together on the everyday food of the negro—corn-meal and treacle—as they sat side by side on the bank of the Tennessee to watch Forrest's troops pass over that great river. His command then consisted of about 10,000 mounted men, well provided with blankets, shoes, and other equipment, everything being legibly stamped with "U.S.," showing from whence he had obtained them. His artillery consisted of sixteen field pieces—also taken from the Northern Army—each drawn by eight horses. The train numbered 250 wagons, with six mules or horses each, besides fifty four-horse ambulances. He had himself enlisted, equipped, armed, fed, and supplied with ammunition all this force, without any help from his own Government. For the two previous years he had drawn absolutely nothing from the Quartermasters' or the Commissariat Departments of the Confederate States. Every gun, rifle, wagon, and ambulance, and all the clothing, equipment, ammunition, and other supplies then with his command, he had taken from the Northern armies opposed to him. His own slaves were his teamsters, and at the end of the war went to his plantation with him, as few other negroes did for their former owners.

His was indeed a freebooter's force on a large scale, and

his motto was borrowed from the old raiders on the Scottish border: "I shall never want as long as my neighbour has." In his many scores of battles and encounters he was always the attacking party.

His defeat of General Sturgis in June, 1864, was a most remarkable achievement, well worth attention by the military student. He pursued the enemy from the battle for nigh sixty miles, killing numbers all the way. The battle and this long pursuit were all accomplished in the space of thirty hours. When another Federal General was despatched to try what he could do against this terrible Southerner, the defeated Sturgis was overheard repeating to himself, as he sat ruminating in his hotel, "It can't be done, sir; it can't be done!" Asked what he meant, the reply was, "They c-a-n-'t whip old Forrest!" General Sherman's report in cipher of this battle was: "He (Forrest) whipped Sturgis fair and square, and now I will put him against A. J. Smith and Mower, and let them try their hand."

In these operations Forrest was again badly wounded; but, notwithstanding this misfortune, he took the field once more early the following August. Unable to ride, he travelled in a buggy. He struck at Sherman's line of communication—tore up railroads, destroyed bridges and viaducts, captured gun-boats, burnt transports, and many millions of pounds sterling worth of stores and supplies of all sorts. Well justified, indeed, was Sherman when he wrote to Grant in November, 1864: "That devil Forrest was down about Johnsonville, making havoc among the gunboats and transports."

He took part in General Hood's disastrous Nashville campaign, and covered the retreat of that General's army from Columbia. This most trying of duties he discharged with his usual daring, ability, and success. No man could have done more than he did with the small force then at his disposal.

Throughout the winter of 1864-5 everything looked blacker for the Confederacy day by day, until at last all hope faded away and the end came. It was a gallant struggle from the first, and, as it were, a pitched battle between a plucky boy and a full-grown man. The history of both armies abounds in gallant and chivalrous deeds done by men who fought for their respective convictions, and from a sincere love of country. If ever England has to fight for her existence, may the same spirit pervade all classes here as that which influenced the men of the United States, both North and South. May we have at the head of our Government as wise and far-seeing a patriot as Mr. Lincoln, and to lead our mounted troops as able a leader as General Forrest!

A man of Forrest's characteristics is only possible in a young and partially-settled territory, where English human nature has been able to show its real, solid worth, untrammelled by old-world notions of conventionality and propriety—where men do what they deem right, but not because of laws enacted for the benefit and protection of the community, or of police-men kept to enforce those laws in the maintenance of order. Acts of cruelty and violence are often perpetrated in a border community, such as that in which Forrest passed his youth. Rough, but on the whole, fairly even-handed justice is admin-istered, though occasionally the inhabitants take the law into their own hands when the ordinary process of law is deemed too slow in its methods, or those who administer it too weak or too timid to enforce it. But it is a great nursery where the right-minded, able, and courageous boy grows into the strong determined man—into the citizen most suited to the social wants and requirements of the wild and self-willed community he has to live in. Forrest possessed all the best qualities of the Anglo-American frontiersman. He was a man of great self-confidence, self-reliance, and reticence; a man of quick resolves and prompt execution, of inexhaustible resource, and of ready and clever expedients. He had all the best instincts of the soldier, and his natural military genius was balanced by sound judgment. He always knew what he wanted, and consequently there was no weakness or uncertainty in his views or intentions, nor in the orders he gave to have those intentions carried out. There was never any languor in that determined heart, nor weariness in that iron body. Panic and fear flew and hid at his approach, and the sound of his cheer gave courage to the weakest heart. There was a fascination about him which electrified the daring, and caused them to gather round this dauntless spirit, especially when a fight was imminent. On the eve of an engagement, men from hospital or just exchanged as prisoners of war, would hurry to report themselves to him for duty. These men never had arms, so Forrest would say to them: "You just follow along here; we'll have a fight presently, and then you can get plenty of guns and ammunition from the Yankees." It has always seemed to me that the great distinctive difference between men of action, between the great and the insignificant, the strong and the limp, is the possession or the lack of determination and of the energy necessary to make that determination felt at all times and under all circumstances. No amount of talent will make a two-legged creature a real man without it.

His was that rare species of courage which is not to be disconcerted by any catastrophe, no matter how sudden or how appalling. Had the earth violently opened in front of him in the stress of battle, the shock would not have disturbed his nervous system; it would only have set his mind at work to devise some plan for passing or getting round the obstacle so created. When in the skirmish line one day—his usual position in action—two messengers from the rear came galloping towards him in hot haste, halloaing out: "General Stanley has cut in behind you, has captured the Rear Guard battery and many prisoners, and has now got into General Armstrong's rear." Equal to the occasion, and determined to prevent this bad news from influencing those about him, Forrest at once shouted out in the same tone: "You say he's in Armstrong's rear? That's whar I've been trying to get him all day, d— him! I'll be in *his* rear in about five minutes! Face your line of battle about, Armstrong; push forward your skirmish line, crowd 'em both ways. I'll go to the Rear Brigade, and you'll hear from me thar directly!" With that he galloped off at the head of his Body Guard, and before many minutes had elapsed they heard the well-known Confederate yell with which he always charged. He retook the battery and prisoners, capturing, in his turn, many from the enemy. The distinguished General who is my informant tells me there is not a private soldier who was then present who does not to this day believe that General Stanley fell into a trap which Forrest had deliberately laid for him. Forrest afterwards admitted that at the moment he thought his whole command was "gone up."

In all his military operations he showed an intimate knowledge of human nature, of man's weak as well as his strong and good points. He was very fond of and clever in devising ruses and stratagems to deceive his enemy. When he found his way barred by a blockhouse or any works too strong to be taken by a rush, he would invite his adversary to a parley, in the hope of persuading him to surrender. Upon one occasion he was thus stopped by a strong body of troops well entrenched. He saw that he could effect nothing against them, and he knew that heavy reinforcements would soon arrive by rail to their assist-

ance. He at once despatched a party to throw off the line the
train by which they were coming, and induced the Northern
commander of the work—who was a German—to meet him
under a flag of truce. In the parley which ensued, he persuaded
this Federal commander to surrender, by impressing him with
the conviction that if obliged to storm the place he (Forrest)
would not be able to restrain his men, who would be as savage
as they had been at Fort Pillow. He dwelt much upon the
inhumanity of sanctioning any such proceeding, and the result
was the surrender of the work and its garrison to Forrest's
inferior force.

General Joe Johnston, one of the most celebrated of the
Confederate leaders, had a very high opinion of Forrest, and
regarded him as one of the ablest soldiers whom the war had
produced. He is still often referred to in the South as "the
greatest revolutionary leader" on the Confederate side. And
although I for one cannot endorse that opinion, I feel that he
was a heaven-born leader of men. An uneducated slave-dealer
he achieved great things during the war, and would I am sure
have achieved far greater had he been trusted earlier, and given
the command of armies instead of the weak regiments and
brigades which for so long were alone confided to him.

The war over, Forrest at once recognised the necessity of
patriotically accepting the fact that the North had won, and
that the South must accept whatever terms the humane Mr.
Lincoln might dictate. He published an address to the gallant
men who had so long followed his plume in battle, and who
were not only personally devoted to him, but thoroughly
believed in him as a skilful and eminent leader. He reminded
his men that the terms granted by Mr. Lincoln were satisfactory,
and manifested "a spirit of magnanimity and liberality on the
part of the Federal authorities." "Whatever your responsibilities

may be to Government, to society, or to individuals, meet them like men. The attempt made to establish a separate and independent Confederation has failed; but the consciousness of having done your duty faithfully, and to the end, will in some measure repay for the hardships you have undergone." The last paragraph of this famous order was as follows: "I have never on the field of battle sent you where I was unwilling to go myself; nor would I now advise you to a course which I felt myself unwilling to pursue. You have been good soldiers, you *can* be good citizens."

Forrest had fought like a knight-errant for the cause he believed to be that of Justice and Right. No man who drew the sword for his country in that fratricidal struggle deserved better of her; and as long as the chivalrous deeds of her sons find poets to describe them and fair women to sing of them, the name of this gallant, though low-born and uneducated General will be remembered in every Southern State with affection and sincere admiration. A man with such a record needs no ancestry, and his history proves, that a general with the heart and military genius he possessed, can win battles without education.

Like most of the planters who had become soldiers, the end of the war found him financially ruined. But, with that pluck and energy which characterised every action of his life, he at once set to work to retrieve his fortune. He went back to his plantation, and from it he extracted enough to keep him from want; he also embarked as a contractor upon some of the railways then being pushed over the Western plains, and although he was never rich again, his gains placed him above poverty.

One of these railways involved him in a tedious and troublesome lawsuit. His lawyer, a General during the war, at this moment one of the most distinguished Senators of the

United States, had practically won the case for him, but his signature was required to some papers which bore upon it. When these were brought to him in Nashville, some seven or eight years after the close of the war, he was already dying. He said to his lawyer who brought them: "I'm a dying man, and have but a short time to live. All my life I've been a man of strife; I now wish to die in peace with all men. I have been converted, and have joined the Presbyterian Church. My mother belonged to that Church, and she was the best woman I ever knew. I hope it may make me good. I won't sign the papers; let the whole matter drop. My son is a fine young man, and will do well in life, and I won't saddle him in the beginning of his career with a lawsuit." He died soon after from the effects of the wound near the spine, which he received at the Battle of Shiloh. He had been four times wounded, and had had eighteen horses killed and ten others wounded under him during his four years of war service. It was well said of him when he died, that he was "Terrible to his enemies and devoted to his friends. To women he was as gentle and chivalrous as Bayard, and to all appeals of distress, as unselfish and generous as Sydney."

It would be difficult in all history to find a more varied career than his. A man who from the poorest poverty, without any learning, and by sheer force of character alone, became a great fighting leader of fighting men—a man in whom an extraordinary military instinct and sound common sense supplied to a very large extent his unfortunate want of military education.

When all the disadvantages under which the South fought are duly considered, it is wonderful what the Confederate Armies achieved. But soldiers who believe in themselves and have absolute faith in their leaders are very difficult to beat in war, where success depends so largely upon the firm inner conviction of military superiority over your enemy. Victories gained over him early in a war engender that feeling of self-confidence which is, in fact, the twin brother of success. Little by little this feeling grew in the force under Forrest, and he knew well how to foster it amongst the wild and restless spirits who followed him.

So much the weight of one brave man can do.

His military career teaches us that the genius which makes men great soldiers is not to be measured by any competitive examination in the science or art of war, much less in the ordinary subjects comprised in the education of a gentleman. The reputation of a schoolboy depends greatly upon his knowledge of books, but that of a General upon what he has done when holding independent command in the field. And it is thus we must judge Forrest's claim to military fame. "In war," said Napoleon, "men are nothing; a man is everything." And it would be difficult to find a stronger corroboration of this maxim than is to be found in the history of General Forrest's operations and marvellous achievements.

CHAPTER TWO

Forrest At Shiloh

Under this title Major Gilbert V. Rambaut published the first, and as it unhappily turned out, the last and only install-ment of what promised to be a particularly valuable memoir of service with Forrest. Read first as a paper before the Con-federate Historical Association at Memphis, Tennessee, on January 14, 1896, it was published on the following Sunday, January 19, in the Commercial-Appeal. *The sudden death of the author cut off further publication.*

Major Rambaut enlisted, at the age of 25, as a private in the company of Captain McDonald, which afterward became part of Colonel Forrest's first regiment. His experience in the hotel business, and his demonstrated capacity in managing the securing and issuance of rations, led to his promotion to Cap-tain by June, 1861, and his assignment to the work of com-missary of subsistence. Through all changes thereafter, he continued at this vital work as a member of the staff of Brig-adier-, Major-, and Lieutenant-General Forrest, with the rank of Major dating from July 21, 1862.

He was twice wounded—once at Shiloh (a circumstance which he does not mention in his account of the two days of

54

*battle there), and again on the march from Pontotoc, Missis-
sippi, to the battle of Harrisburg, or Tupelo, in July of 1864.*

*Upon the return from General Wheeler's futile attack
on Fort Donelson, in February, 1863, Rambaut was captured
at Hillsboro, Tennessee, and sent to Camp Chase, where he
remained in prison for two months until his transfer to Fort
Delaware, from which post he was sent to City Point, Virginia,
for exchange after a total imprisonment of nearly three
months.*

*His account of Forrest at Shiloh is reproduced as it
appeared in the Memphis newspaper, including the erroneous
spelling of the names of General Johnston and of Fort Donelson, and the appearance in one place of Forrest's adjutant,
J. P. Strange, as "K. P. Strang." However, some of Major
Rambaut's lengthy paragraphs have been broken up for greater
ease of reading.*

Forrest having differed with his commanding officers at
Fort Donaldson, they having concluded to surrender their forces
and he declining to do so, asked permission to withdraw his
command, at that time having something over 500 men, and it
was granted. He also stated to them that he considered they
were wrong in their impression of the position of the enemy on
the flank, and if they would follow him he would safely escort
them out. He moved with his command as indicated to the commanding officers and proved his view of the situation was
correct, continuing the march to Nashville. At that point he
found everything in disorder and confusion, a large amount of
stores being sacrificed by our troops and taken possession of by
a mob. He at once assumed control, restored confidence and
prevented this sacrifice of stores, had them safely removed and
saved thousands of dollars to the Confederacy.

He moved from Nashville to Huntsville, arriving there the latter part of February, and, knowing the condition of his men and horses, being tired and worn out from the effect of hard fighting at Fort Donaldson and subjected to very severe, cold weather, he deemed it advisable to grant his men a ten-days' leave of absence, in which to rest up and recruit, with orders to report back on the 10th of March. The men all returned well clothed and bringing with them hundreds of men, who had rallied to his standard. His command was now increased by two companies, having been reinforced by Capt. Jesse Forrest and Capt. Schuyler, each in command of new companies which had been organized during the time. The command had lost one company, that of Capt. Gantt, at Donaldson, who failed to report in time to join in the movement from there.

From Huntsville, under orders, he moved to Burnsville and reported to Gen. Breckinridge. It was at that place that the reorganization of Forrest's regiment took place, resulting in the election of Forrest by acclamation as colonel; Rev. D. C. Kelly, lieutenant-colonel; R. M. Balch, a private, major; K. P. Strang, appointed adjutant, and E. A. Spotwood, sergeant-major. Here also Col. Forrest, under orders from the war department, wrote his report on the battle of Fort Donaldson, being the only officer from whom the department could obtain the information desired, the surrender being under investigation. Nothing of importance transpired here, the command being drilled and educated in soldier life. Two companies (McDonald's and Schuyler's) drilled their movements almost exclusively by the sound of the bugle. The only service rendered from this point until its movement to Shiloh was the detachment from McDonald's company of twenty men, who were sent into the neighborhood of Marr's Landing, on the Tennessee river, to watch and report the movements of the enemy, moving, or supposed to be moving, under command of Gen. Buell to Pittsburg Landing. They learned that Buell with a large force of infantry was moving then in the direction of Pittsburg Landing. It was then, and upon the report, as I learned, that the commanding officer, Gen. Albert Sidney Johnson, replied: "I will fight them, if they have a million men."

It may be well before going into this sketch of Forrest's action at Shiloh to say that little opportunity is offered to portray the skill of the man, being at that time only a colonel, with so many superior officers, yet he made his mark and reputation in this battle. His command knew him to be a man of powerful mind, active and energetic, great will-power, keen perception, quick to act, full of strategy, with cool, daring bravery, his whole soul in the cause, his tactics common sense. Even then he was much criticised for what he had already done and was somewhat conspicuous in the cause. Those of the North claimed he was whipping his fights by "main force and ignorance," and our chieftains said his career would likely be of short duration and mushroom-like, he having had no military education, but we who knew him best felt that all he required was an opportunity to prove his generalship and military genius. He covered the ground of his success when, asked "How do you manage to whip all of your battles?" he replied: "By getting there first with the most men, planning and making my own fight, never letting the other fellow make the fight for me." One should not be surprised, therefore, to find such a man a private in 1861 and a lieutenant-general in 1865.

Under orders the command moved, with Gen. Breckinridge commanding, from Burnsville to Monterey. It was very disagreeable weather, had been raining for several days, and the roads were very muddy, and in bad condition to move an army over. From Monterey we were ordered to the south side of Lick creek and slept Friday night, the 4th, some three miles from its mouth. The next day (Saturday) we had some skirmishing with the Federals, having crossed the Hamburg road at that place, and were driven back. In guarding the ford at Lick creek that night we enjoyed the strains of sweet music from the enemy's band, which we were enabled to hear distinctly while they were unaware of our proximity. A little amusing incident took place, the only thing to break the monotony of the dullness of the occasion, the steady tramp of our picket and outposts. We were awakened by the lieutenant in command, shaking the sleeping men off duty and saying, "Hush! Get up and get to your horses!" We could hear the steady tramp, the pit-a-pat of the enemy's infantry, as we supposed, moving up directly on the opposite bank of the creek. Our videttes and outposts had been withdrawn to our picket line, while our men stood in readiness to fire at command. Gradually and steadily the advancing tramp grew nearer, until it reached the opposite side of the creek at the Ford. While each man stood straining his eyes through the darkness of a cloudy sky, hoping to catch a glimpse of the enemy and awaiting the orders to fire, imagine our relief when it proved to be an escaped artillery horse from the enemy's lines.

The next morning, the 6th, the entire regiment was ordered to this point on Lick creek. We soon learned that the battle had opened, hearing the firing of infantry and artillery. We remained here for several hours, sending scouts in different directions, but finding no enemy. Our army, under Gen. Johnson, consisted at that time of three corps under command of Gens. Bragg, Polk and Hardee, with probably some 4,000 cavalry. We were confronted by Gen. Grant with his three divisions from Donaldson, reinforced by three more—Sherman, Hurlburt and Prentiss—with a cavalry force, with Gens. Buell and Nelson commanding, moving to join him. This was, as I remember, the status of the two armies at this time.

Forrest, as soon as he heard the guns of the battle, threw his regiment across the creek and held it on the right flank, ready for orders, for which he sent to the commander-in-chief. It was about 11 o'clock. The enemy had been forced back to their second line, when he received, or it is said received, the order to move his regiment to the front. (The receiving of this order has ever been to me a matter of doubt, unless it be that Forrest was using strategy to inspire his men.) While in line at this point, having just returned from his outposts, he rode to the front of his regiment, having drawn them in line of battle and addressed them in these or similar words: "Boys, do you hear that rattle of musketry and the roar of artillery?" A yell, "Yes, yes." "Do you know what it means? It means that our friends and brothers are falling by hundreds at the hands of the enemy and we are here guarding a d—n creek. We did not enter the service for such work, and the reputation of this regiment does not justify our commanding officer in leaving us here while we are needed elsewhere. Let's go and help them. What do you say?" A yell, "Yes! Yes!" and with this reply he at once moved his command at a gallop into the fight. Not finding the commanding officer to whom he wished to report where he expected, he pushed his command to a point where the infantry seemed most obstinately engaged. He formed fronting the road and in the rear of Cheatham's division, which had received a repulse from the enemy.

In front of us was an open field, in rear of that field a black jack thicket; to the left of this field a skirt of timberland, with considerable underbrush; to the right a black jack thicket and peach orchard. This was the hornet's nest, and immediately in our front, across this field, there were two or more batteries, one being in the peach orchard. Shortly after our formation on this road the enemy opened fire on us, we being mounted, while a little to our right and partially in our front lay Cheatham's division on the opposite side of the road. We received one or two fires from the enemy, when Gen. Forrest, riding up to Gen. Cheatham, almost directly in my front, asked him for orders to charge the enemy. Gen. Cheatham's reply I can not give to you, but Forrest said: "I can not allow my men to remain here under fire of the enemy. I must either move forward or fall back again." Cheatham answered: "I can not give you the order, and if you make the charge, it will be under your own orders." Forrest responded: "Then I will do it. I will charge under my own orders." He at once ordered his regiment to move forward, McDonald in command of his squadron, composed of his own company and that of Schuyler, numbering some 225 or 230 men, being large companies. These two companies advanced into the open field and soon received a volley with no damage. We could plainly see the enemy arranging and changing their guns as we moved straight forward a little to their left and preparing to open fire.

Quickly at the charge of the bugle we charged front. The enemy fired but did no harm. Bringing from fours into line again, we moved at a trot and the enemy again changed, endeavoring to sweep us. McDonald quickly caught it, and for the second time the bugle sounded and we charged front, still being close to the enemy. The enemy fired, but this movement being so quickly executed, there was no damage. The line changed in a gallop from fours to a company front, the enemy having changed for the third time, endeavoring to sweep us. They fired a little too quick for our movement, one shot striking a column of fours as we moved into line, killing three men and four horses, J. W. Apperson being one of the number, severely wounded, and died the next day. The fourth man, who escaped, was Sam Harson of this city. From this forming the bugle sounded to charge, and we rushed over them, running through and over the batteries, the only one that escaped being that to their right, and it managed to do so by going into the black jack thicket before we got to them, and retreated to their left and in rear of the line. We did not halt, but pressed through into this black jack thicket, riding and firing as we advanced to our right. This we continued to do until, owing to the thickness of the timber of this black jack thicket we were unable to go further and were ordered to fall back.

We fell back over the same ground to the field, bearing to the left. We passed through the skirt of woods on our left and took our position where we were first formed on the road. Gen. Cheatham, I think, took possession of the guns, not knowing the injury we had inflicted on the enemy or the consternation we had caused in their ranks by this movement, and passed into his rear. It was natural for him to suppose we were still there and holding the ground, and that we would be forced to make a second similar movement. We were ordered to mask the battery to our rear and move it up, it being in command of Capt. Marsh Polk. This we did and rested for awhile, until there came an order from our right to bring on the cavalry. Forrest, ever in his proper place and where most needed, ordered the cavalry forward, and we at once charged down this road on the enemy, bearing to our left as we charged, running through the enemy's lines, they throwing down their arms. We continued through, cutting them off from the river, and taking position between them and the river. From the number of men who had surrendered I was of the impression that our forces had captured the whole army.

This charge brings to memory the face and form of Gen.

J. C. Breckinridge, who sat upon his horse to the right of our charge as we passed down, holding his hat slightly above his head, making a beautiful picture of that grand man—he naturally proud that a part of his command had rendered such signal work at that time, while his men were endeavoring in their cheering to outyell us.

The surrender being well over, we continued our march a short distance further up the bank of the river, dismounted and crawled to the edge of the bank. There we could see two of the enemy's gunboats, almost directly under us. The officers and men, crowded on the bows of the boats, seemed perfectly astounded, not knowing what was going on. One volley from even our squadron would have killed every man on the boat, but we had no orders to fire, and the cessation of firing lasted for the period of probably two hours.

From this position we moved down the river and found the enemy in great confusion south of and below us—wagons, horses and artillery in the river and crowding the banks, while the men were endeavoring to escape by climbing up the sides of the transports. The firing was again opened. The enemy had massed many pieces of artillery on each bank of the road which went down to the river, and opened fire upon our infantry line. I can only remember of one other command that had advanced nearly as far as we had and held their position on the adjoining hill. I refer to Gen. James R. Chalmers, with his Mississippians. We both remained there until we received orders to fall back and go into camp. We rested a short distance from and on the camp ground of the enemy and in front of our army. Nothing transpired during the night, save the continued shelling by the enemy's gunboats, which was done, I dare say, to annoy us and prevent sleep.

Early the next morning the enemy advanced, having been

reinforced by Gens. Buell and Nelson with their commands, as we learned by the capture of some fifty men of his advance guard coming up from the river. Being only a private and not being conversant with matters at headquarters, I knew nothing of what was going on as to the movements of our army, save such as came immediately under my supervision as a member of Forrest's cavalry. Sufficient to say we were soon in battle, and it appeared to me that the enemy was firing in every direction, and we soon commenced to fire, retreating and falling back. This continued for awhile until our army was all engaged, we fighting desperately with greatly reduced numbers, and our lines were being fearfully depleted.

Our regiment had rendered effective service during the morning, and about 11 o'clock we were ordered on the right flank, where we soon became engaged again. Three times did the enemy endeavor to break that portion of the Confederate lines, but were repulsed. The third time, during the engagement, Forrest carried his regiment to the center, where he had it dismounted and took part in repulsing them. Before our retreat commenced Gen. Breckinridge, to whom we were attached, was assigned to the duty of covering the retreat and bivouacked that night at a point about four and a half miles from Pittsburg Landing, the remainder of the army being en route for Corinth. Soon after the retreat began Forrest moved with a portion of his regiment, and attended personally to the picketing of Lick creek through the night and to guard against any movement from that direction.

On the next morning Forrest found himself with about 150 men on the road toward Monterey, in the presence of a heavy infantry force advancing in three lines of battle. At the same time a company of Wirt Adams' regiment, under command of Capt. Isaac Harrison, a squadron of the Eighth Texas and some

Kentuckians under Capt. John Morgan, came up and made a force of about 350 men. Our position on the ridge was advantageous, and Forrest determined to attempt to hold it until his regiment could be brought up and formed in line of battle. We bravely stood our ground as two battalions of cavalry and a regiment of infantry were thrown forward to attack us. The infantry advanced handsomely. There was some little confusion in the Federal ranks in crossing the stream, and Forrest, with his characteristic coolness of sight and plan and his wonted hardihood, resolved to charge with his force, small as it was.

The bugle sounded and we dashed forward over the crest of the ridge in good order and spirit, and were upon the enemy before the nature of the movement was perceived or they had had time to prepare for it. At twenty paces we opened fire, a volley of shotguns—a formidable weapon at short distance— and rushed in with pistols and sabers. Instantly their cavalry broke in disorder and fell back, running over their own infantry in a panic, creating confusion and tumult for some moments. Many of their men were cut down and horses pierced by the bayonets of their own infantry. Scores of other horses fell, and there was on the ground and all around a medley of cavalry and infantry, running in every direction, officers shouting and cursing and the hurt groaning. Before the infantry could recover, Forrest was upon them with a sweep of sabers and pistols, and they broke as well as the cavalry. The slaughter was great, and their fleeing command was closely pursued for several hundred yards. The loss was heavy, while we captured some seventy or eighty prisoners.

Forrest himself pressed forward into the pursuit, and within 50 yards of the main body of the force and on a part of those whom he had just routed. Halting, he saw that his men had perceived the situation sooner than he and halted and were falling back with their prisoners, being thus unaware of his perilous position. He was now surrounded and fired at from all sides. A ball from a rifle struck him in the left side, just above the hip, penetrating to the spine, and lodged in the left side, wounding him severely, and, as was thought by his surgeon, mortally. Turning, however, he resolved to escape, while hundreds were bent on his death, shouting "Kill him! kill him and his horse!" His horse was mortally wounded, but, using his revolver with deadly aim, he cleared his path in a moment to the rear, but the enemy, being in easy range, continued to send hundreds of balls after him as he rode over the hill.

Turning over his command to the next in rank, he retired to the nearest hospital for surgical aid, and was ordered to go to the rear, which he did, and soon reported at Breckinridge's encampment, and that general ordered him to Corinth, for which place he started, accompanied by his adjutant, Capt. J. P. Strange.

Owing to the pain from the wound, he was forced to dismount and take passage in a buggy, but in going over the rough roads the pain was worse than on horseback, and he again resumed his place on his horse and rode to Corinth. That night after reaching Corinth (on the 9th) the horse who had borne him faithfully dropped and died a few hours later. Being granted a sixty-days' leave, he repaired to Memphis. There he had remained some two or three weeks, when, having learned of some dissatisfaction in his regiment, he returned to Corinth, and a day or two afterward, being in command of a reconnoitering party, his horse suddenly jumped a log, straining him and caused him to have the bullet cut out. This operation was performed by Dr. J. B. Cowan, his surgeon, and without the use of anæsthetics.

CHAPTER THREE

As Wm. Witherspoon Remembered It

William Witherspoon didn't write his Reminiscences *as a connected or chronological account of his experiences. The last part was written and published first, and dealt with events which were latest in time. A little pamphlet,* Tishomingo Creek or Bryce's Cross Roads *was "published by the author" at Jackson, Tennessee, in 1906. The purpose of publication, according to the author's son—who bears the name of Forrest—was to make some money on which the author might go to Confederate reunions. But most of the copies remained unsold and were lost when the old Witherspoon home place in Madison County burned. The result is that in its original 1906 form,* Tishomingo Creek *is what some book catalog writers call "excessively rare."*

But the material, slightly revised, was again used by the author as the third and final chapter in his Reminiscences *of a* Scout, Spy *and* Soldier *of Forrest's Cavalry, published at Jackson, Tennessee, in 1910.*

In addition to the chapter on Brice' Cross Roads, this pamphlet consists of two chapters. The first arose from the coincidence of attending in 1908 a Confederate Memorial Day exercise in the same room in the Madison County Court House in which the author had been confined as a prisoner, charged with being a spy, just forty-five years earlier. The chapter gives in amusing fashion an account of the wiles and ruses by which he secured his acquittal and release, and continues with accounts of the "Armstrong Raid" into West Tennessee, culminating in the Battle of Denmark, or Britton's Lane, on September 1, 1862 —more than a year before Forrest took command in that quarter. The chapter closes with further observations of the battles of Okolona and Brice's Cross Roads.

The second chapter in the Witherspoon volume of 1910 recalls the manner in which the Seventh Tennessee Cavalry (Confederate) bluffed and bamboozled the Seventh Tennessee Cavalry (Union) into surrender at Union City, Tennessee, with the magic of the name of Forrest.

William Witherspoon, the author of these entertaining and illuminating recollections, was born in Madison County, Tennessee, on March 17, 1840. He enlisted in a Madison County company which became Company L of the Seventh Tennessee Cavalry, the regiment commanded first by Colonel William H. Jackson and afterward by Colonel W. L. Duckworth.[1]

---

1. Another Madison County soldier, John Johnston, an infantryman who had been discharged for sickness and had spent most of the winter of 1862-3 at home, started back to rejoin his command in the spring. On the way he fell in with the Seventh Cavalry at Wyatt, on the Tallahatchie. Ex-infantryman Johnston gave his first impression of a cavalry camp as "unpleasant." The men and horses all camped together and the odor and filth were not agreeable and then the men . . . seemed more profane and wicked than the old soldiers of the 6th Infantry . . . But I soon found some good friends and altogether the 7th was a very fine regiment." Among the friends he found were "Hewitt Witherspoon and his brother Billy" in Company L. Private Johnston stayed on with the 7th Regiment and was back home in November, 1863, to get clothing and a horse. At that time, he recalled, there were a "number of Confederate soldiers scattered through the country and a number of officers who had been commissioned to raise companies and regiments and to gather up stragglers." When the news came that "Gen. N. B. Forrest had come to take command of all the cavalry, we were thrilled." Pages 84, 102, 104, 105 of typescript "Personal Reminiscences of the Civil War: 1861-1865" by John Johnston, Memphis, Tennessee, dated November 8, 1900, in the possession of Mr. Roy W. Black of Bolivar, Tennessee, through whose kindness it has been made available.

*Witherspoon, in his own words, was "high private two years
and lieutenant two years."*

*In 1881 he married Miss Bettie Rodgers Weir. Through
the kindness of their daughter Jennie Vie (Mrs. E. R. Eikner)
of Memphis, it is possible to reproduce two photographs, made
about 1910, which testify to another of Mr. Witherspoon's
absorbing interests—the game of chess. In these photographs
made for a magazine devoted to chess he has as partners, in
the picture in civilian dress, G. R. McGee, through whose school
History of Tennessee a whole generation of young Tennesseans
were introduced to the story of their state, and in the picture in
uniform, his old comrade in arms Milt Hurt, also of Jackson.*

*"Captain Billy" Witherspoon, as he was known in Jackson,
died November 10, 1923, in the eighty-fourth year of his age,
and is buried in Andrews Chapel yard at Huntersville, Madison
County, Tennessee.*

The first two chapters of his Reminiscences *are reproduced
from the 1910 publication, with the title page of that date. The
third chapter is reproduced as it appeared in its first printing,
in 1906, with the separate title page it then bore. Combined,
the three chapters present the recollections of one who never
lost his pride as a Rebel. "My grandfather was proud of the
term 'Rebel'," he wrote. "I may have the love for the term
'Rebel' by inheritance, yet, I love it and will so teach my children. I simply look at it that grandfather in 1776 and myself
in 1861 were standing in the same shoes."*

REMINISCENSES OF '61 AND '65

While sitting in the Court House at Jackson, Tennessee,
June 3, 1908—Memorial Day—exercises held there on account
of the inclemency of the weather, when reminiscences were
called for from the old Veterans of the Gray I felt impelled

REMINISCENCES

OF

A SCOUT, SPY
AND SOLDIER

OF FORREST'S CAVALRY

BY

WM. WITHERSPOON
JACKSON, TENN.

1910

McCowat-Mercer Printing Co., Jackson, Tenn.

69

to relate this story, but not accustomed to speaking, I was halting and hesitating what to do, although I had on many occasions faced the mouth of the cannon hurling grape shot and cannister amidst our ranks, charging the line of Blue armed with the rifle of the best that Yankee ingenuity could devise. Sometimes behind formidable breastworks and at others lying behind some advantageous position of the ground or meeting them in a charge with that terrible awe-inspiring Rebel yell that never failed of victory. Strange as it may appear, after having undergone all this in following the fortunes of the wizard of the saddle, N. B. Forrest, my heart failed me, although every face, eye and heart in that assemblage were beaming with admiration and love for the cause that went down at Appomattox.

Then the chairman, Mr. R. R. Sneed, turned to other parts of the programme, I was so impressed with the environments on that occasion, for it was in that Court House and in the same room this occurred just forty-five years ago, two young boys of the 7th Tennessee Cavalry were marched into that room prisoners of war about 1 o'clock A. M. (having been captured at Capt. Jones, some twenty miles west of Jackson, on the Forked Deer River, early that night) with the charge of spy entered against one of them.

Of that charge, of course, neither knew. But one was terribly uneasy in regard to himself and so was the other feeling bad for his friend's situation. It was this, one had been wounded, shot in the face, was discharged from the army. At that time, 1861, a discharge was easy. The Confederate authorities were not particular in having disfigured, maimed or any kind of cripples on the fighting line.

It was then you so often heard the expression, "One Southerner could whip one-half a dozen Yanks just for a breakfast appetite." After the discharge was given, he said he would not quit the Confederate cause, but would act in other ways, which he did. He became spy and scout, and in that capacity acted for the South.

He gave the enemy so much trouble, and they had an inkling of what he was doing. A reward of $500.00 was offered to take him, dead or alive, by the Federal commander at Jackson.

Now, to make my story better understood and complete, I will go back to the beginning of this adventure. The prisoners alluded to are Allen Shaw and William Witherspoon, the writer of these Reminiscences. A few days previous to this General W. H. Jackson's brigade, consisting of the 1st Mississippi Cavalry Regiment (Pinson's) and the 7th Tennessee Cavalry, were encamped on Cold Water Creek, about five miles north of Holly Springs, Miss.

I (William Witherspoon) received an order from my Captain, James Taylor, with an explanation of my expected services to report immediately to General Jackson. I did so. General Jackson explained to me the nature of the duty he wanted me to perform, but said it was out of the usual line of duty for a soldier to perform and it would have to be altogether voluntary on my part. He stated he preferred a Madison County man (Jackson is the County seat of Madison County) as he would be better qualified to do the particular work he wanted done, acquainted with the country and people. "The enemy are fortifying at Jackson, Tennessee. I want all the information I can get of their strength, amount of work they are doing, in fact any and everything in regard to them." He (General Jackson) then explained to me if I should undertake the duty and should meet with the misfortune of being captured and it was known what my errand was, it would be short shrift

with me. A drum-head court martial and hung by the neck at
sunrise the next morning. He would not order me to do this,
but it must be a voluntary act on my part. I told him if he
considered it of any importance, I would undertake it. But boy-
like I did not realize the big job I was about to undertake or
its fearful consequences in case of a mishap, although in my
limited reading as a schoolboy I was aware of the fate of
Nathan Hale and Andre of Revolutionary times. General
Jackson wanted to know when I could start. I replied, as soon
as I could saddle my horse. I had a tip-top thoroughbred
Kentucky saddler. It was about seventy-five miles from Cold
Water, Mississippi, to my father's, who was then living ten
miles west of Jackson. Accompanying me on that trip was my
old schoolmate, bedmate and comrade, Henry J. Fox, then of
Carroll County, now a resident of Humboldt, Tennessee. He
in no wise was connected with my expedition, but was coming
to get a better horse than he had. I got to my father's about
1 o'clock in the night. My father and mother were much
excited on my arrival. Father wanted to know where was my
command, I told him I was alone and the command was in
Mississippi. He said, "Great God, Will, you have not deserted."
My father would much have preferred my filling an honored
soldier's grave, than to be in life at home a deserter. I told
him no, but I had come on business. "What have you done
with your horse"? he asked. I gave him to Wash (a negro who
was a house servant) to attend to. "Yes, and that negro has
gone to Jackson on your horse and you will be captured in two
hours." I said to him I was not afraid of Wash betraying or
the Yanks taking me. How well was that confidence and trust
the South placed in the negro, slave though he was. In the four
years of conflict, all over the South the negro—then a slave—
although Mr. Lincoln's emancipation proclamation made him

free, was loyal to his master and family. That fact being so universal we can not honor and love too much our old time before-the-war negroes and that we certainly do. My ride of seventy-five miles that day with one-third of it in the possession of the enemy, made me hungry, tired and sleepy. "Give me something to eat and let me get to bed and we could talk it over in the morning." I did not and could not realize what had taken place in my home in such a short time. Its condition before the advent of the Yanks and now their possession of my home. While eating my supper father and mother were telling of how affairs were going on. The negro men, about twenty in number, were impressed to work on the fortifications at Jackson, Tennessee. The Yanks were coming there every day, would make the two housemaids (negroes) go in the parlor, sit there and amuse them, insist on their playing on the piano and singing and order my mother and sisters to cook their meals. I went to bed—but tired and sleepy as I thought I was, could not sleep. I saw that my situation there rendered my parents miserable, I got up, mounted my horse (good and faithful old Wash had not carried him off as father predicted, but gave him a good feed and rubbing down) and camped in the river bottom some two miles off, the remainder of the night. I was two days getting the information about Jackson and then I was requested by General Jackson to hunt up Shaw and get what information he had, for he was acting in the capacity of spy and scout for the 7th Tennessee Cavalry. Shaw's father lived below Jackson on the river some eighteen miles. I went there, and although his father knew me, when I inquired for Allen Shaw (his son) he knew nothing about him. I felt satisfied, he was suspicious, and the times justified him, you knew not who to trust. Our people were almost a unit in their loyalty to the Southern cause, but we had some black sheep. I finally convinced Mr. Shaw that

I was all right, and he piloted me to where Allen was camping
on an island in the river bottom. As he was very comfortably
fixed and pretty secure, I, tired and worn out, concluded to
spend a day or two with him before returning to my command
and especially when an attractive little miss whom I claimed as
a sweetheart was living near. My comrade proposed we would
go to Captain Jones' for supper. Before going he took the precaution of sending a friend to notify Mrs. Jones we would be
there for supper and also to see if the coast was clear. The
friend reported everything clear and Mrs. Jones would be
delighted for us to come. We went, but instead of enjoying the
hospitality and good supper at Captain Jones' we were suddenly
taken in by a company of the 2nd Illinois Cavalry. They were
on a scout and became lost and had gotten to Captain Jones'
about ten minutes after our friend left. As we rode up to the
front of the house I heard a sabre rattle, and remarked to Shaw,
I did not like that sound. He said, "That's nobody but Dan
Jones. He is at home on a furlough and he has a sabre and
knowing we were coming to supper he has rattled it to see us
run." I remarked I didn't like such jokes. We dismounted and
as we were hitching our horses to the palings a half dozen
rifles were thrust over the palings within six inches of our heads
demanding a surrender, and were asked the question if we were
citizens or soldiers. Shaw replied, "Citizen." But for myself,
how should I answer. I had on my uniform, a short jacket with
brass buttons and pants to match, made at home, with white
and black wool mixed, which gave it a gray color. With two
navy sixes belted around me and a pair of C. S. spurs, the last,
the only thing I ever received from C. S. government in the way
of accoutrements; but over all was a citizens' overcoat.

Lightning is pretty fast, but my thoughts were traveling
such a gait lightning would have been a slow coach in com-

parison. To say citizen they might turn me loose, but if they should search me and carry me to the light, I would be in a dilemma. To say soldier with that overcoat on and knowing my errand, and being captured with one they had been hunting and having an inkling of his business with the heavy reward for him dead or alive, made it look more than a dilemma. Yet with it all I had to answer promptly or there would be suspicion created. I fortunately thought of the admonition my old school teacher so often gave us boys at school. "In all things be honest and truthful." I answered, "Soldier." "Are you armed?" "Yes." I started to lower my hands. (I was in the act of hitching my horse when captured). "Hold your hands still." They sent one to disarm me, after unbuckling my belt and securing the pistols he ran his hands through my pockets. I had about $400.00 in my pocket, a mixed lot, gold, greenback and Confederate, given my by the parents of the boys in my command. I said to him when he touched the money, you are not going to rob me. He said he was no robber, but would take my knife. After he did not take my money, I felt buoyed up.

They were pretty clever fellows, if they were Yanks. The Captain gave an order to mount. I spoke up quick in a heartbroken and much disappointed tone, "My God, Captain, won't you let a poor hungry fellow get his supper, and more than that won't you let him get one glance or say one word to his sweetheart?"

They had eaten the supper that was prepared for us. I told him it looked cruel and bad for him to rob me of all. The fellow that searched me plead for me and the Captain finally consented. Captain Jones, Mrs. Jones and daughter (the sweetheart) were on the gallery hearing all I had to say. They have told me since the unpleasantness was over (since the war) how terrible were their feelings. They knew if we had any chance to escape we would undertake it and what would be the certain result, would be shot down in their house. Our captors took the precaution to separate us as we were marched into the house, placing Shaw in front and myself about middle way the line. After reaching the dining-room we were seated at the table and the Yanks began to wait on us. I protested, told them I was not accustomed to such waiters, for heaven's sake let my sweetheart and her mother attend to the table. They good naturedly acceded to my request. After supper we started for Jackson. Our captors did not know the way, but halted at a house and impressed an old citizen as pilot. In sympathy for the old man, whom I knew well, I called to the Captain, "Let the old man stay in bed," I knew the way and wanted to go to Jackson anyway and I could pilot him. He (the Captain) remarked, "I don't want your kind of pilots." Getting to Jackson about 1 o'clock A. M. we were marched into the Court House, at that time used as a prison. In there we found about twenty prisoners, but did not know any of them. Some were dressed as citizens and others as Confederate soldiers.

Since our capture Shaw and myself had not been able to exchange a word, so we soon got together in the center of the large room, to be as far away from every one as we could get. We commenced concocting stories of who we might be or anything for our good. Shaw was quite uneasy, afraid they (the Federals) would find out who he was. I was not so troubled as I claimed to be a soldier and with the overcoat off looked like one. We would concoct one story, pick it to pieces, form another and do the same with it. We were thus planning and scheming for some little time when one of the prisoners in Confederate garb approached us and asked who we were. I replied, "Just boys." "Oh, that is all right, you don't know who may be talking to you. It's best to be on your guard, but I will tell you something. I have been here two weeks and this is the first time it has been so since I have been here. They (Federals) have some one here they propose to keep." "What is it?" I asked. He replied, "Don't you see the guards are walking the walls of the rooms, and the guards are doubled at the door." Of course we noticed that shortly after we were incarcerated, but thought it was usual and indicated no more than a safe and strict guard.

That information was a bombshell exploded in our midst; we both felt sure they had been informed by some traitor who Shaw was. We continued this planning and concocting stories, to be picked to pieces, up to 8 o'clock in the morning, when a guard came in and carried me into another room (the room now occupied by the trustee) where I found three officers seated behind a table. One of the officers inquired of me if I was one of the prisoners brought in last night. I replied I was. He said, "You claim to be a soldier, don't you know when a soldier is captured in citizen's dress in the enemies' line he is regarded as a spy?" Another bombshell in camp. It was not Shaw in jeopardy and had been recognized as a spy, it was not Shaw for whom the guards were walking the walls of the court room, it was not Shaw for whose safe-keeping the guards had been doubled at the door. It was the one who felt somewhat easy and placid, in that he had followed his old school teacher's advice in answering a question "truthful and honest."

For the nonce the old teacher and his advice will take a back seat and King Ananias and his cohorts will step to the front. I had made a plan for myself, my whole bent and energies were for the protection of my comrade. A stick of dynamite would have been a lame plaything to me at that moment, my mind in its mad race for some sane and sure plan of escape from my dangerous position, outstripped the lightning in its vivid flash.

My plan was formed on the instant. I would play the ignorant, poor country lad who had been forced away from home into the Confederate Army, by the conscription act. I replied to the Major who addressed me, I didn't know what he called spy. My name is not Spy, but Bill Witherspoon. Pa and Ma are poor folks and I am the only child they have got. The major was determined I should know what a spy was, so he repeated, one who claims to be a soldier and is caught in the enemies' line in citizen's dress. I didn' know anything about that, I was caught at home. I was equally determined the Major should know I was a poor, ignorant boy. I repeated, "Pa and Ma are poor folks and I am the only child. Pa didn't want me to join the army, said he didn't know what it's for, but the rich folks kept after him to let me go and they would take care of him and Ma, and they (the rich folks) told him I would have to go anyway, I would be 'scripted.' So Pa said to me, 'Will, you had better go, I don't want you to go, and they (the rich folks) say they will take good care of us.' So I took old Charley, the only horse Pa's got, and joined the army." The Major wanted to know how come me to be here and where was my command. I told him the command was near Holly Springs, Mississippi, and I had come home because, since you all have been here, the rich folks have quit taking care of Pa and Ma. So I took old Charley, he is a mighty good plow horse and all the horse Pa's got, and I want you to turn me loose and let me have old Charley to go home and plow. The major wanted to know if I would not be satisfied to get loose myself and leave Charley. I told him "No, Pa and Ma are poor and old Charley is nothing but a good plow horse, and I wanted old Charley to make a living for Pa and Ma." The Major wanted to know if

I knew what was the cause of the war. I told him no, I couldn't read much and that Pa said he heard it was a rich man's war and a poor man's fight. The Major wanted to know who Shaw was and how it was we were together. I replied, "He was Dr. Allen (Allen is Shaw's given name) a young 'sorter' sickly doctor. I met him in the road near where we were caught and he told me old Granny was mighty sick. "Don't you know old Granny?" I asked the major. With that question the officers clapped their hands, stamped with their feet and bursted out in a big Haw! Haw! They had been before very much amused at my ignorant and uncouth ways. The more they laughed, the better I felt. If I could keep up their hilarity I would win out.

I was asked what did Jeff Davis and the Confederate government give me when I joined the army. I was standing in front of the table they were sitting behind, I whirled around and placed my toe on the table, pointed to the pair of C.S. spurs I had on. That brought forth another hearty cheer and laugh. They wanted to know where my clothes came from. I said, "Ma she mixed white and black wool, carded, spun and wove it. Ma makes all our clothes, and old Granny was a good weaver too." I said. The Major said, "You seem to think a great deal of Granny.?" "Yes," I replied, "I love her, for she grannied me when I came in this world." Another big laugh. As serious as a judge would be in pronouncing a death sentence, I asked them again if they did not know, or had not heard of old Granny. I seemed to be simply astonished that everybody who was anybody did not know or had not heard of old Granny. After they had gotten through laughing, one of the officers remarked, "I believe he is a good boy and will go home and take care of his Pa and Ma." I said that was just what I was going to do, but they must let me have old Charley. I seemingly took it for granted they had nothing to do but to turn me loose and give me old Charley.

I was then sent back into the prison room. I went immediately to Shaw and told him what had happened. Fortunately they were about fifteen minutes in sending for Shaw. I suppose they wanted to get through with the jocular condition I left them in, before they would be prepared to try another prisoner.

Shaw was sent for, told them his name was Allen, a young doctor, who practiced in the neighborhood where we were captured. That he met me in the road and told me about an old midwife who was very sick, for he knew I thought a great deal of her and he was on his way there and I concluded to go with him. He stopped at a neighbor's to get supper when your men picked us up. He thought he would not have been molested for being caught in the company of this poor boy who belonged to the army. He told them my parents were old and poor, that I was the only child and they necessarily looked to me for support, and he thought from the surroundings and the way I talked to him I was done with soldiering.

He was asked if he had ever taken the oath.

It was required of all the citizens in the South where the Yanks had a foothold, to take the oath of allegiance to the U. S. government. But there were some who would not, my father among that number. He was imprisoned for six weeks and through the kindness of General Logan was released. He was sent to prison by General Sullivan for refusing to take the oath of allegiance to the U. S. government. He was transferred to another prison where General John A. Logan was in command. He told General Logan he had seven boys, five in the Confederate army, and to take an oath that he would not give aid or assistance to one of those boys if he needed it, he would rot in prison first. Logan replied, "I would not have any confidence in a man that would take it," and set him free.

Shaw answered "No. I live twenty miles from here, am a Southern raised man. My health is too delicate to be in the army. I don't know that I would have come all the way here to take the oath, but since you have me here, and require it of me I don't object." They administered the oath and told him he was free, but did not offer him his horse. He was too overjoyed to think about his horse, and he had a good one. When Shaw came back in the prison smiling and said he was free it made me feel glad, although I was not out of their clutches. I was immediately carried back to the trial room and whom should I see sitting behind that table with the three majors but my father's lawyer, a prominent citizen of Jackson, who well knew every word I had said was a lie of the whole cloth. Another bombshell, would they never cease coming. I had managed the others, I will manage this, although it appeared larger and more serious than the others. My heart all but leaped in my mouth, but I went running up to the lawyer, called him by name and said, "Don't you know all I have said to these men is true. Pa and Ma are poor folks, and I am their only child. The rich folks promised to take care of Pa and Ma and they are not doing it and that is why I went into the army and it is why I am leaving it, and here at home." He said, "Yes, Billy, I know it all to be true." I turned upon the majors in a second, "Since he tells you all I have said is true, give me old Charley and let me go home." They assented. I asked if they had given the doctor (Shaw) his horse. "No," they replied. "Well, you must give the doctor his horse for it is a long ways to old Granny's, and she will die if the doctor don't get there quick." For my seemingly great love for old Granny and anxiety for her health, the Majors with a laugh said the doctor should have his horse too, and they hoped the next time they heard from Granny she would be much improved, as she had, certainly, two good friends in myself and the doctor. They gave me an order for our horses, but to find them it was like the old proverbial saying of "finding a needle in a haystack." In Jackson with its 20,000 or more troops it would be difficult to locate a scouting party that had come in late in the night before. They said they did not know where I would find them. Having the order I would undertake it. It was a forlorn hope. If successful and mounted on our good horses, our chances of escape would be doubly sure. To attempt to walk away we could have been picked up easily by any kind of a scouting party. And besides we both knew how to ride and were not much on walking. As I was going in to stand my second trial and Shaw was gathering up his belongings in the prison room, I whispered him to wait a while near the Court House and see what would be my fate, as I thought it would be one way or the other shortly. He did so, and when I was adjudged a good boy and would go home and plow old Charley and quit soldiering since Jeff Davis was so chary in his equipment to his soldiers, as he had given me only a cheap pair of spurs, which their men would be ashamed to wear. One of the Majors jocularly remarked he had heard of the "Georgia uniform" and if I had had a necktie in addition to my spurs given to me, minus what my mother gave, I would have had a complete "Georgia uniform."

The sneers and squibs they indulged in at the poverty of the Southern Confederacy, were a little stinging, but prudence was the better part of valor at that particular time, and acting the poor, ignorant and unlettered boy of the South, their jibes and sneers fell as harmlessly as water on a duck's back. Finding Shaw in front of the Court House and showing him the order for our horses, he did not think it practicable to endeavor to get them and besides it would be dangerous. "The quicker we get out of here the better," I demurred. It was not old Charley, the good plow horse, but Charley the Kentucky thoroughbred, that cost me $250.00 and had never looked through a collar, I was so anxious to get, not only for his particular value, at that time, but might be in the future, as such horses were scarce in Dixie. Charley full sustained the estimate I placed upon him, for at the surrender of Gainesville, Alabama, May 11, 1865, we were both honorably paroled. He had the help of two other good horses. It would be saying too much of a horse, however good, to say he was able to endure the peregrinations of the wizard of the saddle four years.

Shaw was right, we encountered some risk the longer we tarried in Jackson. But I was so adverse to the footing process, I insisted we should make an effort and went back in the trial room to beg of the Majors if they could not possibly find out where the party who captured us might be. I was so anxious the doctor should get his horse for Granny's benefit. They said "No." But while pleading with the Majors, I saw, drawing water at the old well northeast of the Court House, the man who rode at my side (my bodyguard) from Captain Jones' to Jackson. I remarked to the Major, there is one of the men at the well. He directed me to bring him in. I did so, he was asked if he was one of the party that brought in two prisoners last night. "This," pointing to me, "one of them"? He said "Yes." "Well, we have found them to be pretty clever fellows and have turned them loose, with an order for their horses. Let them have them."

One happy boy I was. My Yankee partner on that ride of twenty miles the night before was glad too, so he expressed himself. I believed him then and so do now more than forty-five years afterwards.

We Southerners generally term all in the Federal army Yankees, but the troops of the Central States, Illinois, Indiana, etc., were as different from the genuine New England Yank as the noon day sun from midnight. A great many of the first settlers in those States were from the South, for instance, Lincoln from Kentucky. I took my Yankee partner by the arm, walked out of the Court House. Outside we found Shaw, who gathered our Yank friend by the other arm. We went that way through town up to the old Manassas house, one mile. We were a jolly set. I passed a couple of my neighbors, Joe Henning and Parmenia Transou, on the street. I did not know them, they were entire strangers, yet a few days before, knowing them to be true to the South, was getting what information they possessed in regard to Jackson.

Both told me afterwards they were completely dumb-founded, didn't know what to think. The day before giving me what news they had, and the next in Jackson arm in arm with a Yank, apparently contented and happy, if so, they had said too much.

The scouting party, with our horses were encamped just back of the Manassas house. In passing in front of the saloon at the hotel, seeing the fancy bottles on the shelf behind the bar filled with all kinds of drinks, wine, whiskeys and brandies, that give cheer to the consolate and disconsolate, I proposed to treat. My Yank friend and Shaw accepted. But no sooner was the proposal offered than I thought of the dangerous position I had placed myself, the $400.00 I had in trust for the boys in my command was in one package and some Confederate money loose in my pockets. Confederate money would not pay for drinks at a Yankee bar and to have to pull that $400.00 out to get a greenback bill would have looked awkward and suspicious for a poor, ignorant country boy to have. I felt like sinking to the ground. With my escape about accomplished from a military prison or worse, the fate of a spy, both for my comrade and self, to let an insatiate appetite for drink ruin all. I was in that miserable situation in mind and body. As we were just entering the barroom, we met the Captain of the squad. Our Yankee friend said to him, "Here are our boys, they are all right and I have an order for you to give them their horses. Johnnie (all Reb's are Johnnies with the Yanks) is going to treat. Will you join us?" "Yes. But Johnnie can't treat, I will do that myself, for I brought him here." Well, I could have shouted as lustily as any good old Methodist sister, "Glory Hallelujah!" but for the environments, a bar-room would have been a little out of the usual order, but to say I felt good and happy don't half express my feeling. The sudden transition from a miserable, uneasy condition to one of security, was a joy indescribable. After the treat of the Captain, we went back of the hotel and there we found the remainder of the scouting party and our horses. As I had just committed a foolish and indiscreet act, in proposing to treat, and by an accident escaped probably an exposure, it seems I was bound to commit another equally as much so. The Yanks were playing cards, being a good player myself, I asked one of the Yanks to give me his hand, I would show him what a Johnnie could do. My idea was to get back my pistols. Shaw was standing by but on "tentre hooks" kept saying "Come on Bill." I told them I was going home to stay there and as they did not particularly need the pistols, could they not let me have them? "Oh! no, Johnnie, you might change your notion. We will trade spurs with you." I got the best they had. Wanted to send mine home as souvenirs. We mounted our horses. Shaw remarked, "Now Bill, what other fool thing are you going to do before getting out of this place?" "Maybe I have acted the fool," I replied, "but for my

fool deeds we would be tramping out of here *foot-back*." We
rode through town leisurely, when reaching the timber land
joining the bottom, we traveled pretty fast until we got into
the cane. It was then we could draw a good long breath. We
were safe. Encamped on Shaw's island that night, I started
before day for my command at Cold Water. It was safer traveling in the night than day time. I reached Dupree's Landing on
the Hatchie River just as the sun was rising, preferred crossing
on a boat than swimming the river, if possible. Saw a man
wildly motioning with his arm in front of Dupree's house,
could not understand whether he wanted me to come on or go
back. But as the country behind me was full of Yankee scouting
parties, it would never do for the ignorant, unlettered and only
child of poor folks, who was expected to be at home plowing
old Charley, to be caught so soon on his way back to the army
with a good pair of pistols belted around him, mounted on a
noble Kentucky thoroughbred. It would indeed have been
short-shrift with *the only child*. So I tickled Charley in the sides
with my spurs, who responded in a full gallop. We were soon
upon the man gesticulating, who turned out to be Mr. Dupree.
He said, "My house is full of Yankees." The boat was near in
a run, he went with me and we were soon pulling our way
across. We were both expecting to hear a bullet whizzing, but
fortunately they were all asleep or fearful I was only a forerunner of others like me somewhere near. He told me afterwards they had nothing to say when he got back to the house,
but seemed to be somewhat nervous and anxious for an early
breakfast. One remarked he thought he heard a horse galloping. "It was a boy who was going across the river for a doctor,"
Mr. Dupree replied coolly.

From there on to my command the way was practically
clear. I gave General Jackson what information I had gathered.

He said to me, "You are talking like you had been in Jackson."
I said it was true, but I was honored by an escort of thirty men
of the 2nd Illinois Cavalry. He said he was uneasy about me,
but was glad everything turned out well, was heartily amused at
the poor boy's trick I played upon the court martial, but astonished at the "cheek by jowl" position of the prominent lawyer
with the majors.

This scout was more than likely in anticipation of the
Armstrong raid in West Tennessee, for shortly afterwards,
Jackson's brigade was joined by Armstrong's making a force
of 3,000 men, which I believe to be a low estimate. What regiments composed Armstrong's brigade I do not know, but on
that raid it was generally thought by the boys in Jackson's it
was as strong or stronger than ours. We had a skirmish at
Toones, following up the I. C. railroad, at Medon late in the
day another. These skirmishes were with the small guards stationed at those places, which amounted to not much damage
to either side. Leaving Medon about sundown, we turned our
course towards Denmark and went into camp. My regiment,
7th Tennessee, was encamped near a cornfield, was without
rations for man or beast. How different when following
Forrest we often started without either, but Forrest knew where
Uncle Sam had a bountiful supply and of the best, and at his
disposal when giving the proper "password." It was sometimes,
all hands "Charge" or "Surrender." One or the other rarely
failed. But under West Point tactics we marched all day without rations for the men or provender for the horses. At a time,
1862, when the whole country was full of both. We were
ordered not to make any big fires, we gathered the brush and
started our fires, not that it was cold, but the corn in the field
was getting hard, September 1st, and we wanted to make
embers and ashes to roast the corn. Our horses fared well and

we did not grumble, like philosophers it was what would happen sometimes in a soldier's life. Our supper, exclusively a parched corn diet, breakfast ditto. Early we mounted "en route" to Denmark. Seventh Tennessee was in the rear, one company had been left near Medon on picket. We entered a lane, a rail fence on each side of the road, at that time usual before the day of wire. Heard some firing in front with an occasional boom of cannon. We were ordered to dismount, throw every other lock of the fence, mounted again, went but a short distance, ordered to load, were armed with the double-barreled shotguns that we formerly shot squirrels, rabbits and the wild game that was common to the country. Now it was for different game, a two-legged biped, who had come down in our Southland, regarding us as barbarians, one type removed from the wild horde of Aborigines that once roamed our country, teaching what constituted a higher civilization, by entering our homes, abusing and insulting those we had left at home, unable by the decree of nature, unable on account of sex and age (our mothers, daughters, sisters, and sweethearts, our fathers decrepid with age and boys too young) to shoulder the musket to defend what is dearer and first in the heart of every true citizen, his home. As the game we were to meet was different, so was the load, rammed down those shotguns, buck and ball, an ounce ball and three buckshot. Although an ordinary hunting weapon, it did terrible execution at close quarters. After loading we took the walk, shortly ordered to the trot, then to the gallop. The firing in front became more prominent and frequent. We came upon General Armstrong sitting on his horse, near the mouth of the now famous Britton Lane. The regiment, save my company and Company F at Medon, with General Jackson at its head, was ordered to the right, dismount and charge the enemy. That was through a cornfield, my company halted by General Armstrong. Sitting there on our horses, it was but a few minutes the enemy, not far from the west end of that short lane, espied us, began to fire on us with artillery. Their first shots went above the black-jacks we were under, the next a little lower, too much so to be comfortable.

General Armstrong ordered us to form fours and charge. Now an explanation of the position, the point where we charged from was north not more than 200 yards from the lane. The road turned south across a pretty deep ravine and then up to the lane going due west so at the mouth of the lane (east end) we made a right angle. With a yell we charged, going at full gallop. In that hollow, from some inexplainable cause, the rear of the company became tangled. Those in front, twenty in number continued on, turning into the lane. It was an ordinary road fourteen feet in width with a deep gulley on either side between the fence and road. We were four abreast in entering the lane, we were in plain view of the artillery men, as they had been shooting at us in our former position, as we made the right angle at the lane it was necessary for them to change their pieces to do us any damage. That necessity was our safety, although it required but a short time, we were too close for them to adjust the cannon, load and fire. As we got fairly started down the lane, we noticed they were ramming down the load. With a general impulse, that cannon had to be reached before it could be fired. We drove in our spurs and in a mad bound were upon them. It was then and there the old much-derided double-barrel as an army gun done its work perfectly. In a second of time, we twenty, not one hurt, were all that were left alive with the two brass cannons. We dismounted, the smaller boys, four in number, I being one of them, holding horses, the others divided eight to a piece. The enemy were in the woods southwest, still firing at us. The balls would hit the cannon and shiver the spokes of the wheels. Yet, strange to say, we did not have a man or a horse hurt. The boys started off with the pieces, did not go far, had to stop, two dead horses were lying across the road and they had begun the ascent of the hill. Noticing help was needed, high private though I was, I ordered one of the holders to mount, tell the others of the company the "monkey was caught," for God's sake come and help us. They were there in a few moments and with the dead horses rolled out of the way, the cannons were soon carried to the east end of the lane. As Company F, who had been at Medon on picket, rode up, we were ordered to turn the artillery over to them, mount our horses, and report to Gen. Armstrong, who was sitting on his horse at the same spot we left him on the charge. He with a wave of his hand and lifting his cap, complimented us for the gallant action. Noticing the wounded and probably dead were being carried to a small log house east I dismounted to go and see who had been killed or wounded, had gotten off but a few steps when ordered to mount. We then turned north and went in a northwest course, leaving Denmark two miles south, crossing the Hatchie River at Estanaula, where we encamped that night, paroling thirty-two prisoners the following morning. Whether they (the Yanks) paid any attention to that parole I consider very doubtful. This is the extent of what Company L, 7th Tennessee Cavalry, did at Britton Lane. In about fifteen minutes time Company F destroyed the artillery (at least thought so), spiked one piece, cutting down the wheels and throwing the other in an old well. *Terrible destruction.* Why the Yanks had that artillery in less than twenty-four hours, ready to destroy the young manhood of the South. The defense of its cause, why was it so? When we stood so much in need of it. We waged that battle with all we then had, double-barrel shotguns. No doubt both Colonel

Dennis (Federal) a force 1800 infantry and two pieces of artillery and General Armstrong (Confederate) with two brigades of cavalry 3000 strong, were equally surprised. The Federals were whipped several times in that fight, had hoisted several times the white flag, certainly an index of defeat. Why having that battlefield in less than ten minutes after their artillery was captured and not a gun fired or any demonstration of the enemy to recapture it. When, in fact, as told by the citizens of Denmark, over 200 of the Federals had returned there and were anxious to find some one to surrender to. Some four miles from the fight, fortunate for Armstrong, they did not go two miles farther north, display some pluck and have captured Armstrong. We were certainly on the run, to say the least, a forced march, not halting or stopping until we were ferried across the Hatchie, sixteen miles distant, on a ferry boat. Where does the blame lie? Certainly not with the men, they carried out every order and executed it as completely as the 7th Tennessee did.

When the plan of erecting a monument to our noble dead, lying there in unmarked graves, was agitated in the newspapers, heralded all over the Southland, there came a response from an Alabamian, grateful that a mark of respect would be shown to the sons of Alabama who had fallen there, giving his version of the battle, claiming Alabama troops had captured the artillery. In a short time a Texas trooper replied, "My 'comrade' from Alabama is certainly mistaken, for the Texas Regiment captured the artillery." All this was a great surprise to me, of the 7th Tennessee, living within sixteen miles of the battleground, when I, one of the twenty who captured it. I had surely not been in a dream for more than forty-five years. Going to Jackson one day, a short time previous to laying the cornerstone and telling my company, Company L of the 7th Tennessee

Cavalry, captured that artillery, my statement was met with a counter statement that Captain Deupree, a professor at that time in the now Union University, of Pinson Regiment, 1st Mississippi, read a letter before the John Ingram Bivouac giving a history of the battle, stating his Company captured it. Why all this seeming contradiction about capturing two pieces of artillery in an engagement that no history of the Civil War on either side has thought of sufficient importance to mention. Strange will appear the explanation, will justify the claim of the Alabamian, Alabama did capture it; will justify the claim of the Texan, Texas did capture it; will justify the claim of the 7th Tennessee, Tennessee did capture it. On the morning of laying the corner-stone I met with Captain Deupree, went over the battlefield together, followed with twenty or more citizens, who knew us both well, wanted to hear what two old soldiers, participants in the battle, had to say. In reaching the east end of the lane, Captain Deupree remarked, "there was a house over there," pointing south about twenty yards. I told him I thought so too. It was our first visit to the place since the fight. We will go and look if there is any sign of a house having been there. We found the brick bats, indicating where the chimney was. He remarked, "here stood the house, it was enclosed with palings, my company was over there," pointing southeast. "We crawled to this house, I (Deupree) ripped off the palings, crawling through, and here was a sweet potato patch; we kept crawling on all fours over there about 100 yards southwest, when a company of cavalry charged on the artillery and captured it."

Captain Deupree said he did not state in his letter that his Company had done so, but said they assisted in its capture. Captain Deupree's Company was near enough to render good assistance and no doubt was. How could it be possible for so many captures of that artillery and some one not be mistaken. By applying the mode so many West Pointers make their fights, fighting their commands by detail, and holding back a large reserve. The paramount idea, not to be whipped, and routed, instead of the Forrest plan, when he (Forrest) went into action, to win with no thought of defeat and with every man on the firing line. On Sand Mountain, following Street, he ordered his men tie their horses to the bushes and every man to the charge. When remonstrated by one of the men, we might fail, and our horses captured, he replied, "If we are whipped we'll not need any horses," implying the full determination to do or die. Commanders of armies, like poets, are born, not manufactured. With a superior force and men all volunteers, no substitutes or bounty jumpers, springing from the loins of sires and grand-sires, the best fighting element on the earth. What did Armstrong do, put in a regiment at a time, no more than one-half of the enemy, charged, went through, hoping on, no more in the fight, followed by another regiment doing the same, until the rear regiment came up and the same program followed out to the letter, save we make a pretense of destroying what had cost the lives of so many good men, the triple capture of two pieces of artillery. The estimate generally by the members of the 7th Tennessee up to the time of erecting that monument, our total loss not more than ten or twelve killed and about the same number wounded. Captain McNeil, the leader in erecting the monument, asked me what I thought was our total loss. I replied as above stated. He said, "You are far wrong." From his investigations and correspondence with the different regiments, our loss will in killed and wounded be near 115. Is it not shameful that our troops were so managed as to suffer a loss of such magnitude with no corresponding good. What if Forrest had been there, instead of Armstrong. Colonel Dennis would have been crushed as easily as an eggshell, with not probably the loss of one-half a dozen men. Forrest's and Stonewall Jackson's mode of fighting was similar. An innovation on military strategy, at that time, which so excited the wonder and admiration of the different nations of the world, sending their military men here to study their mode and since in the battles of Europe, has to a great extent been followed, particularly by Germany and Japan. One of the Federals in that engagement from Illinois came down several years ago to go over that battle ground and was carried out there by one of the 7th Tennessee (Bill Campbell) who also was in the fight. The Federal told Mr. Campbell, "we were whipped badly, did our best to surrender not only once, but several times, but you boys seemed to think we were not worth the trouble. We wended our way back to North Mississippi and then rested from our *arduous* campaign in West Tennessee." When our scouts reported the enemy in Memphis were issuing six or nine days' rations we would be issued like amount, as they (the enemy) marched in our direction, we would start south. Not by any *hocus pocus* (I would say strategy but not deserving of that name) could they get any nearer to us.

Grenada, Mississippi, was our usual destination and occurred so often that we boys called it our Methodist Circuit, so similar to the circuit rider of that church. The exigencies of the South were becoming too great to allow of its soldiery playing circuit rider. So Forrest took us in charge, after which when several days' or more rations were issued, it was not from, but towards the enemy, we marched, and often without rations. But Forrest, as I have before stated, knew where Uncle Sam had them stored away for us. Believing, too, that a change of diet would be good for his boys, not that we did not have good enough, but Uncle Sam's was a greater variety and of something we were deprived on account of the strict blockade he kept on the South's ports. Whether his soldiers fared any better than ours I can not say, personally, for the short time I was in his hands I left before meal time, but what we boys got from his commissary department nolens-volens was superb. Forrest did not confine his demands on Uncle Sam's commissary department alone, but for arms and ammunition. We had early discarded the old double-barrel, after following a short while the fortunes of the Wizard of the Saddle, as obsolete, took up the sharp carbine, at that time a splendid, reliable breech-loader rifle which would kill 1000 yards. A Yankee rifle, it demanded Yankee ammunition, after getting the gun in our hands and one supply of cartridges, it was a sure matter to get more.

I was much amused at one time going to one of our Reunions, I offered for sale my little book, "What I saw at Bryce's Cross Roads," to a citizen, saying, "I vouch for all in that book to be true." He took the book and in a few moments, beckoning to me said, "What do you mean when you say Uncle Sam?" I replied, "The United States government." "You do not mean to say and for it to be true that the United States government furnished the Rebel Forrest and his men arms and ammunition?" "I do." "How is it? I was a soldier in the Federal army in the Civil War, I do not understand it, although not in this department." Strictly a case of "nolens-volens." Uncle Sam could give to his boys willingly, to Forrest and his men he would have to give unwillingly if not otherwise. No difference in the doing of the act, whether willing or unwilling, and that we drew on Uncle Sam for more than we could use. We had your guns necessarily we had to have your ammunition. The light began to dawn on his obtuse mind, when he remarked, "That Forrest was a terrible fellow."

At the Louisville Reunion, in the lobby of the Galt House,

General Lyons of Kentucky (who started the Bryce's Cross Roads fight) belonging to Forrest's Cavalry, and myself were discussing war topics and the histories that had been written of our different battles. There were a half a dozen gentlemen standing near, apparently interested, in our chat. When General Lyons remarked to me, "My daughters are here in this hotel and they wish to see you, you remain here until I get back."

As General Lyons left one of the gentlemen of the group, above mentioned, said to me, "We have been listening with a good deal of interest to your's and the General's talk," introducing himself as a Lieutenant Colonel of an Illinois Cavalry Regiment in the Civil War. He said, "I am very fond of reading the histories on both sides, and I see you two are not any better pleased with your historians than I am with mine. In all the battles I have participated in our historians are so wide of the mark, as true accounts, that I could not realize in view of what they said and the true facts as I knew that I was in the fight. But there is one question I wish to ask you. I see on your hat 7th Tennessee Forrest Cavalry (I carried that insignia not alone that I was proud of being one of Forrest's indomitable riders, but as a means of recognition by my old comrades). I have read your (the Southern) side of the Okolona battle. In that version it speaks of that regiment, 7th Tennessee, resisting and repulsing successfully three charges, made by our cavalry in greatly superior numbers. I was in those charges. You did resist and more than repulse, you came near annihilating us and night— blessed night, too, the only thing that saved us. Your version gives the strength of the 7th Tennessee about 350 men. Now what perplexes me is how 350 men in an open field, dismounted, could do what they did. We brought against you in the first charge, mounted, 1000 men, you drove us back. We then reinforced to 1200, charged the second time, with the same result, driven back, after getting as we did in the first charge in about seventy-five yards of your line. We reinforced to 1500 strong, and at the sound of the bugle charge we went at you, with a full determination to win, but met with the same repulse. Not only a repulse, but an almost annihilation. That is what I can't understand, that 350 men can be so constituted, out in the open ground, as to be able to do what they did." I said to him let me give you my side of it. "The 7th Tennessee Cavalry was chosen by Forrest as one of the two charging regiments of his command, not probably any better than other, viz.. 2nd Missouri, Biffle, Pinson, Kelly or any of the Kentucky regiments, but Forrest selected two regiments, Wilson and 7th Tennessee, an honor over their worthy competitors. There were no laggards or slouchers in Forrest's command proper. There are plenty who claim to be Forrest men, never saw Forrest or fired a shot even in the four years' war. This regiment was composed of twelve companies, numbering at the beginning of the war near 1200 men. Three companies were at that time on escort duty, away from Forrest. Now Colonel, would not 350 men, actually in line of battle, be a big number for one regiment to have in 1864 with three companies off?" He said, "Yes." "You remember it was a long narrow branch field. We were placed in that field, it was our center, to extend across, we opened ranks to extend across the field. As the line was formed, Forrest rode into the field, in our rear, saying to us, 'I think they are going to charge you, boys, hold this line for me.' He passed on down the line, repeating it. With but one response from his men, 'We will.' Now, Colonel, when you charged that line, it was not one Forrest you were contending with, but every man in that line was a Forrest. Let us look at the morale of the two forces. You said, Colonel, you had fought Forrest frequently, and I suppose a good many of the men in that charge had done so. Now did you ever whip Forrest in any of those engagements?" He replied, "No, unless I might claim Parker's Cross Roads, but I think that doubtful." "Was it not that Forrest decidedly got the best of you?" "I think so," he admitted.

"Now two forces, meeting in combat one, invariably successful, the other meeting, as invariably, defeat. The one buoyed up with its former good fortune, the other disheartened to the same extent at its misfortune. In that condition, Colonel, man for man, they are not equal. You were forming your line in the edge of the woods bordering the field. You made a formidable appearance, mounted, with your charges well reined and sabres drawn, you looked fearful and to raw troops would have been so, but it had no effect on the seasoned veterans before you, we had seen 'the monkey before.' At the sound of the bugle you dashed forward, holding your horse with the left hand and sabre grasped by the right. We were meeting each other, you in mad gallop, with us a walk. Forrest's style always to meet a charge, with a counter advance, we had the same arms, when you were near enough for our rifles to do good work we commenced pumping lead, some of you were firing occasionally, but the greater part of you were intent on holding that rein and sabre. As you got within seventy-five yards we dropped our carbines (which were strung by a strap across the shoulder) drew the navy six's, one in each hand, then we fed you on lead so furious and fast you whirled with your backs to us. Then it was again with the carbine until you got back into the woods and we saw you were forming again. 'Well, boys, we whipped the first charge, and we can whip the next,' was the universal remark with us.' We had been soldiering long enough to know you would increase your number, but number was not what we considered, it was making good the pledge we gave Forrest.

"You came on us the second time as you did the first. In the interim, while you were forming, we were reloading our pistols and attending to any mishap to our arms. At one time we had sabres, but had discarded them as a fighting weapon, useless, only good on dress parade in the hands of the officers, making them (the officers) feel they might be a little better or different from the men.

"In your second charge you got within the same distance as the first (seventy-five yards) when the navy six's began their music you whirled, it was another play on your backs. It was soon evident to us you were forming your third line, and it would be greater still, if you had the men to make it so. You say the first was 1000, the second 1200 and the third 1500 men. We saw you were determined and admired your pluck, but we were more confident still in holding that line. We had confidence in our leader and when he left us we knew Forrest would soon be heard from and if we needed help would get it. You came on us as you had previously done, but we failed to halt you with our navy six's. Just before you charged the third time we had crossed a deep gully, a wash through the field. As you rode upon us, you cried out, 'Surrender! Surrender!' Now, Colonel, how many of us paid any attention to that demand. Not one. It was a word not in Forrest's vocabulary or in his *manual of arms*. As you rode through us no one gave any heed to your cry, 'Surrender! Surrender!' We could handle ourselves, dismounted more easily, better and quicker than you mounted. As you rode through us the firing with no let up, but more furious and terrible, than ever before, and espying that gully in your front, you were forced to come back through our line or yourselves to do the surrendering. You passed back through us, and it was then the 2nd Missouri came up on the side of the field, giving you a broadside, coupled with our volleys in your backs. That, as you say, was not only a repulse but an annihilation and night, good night, is all that saved you."

One of the Colonel's friends remarked, "Can you not now, Colonel, understand how 350 could possibly do the work?" He said, "Yes," extending his hand, thanked me for the explanation. Our loss was very light. My company of forty men, one badly wounded, shot in the thigh, ball ranging downward, who died third day afterwards. Other companies comparatively about the same loss. This engagement certainly showed the great foresight in Forrest in discarding the sabre, and to which the Federals, to a great extent, owed their defeat. Reverse the forces, with 1000 of Forrest's riders mounted charging 350 dismounted on open ground. It would have been like a cyclone ridding a farmer's field of his wheat shocks. I do not say this in a spirit of bravado or zealotry. We were better riders, more expert with the gun, had been trained to both, almost from infancy, and were about as expert mounted or dismounted. This achievement of the 7th Tennessee on open ground, successfully repulsing three distinct efforts, following immediately each other, three to four times their number, and inflicting such terrible loss upon their assistants, is all but incredible. The Yankee Colonel was justified in doubting. Incredible and out of the ordinary are nearly all of the exploits of the Wizard of the Saddle. General Forrest considered this as the most brilliant deed of the many enacted by his men throughout the war. As great and brilliant as this exploit may be, I think, as a participant in both, the 7th Tennessee charge at Bryce's Cross Roads superior, particularly in results.

Forrest would have whipped Smith the next day anyhow if he had failed in holding that line. At that time Smith was on the run and badly discomfited. It was here resisting men mounted, with both hands occupied, one holding the reins to control their horses, the other their sabres (all but a useless weapon) as our small loss showed. At Bryce's Cross Roads, as in this, in an open field marching upon men, dismounted, lying down behind breastworks, as in this in a walk, within seventy-five yards of their line, withholding our fire until we received theirs, then with a yell and fusillade, whip three times our number.

Both positions were the center of the opposing forces. In this the 7th Tennessee was holding what it possessed. At Bryce's possessing what was held, a failure there would have been irretrievable, our success in that charge, magnificent as it was, did not make a victory, but a forerunner of the great and unparalleled victory that did come a few hours later. Compare the loss of the two charges: Okalona small; Bryce's great.

The official report of Rugger's Brigade, 23 per cent of it was composed of 18th Mississippi and 7th Tennessee, and the storming of that fence and log barricade with that terrible hand-to-hand encounter was performed alone by the 7th Tennessee, consequently its loss was much greater than the 18th Mississippi, which would make the official report here heavier than 23 per cent on the 7th Tennessee.

THE SEVENTH TENNESSEE CONFEDERATES VS. THE SEVENTH TENNESSEE FEDERALS

In the Spring of 1864 Forrest was at Jackson, Tennessee. One morning early, we were formed into line on Liberty Street, mud fetlock deep. General Forrest came riding up the line, saying, "You d—n boys have been bragging you could whip half a dozen Tennessee Yankees. You are the 7th Tennessee Rebs, the 7th Tennessee Yanks are at Union City, I am going to send you there to clean them up, if you don't, never come back here." All he had to say, but enough. We all felt if by any chance we were unsuccessful, we would be the laughing stock of Forrest's command, regardless of what we had previously done. On our way there we got to thinking of the situation. Hawkins and his men were West Tennesseans, raised as Southern men. Some of his men were neighbor boys of our boys. Had, no doubt, a full quota in his regiment, had not been fighting to any extent, were more marauders and pilferers than fighters, which had a tendency to increase rather than decrease his numbers among that class of mankind. While we 7th Tennessee Rebs had been constantly fighting, numbers greatly reduced, would probably be outnumbered by more than 100 men. They would have all the advantage in position, as we would be the attacking party. We all felt and said to each other, on that sixty mile journey, "Boys, maybe we have been talking too strong. But Forrest has called our hands. If they fight we have a job on our shoulders. We are in for it, and with any showing will clean them up." We got as far as Trenton, when we discovered that Forrest in his goodness of heart added to our force seventy-five men of Faukner's command, good men, too, which gave us a force of 475. The nearer we approached Union City the more numerous were the bushwhackers (a bushwhacker is a fellow who will not fight in the open, face to face, but will lie in ambush on the roadside, shoot and run). It made us feel a little uncomfortable, not knowing when, or where, the deadly missile would come. We put out a good squad of flankers, regular daredevils, well mounted, and it was not many of the bushwhackers, after firing his shot, that escaped. They did not give us any more trouble after capture. Were simply planted to stop the increase of such vermin. We got to Union City with the advanced guard about daylight, captured their pickets, but Hawkins was on the lookout for us. He had gathered his men inside of a stockade, this was an enclosure with walls of dirt thrown up about ten feet high, with logs placed upon top and small portholes underneath the log, every few yards apart. It was probably seventy yards square, the timber cut down, felled from the stockade with the limbs and branches trimmed to a sharp point. We dismounted and advanced on the stockade, reaching the fallen timber we got down on all fours, crawling our way, firing occasionally as a head would pop up above the logs. It was all we had to shoot at, they (enemy) would fire through the little portholes, not of much advantage to them, our lying down in the timber made it difficult to see us. This hap-hazard fighting was indulged in about one hour, with several wounded on our side, among that number my comrade, Henry Hammerly, now a citizen of Jackson, Tennessee. The enemy's loss was five killed, none wounded, all shot in the head, through curiosity or something else that prompted them to pop up their heads above the logs. Our close watch for something to shoot at, when a head did appear, a dozen or more rifles would bang away and the owner of that head would be put out of service. Foreseeing no result from such fighting Lieutenant Livingston of Company D, now ex-Judge Livingston of Brownsville, Tennessee, (I think the author of the strategy, others claim it was Adjutant Billy Pope, who was killed at Bryce's Cross Roads), proposed the plan of playing Forrest's demand of a prompt and unconditional surrender or accept the dire consequences, if necessary to take them by storm. Be as it may by Livingston or Pope, both unexcelled as soldiers, a white rag, where it came from I and a good many others of the 7th have never been able to learn, was tied to a pole and hoisted. A flag of truce now, firing ceased, Livingston or Pope the bearer of the flag went up to the stockade demanding of Colonel Hawkins a surrender in Forrest's name within five minutes, "That he, Forrest, didn't care if they did not surrender. He wanted to turn loose all his artillery on that stockade, blow them to hell and not leave a greasy spot." Colonel Hawkins wanted ten minutes to consult with his officers. Could not be granted, Forrest was peremptory in his demand. No dilly-dallying. Was not particular for a surrender, wanted to wipe such traitors to their State and the South from off the face of the earth. Hawkins was pleaded to in the name of humanity to yield. He (Hawkins) knew Forrest and it was a large force of Tennesseans principally he was surrounded by, he knew the feeling of hatred between Tennesseans of opposite sides, finally five minutes was yielded to consult his officers. He went in, called his officers together, told them of the demand put it to a vote. All voted surrender except Captain "Black-Hawk" Hays. (This was told me the next day by Captain Hays). He (Hays) did not believe Forrest had any artillery there and wanted them to hold out until that was shown. It was then Colonel Hawkins replied to Hays, "be too late, for Forrest would not leave of us a greasy spot." He (Hawkins) then came out, agreed to surrender, but wanted to surrender to Forrest in person. Hawkins knowing Forrest, having surrendered to him before, was told he was asking too much, General Forrest would send him a man of his rank. Colonel Duckworth, the only Colonel we had along, was sent to receive the surrender. When the flag of truce plan demanding a surrender was adopted our buglers (each company had its bugler, besides the regimental bugler) horse holders (every fourth man was horse holder in fighting dismounted) and our negro cooks (most every mess had a cook, they were slaves at that time), were all sent around to different positions. The bugler would sound the artillery call, we boys lying in the cut timber would yell lustily, feeling good all over for it was artillery we needed. A hope, however slender, the thread by which it hangs gives a corresponding gladness to the heart. Another artillery call, at a different point, more ringing cheers from the boys. Another bugler would sound in other quarters, more cheers, lustier than ever. The boys began to actually feel as if Forrest had changed his purpose and was really there with all the artillery. While those artillery calls sounding here and there were making our hearts glad, they did the unmaking for Hawkins and his men. Word was passed around to those nearest the stockade, when they were marched out, stacked arms, they were to rush with a yell, get between them and their arms.

It was a surprise and shock to the enemy, could not understand it, were not long left in ignorance. The buglers, horse holders and negroes came bounding in when they saw the surrender was accomplished. The negroes in the lead, yelling here is your artillery, Toot! Toot! Toot! with all their thumbs stuck in their ears, working the hand like a mule's ear. Our negroes, that followed our fortunes through the war, as cooks and servants, were truly as jubilant at success as we, their masters, and as sorrowful at reverses. There are some yet left to join with us in our reunions and they meet with a hearty welcome from all.

After the capture, we raided the stockade, it was pretty bountifully supplied with army supplies. Took what we could carry well on our horses and set fire to the balance and marched off with the prisoners, their officers riding, the privates walking four abreast with our men in single file on each side. It soon commenced a gentle rain. The prisoners equipped themselves with a new outfit of clothing and blankets from their store. With the rain and forced march they were soon jaded and overburdened with the weight of their clothing, began to throw aside first one thing and then another. Some in dropping their heavy U. S. blankets would take their knives and cut and tear them to pieces. At that we boys would laugh, tell them we were well supplied, and if we should run short all we had to do was to find the Tennessee Yanks to get all we wanted without even a fight. In casting aside their clothing we discovered inside their vests a breastplate, the first and only time I saw one during the war. We had our fun at their expense. With breastplates, behind a ten-foot wall of dirt and logs, and then could not fight. We captured 525 rank and file, all could fight, no horse holders. Our strength 475, one-fourth holding horses, a victory of 350 on the firing line, against 525 behind breastworks and breastplates not a victory, "Vi et Armis," but strategy and name of Forrest. In the capture, we noticed we did not get any flag, for it was usual for all commands to have a flag, but supposed they probably did not need one as they would not appreciate it enough to defend it. We were not left long in suspense about the flag. We had not gone more than a mile when Ab Estes the flag-bearer of Company D came riding up with the enemy's flag inverted trailing below our flag. They were somewhat surprised at its appearance, having given it to a negro to bury and were sure it was safe. Estes was about the last of our boys in the stockade, he noticed a negro to be somewhat excited and nervous, watching him pretty close. He (Estes) drew his pistol, with it pointed near the negro's head, ordered him to go and get it, not knowing there was anything hid, but a guess. The negro begged him not to shoot, he would get it, dropping on his knees he went to scratching in the dirt and soon unearthed the regimental flag and a pair of pistols. In camp that night the prisoners were kept under guard, except the officers, they were paroled on honor, a mark of respect at times given the officers, but which seven of them that night violated. One of the officers that night approached Estes, the captor of their flag, wanted to know what he would take for it. Estes replied it was not for sale. The officer stated why he was anxious to get it, his sister made it, presented it to the regiment in a speech at Huntingdon, Tennessee. Estes, a splendid soldier, quiet and not of many words, said to him, "Your sister in that speech said or at least thought she was going to give it to men that would defend it, as she is now mistaken, if she is good looking, after this unpleasantness is over will come to Haywood County, where I live, she and I can probably make a trade, but you and I never. Say to her it is in the hands of men who know how to defend such emblems."

Since the restoring of flags has become a fad and no doubt commendable, I at our annual reunions have consulted with members of the 7th Tennessee Cavalry in restoring this flag to the 7th Tennessee (Federals) which met with a hearty approval. But so far have been unable to locate it. Ab Estes, the captor, having died some time ago and his family not knowing what has become of it. Getting to Jackson safely with our prisoners, we there met General Forrest, who had just returned from the Paducah, Kentucky, raid. We were more successful than Forrest. So the laugh and ridicule we anticipated might happen did not occur.

When General Forrest was informed of the seven officers violating their parole of honor he was furious and made Colonel Hawkins and the remainder of his officers (who were still allowed to ride) dismount and foot it, in mud ankle deep. But Forrest, easily made mad, did not remain so long. After tramping afoot for a mile or so they were remounted. At that time in Jackson we had a few Union men, one of them Jas. McCree, who took it upon himself to notify the Federal command on Tennessee River of Forrest being in Jackson with 600 or 700 prisoners and his force not much more; that he could be intercepted en route South, the prisoners released and Forrest probably captured. This Forrest by some means found out, had McCree arrested, carried him just across the river near Jackson, with the full purpose of shooting him. McCree was looked upon as a clever inoffensive man by the citizens of Jackson and they were surprised at his arrest with the charge brought against him. Knowing of Forrest's purpose, several of Jackson's best citizens followed on across the river where Forrest had halted to carry out the execution. The citizens pleaded and begged, could not but believe there was a mistake, and terrible it would be to summarily execute a good citizen if it should finally prove to be so. Forrest yielded, turned McCree loose with this admonition, "I know you to be guilty, through the interception of these good men you are free, but never let me here any more of your crookedness." Mr. McCree, years after the war, when he had been honored to the position of Trustee of the County, told me it was the closest shave of his life. Forrest was right, he was guilty. After that I did not dare to think, let alone act disloyal to the South. Late in the evening on our way South, the enemy were reported in strong force at Purdy (thirty miles south of Jackson). We had discovered a small force on our flank and rear. Forrest came riding down our line with his escort, going back to the rear saying, "Boys, if we are attacked save your prisoners and then we will clean them up" (the attacking party). I was riding along with Captain "Black-Hawk" Hays (prisoner) and he heard Forrest. He said to me, "What does that mean?" I said, "You understand the English language, Captain, it means exactly what it implied, you are not to get away." He answered, "That's hell, but I suppose it's right, I would do so myself if our positions were reversed." It proved to be a false alarm, the enemy, as Mr. McCree told me, did receive his dispatch but were too faint-hearted to attack Forrest.

From there on to Andersonville prison the way was clear, it being the finis of 7th Tennessee Federals for the remainder of the war owing to the cruel and heartless edict of Grant and Lincoln, "No exchange of prisoners."

Our flag of truce was fired on by three of Hawkins' men, one of whom is living in Jackson, or was a short time ago. We have had several chats over this fight, I should say capture. He says, "Hawkins and all the others of his command, save the three who fired upon the flag of truce, were terribly *hacked* and humiliated that Forrest was not there in person, but we three were the happiest fellows in the world at his absence. Colonel Hawkins had notified us Forrest would be certain to call for the men who had fired on the flag of truce and he (Hawkins) would have to deliver them up. Being a dastardly act, Forrest would make quick work of our execution." Fortunate indeed, for them. Forrest would have noticed such an act and its punishment would have been fully carried out, so Jackson would at least be minus one citizen by count if nothing more.

The days of chivalry can not be confined to the past, in the times of the knight and knight-errantry. In the stirring events of 1861 and 1865 were the exploits akin to the acts of the Knights Templars of yore.

In the raids of the Federals on the rich prairie land of Northeast Mississippi, the Federals had sent out a scouting party of near 100 men in the vicinity of Aberdeen, Mississippi.

Two companies of the 7th Tennessee Cavalry about the same number were on a scout in the same territory. Being a level country, interspersed with groves of timber a party could be seen some distance. It so happened with these two scouting parties, they recognized they were about equal in force and their mission the same as scouts. They continued their advance toward each other, with no firing. When with several hundred yards of each other the Federal commander halted his party, advanced alone; as he did so our men halted. When in distance to be heard, he stated, "as they were about equally matched and both on the same errand, instead of a general engagement, would leave the issue to one of each party in a sabre duel."

This officer was a German, and the Germans as a nation were experts in the use of the sabre, dueling common then and in vogue to this day on the field of honor decided by the sabre, their favorite weapon.

It was out of the rules of dueling (at that time not obsolete in the South) for the challenger to choose the weapon. No doubt it was a bloodless victory he desired, knowing too that the sabre was not our strong arm, but the pistol, which if used, someone stood a good chance of being placed hors de combat. Our boys did not demur, for with them was a Polander, an expert with the sabre, Poland, like Germany, used the sabre. Our Polander, a regular athlete, six feet in height, weighing 180 pounds, with no surplus flesh. He was eager to accept the challenge, did so, understanding the vanquished party to stop scouting and retire to their command.

They met on middle ground, mounted—a horseback duel. It was but an instant after they clashed the sword of the German went flying from his hands. The combat was over. The two parties came together, cracked jokes and chatting, not as a few moments before enemies, but the best of old friends. This lasted about an hour, when the German mounted his men and returned to his command. Ours continued their scout without molestation.

A gallant way to decide who should be top of the situation, better than a bloody conflict that would have no effect either way on the impending battle.

TISHOMINGO CREEK

OR

BRYCE'S CROSS ROADS

BY

WILLIAM WITHERSPOON

———————

JACKSON, TENN.
PUBLISHED BY THE AUTHOR
1906

TISHOMINGO CREEK OR BRYCE'S CROSS ROADS

I was a member of the 7th Tennessee, Company L, high private two years and Lieutenant two years.

On June 8, 1864, the 7th Tennessee (cavalry) met the advance of the Federals near Ripley, Mississippi, and skirmished with them that day, going into camp late in the evening at Booneville, Mississippi, where we met General Forrest with a part of his command. The next day three men were to be shot for desertion. Two were shot—one, a mere boy—was reprieved. This was the first and only time I ever witnessed a public official execution. That night about midnight, as near as I can come at it, for we had some time before crawled into our "chebangs" (a "chebang" is an oil cloth which "Uncle Sam" furnished all of Forrests cavalry, 7 x 4 feet, stretched over a pole on two forks about two feet high with the sides pinned to the ground) and were fast asleep, when an order came to me to send L. Tanner, a member of my company, to General Forrest. Tanner was formerly an engineer on the Mobile and Ohio Railroad (Booneville is on the M. and O. R. R.). Now this is what I get from Tanner: He carried General Forrest on an engine to West Point, where General S. D. Lee was with about 3,500 men. Generals Lee and Forrest consulted on the engine, in the presence of Tanner, swearing him to secrecy in regard to the impending battle. Not far from day, Tanner came to my "chebang" and said he had something to tell me, and that he knew I would not give him away. He then told me the plan of the battle, Forrest was to fall back toward West Point until Lee and Forrest could unite their forces, and then the fight should begin. Now, remember, that General Forrest had, all told, only 3,200 men and Captain John Morton, with the celebrated four "Bull Pups" (as Morton's artillery was called by the boys). General Lee, with 3,500 men and some artillery, how much I don't know, nor is it material, as it nor General Lee, either himself or men, were in the battle. General Sturgis (Federal) had 9000 infantry, 3000 cavalry and twenty-two pieces of artillery.

Does not Tanner's story, of the plan of the battle told on the engine, look reasonable? Consider the forces on each side and what "West Pointer" would not have decided to join the Confederate forces before giving battle? I do not say this in disparagement of West Point Generals, but old "common sense," a rare commodity, would have so advised, but it was a reckoning without the host, for Forrest never did anything as anyone else would have done, or even thought of doing, in regard to a fight. He was all alone, none ever came near to him or his like, but Stonewall Jackson. I am somewhat digressing, but it can be excused in an old Veteran, a follower of the "Wizard of the Saddle." About sunrise "boots and saddles" had sounded—we were forming into line by companies, when General Forrest came riding by and remarked to us, "You boys had your fun the other day (alluding to our skirmish with the "Yanks" at Ripley) and I am going to put you boys in the rear." As he called skirmishing fun, we boys did enjoy it from the manner in which we acted—were not in any great danger, either to man or horse, and as it resulted in that day's skirmish, neither were hurt. Our plan was this, we were about 400 strong, 100 of this number were sent around the flanks and rear of the enemy to gather reliable information of their strength. General Forrest never placed much reliance on the "featherbed scouts" as he termed our scouting companies, when a battle was pending. We then divided the 300 left in two parts. The road from Ripley, Mississippi, going southeast on which the enemy was traveling runs upon a ridge with deep hollows on each side, the tree-tops in the hollows not more than on a level with the road. Just before meeting the enemy their cavalry, 3000 strong, was marching in front. One of their division (150 men) would select a good place for ambush, the other (150) would fall back to the next suitable place for an ambuscade. As the enemy got near enough for good execution with our rifles and pistols, our boys would pour into their ranks a deadly volley, mount their horses and scamper back beyond the second part lying in ambush, hide themselves at the next suitable place. I don't care how brave and well disciplined troops may be, a sudden deadly volley, poured into them will temporarily "knock them up," throw them into confusion, and before a rally can be made our boys are out of reach of their shots, galloping merrily on to the next rendezvous. This was kept up pretty well all day, leaving them in time for us to reach Booneville about night. So we were placed. General Lyon (Confederate) was ordered to go out and meet the Yanks and see what they were doing. Captain Morton with the "Bull Pups" started towards West Point. Does not this look like Tanner's story was true? What changed the program?

Forrest, riding along with General Lyon or Rucker, remarked, "It is hot and dry; Sturgis is not expecting a fight and he (Sturgis) is stretched out on the road seven miles and I can whip him as fast as he can get his men up." Ordered General Lyon when he met the Yanks—"Charge and give them hell, they (the Yanks) will fall back and for him (General Lyon) to keep charging and giving them hell and I'll soon be there with you." And that is just what happened. By 9 o'clock a.m. the fight was on. We moved out from camp that morning, in the rear, marching quietly and orderly, and from what I thought I knew of the doings for that day, felt satisfied I could go another day with a whole hide, but what tranquility and peace of mind I had soon vanished. The order load, trot,

and soon enforced to the gallop and into the run, by the right
we wheeled, fronted into line, dismount, action front. We were
near a field in corn about knee high. In that cornfield was a
Yankee skirmish line. Fifty volunteers were called on to form a
skirmish line to drive the Yankee line back; 100 men jumped
forward; fifty ordered back to our main line. This field was
long and narrow; the timber about it was scrub oak and black-
jack. Over the fence we went, following our skirmishes—none
firing but the skirmish line. General Rucker was with us and
our field officers mounted. About midway the field our mounted
men were dismounted (horses shot). Nearing the opposite side
of the field we discovered the Yanks had doubled down the
rail fence, with logs on top, behind which the Yanks were lying,
with a bright line of steel shining in front (their guns poked
through the cracks of the fence). Their (the Federals) skirmish
line got over behind the fence. Ours halted until we walked
(all across that field was a walk) up and got into line. We
were then not more than 200 yards apart. Up to this time firing
was kept up by the skirmish lines; after their getting over the
fence they ceased firing and so did ours. All at once as if by a
preconcerted signal a silence fell over the battlefield. In its deep
stillness it was awful. More trying on one's backbone and grit
than any charge on hill or breastworks, amid the bursting of
bombshells, the sharp crackle of grapeshot and cannister
mingled with the more dangerous and fatal sharp zip, zip, of
minnie. A calm, that happens now and then in battle, and
which portends such awful and direful calamities to the participants facing each other, it is then a man's (I should say a
boy's, for most of us were boys) whole life becomes a living
panorama before him. I could see my father and good mother
and myself, a little tot, playing upon her lap—my schoolhood
days—romping and frolicking with my schoolmates. In fact, a

man's whole life is before him and all in a moment. Look up and down the line. Not a word spoken. All with as but one thought: Where shall I be in a few moments?

Just in front of us was a slight rise, thinly covered with broomsedge. We had been soldiering long enough to know what to expect and when. This rise was about seventy-five yards in front of their hastily improvised breast works of fence rails and logs. Now I shall relate what was a strange coincidence and to what we owed our salvation, personally, and the success of our arms in that fight. It will explain itself further on. Word was passed down the line in a whisper, "hold your fire and at the flash of their guns every man to fall to his face, and then up and with a yell and volley, and over that fence go." As we got up on that rise the Federal commander's voice rang out: "Make ready! Take aim! Fire!" I can hear that voice even to this day (over forty-two years ago) when I look on old Time. In that volley, we lost out of 350 men, 75 killed and disabled from any more service and a great many only with temporary wounds. Why they did not kill all of us I can not say, only the Yanks could not shoot as the Rebs did. Over the fence we went and then, as can be seen, correctly pictured in Dr. Wyeth's History of Forrest and His Men, took place a hand-to-hand fight, Yanks and Rebs terribly mixed, but it did not last long— just possibly couldn't, for there would have been no one left to tell the tale. I was near Sergeant-Major Huhn when he was clubbed with a gun by a stalwart Yank. My old school-mate, bedmate and comrade, Henry J. Fox (now living at Humboldt, Tennessee), was upon the other side of Huhn about the same distance as myself, shot the Yank dead with his navy six. He was not more than three feet distant, if that. Other histories of that fearful holocaust give credit to others of killing Huhn's assailants, which they probably did, but the killing of the one who clubbed Huhn was certainly shot dead by Fox. We (Fox and myself) were somewhat in the rear of Huhn, but near enough to have touched him with our hands. Huhn was a brave and fearless soldier. It was there the sabre and navy six decided who was boss. The Yanks had seven shooting Spencer rifle and sabre; Forrest's men the old Sharp carbine and two navy sixes each. Dr. Wyeth in his history (and I gather the same from Federals I have met who were there) places three regiments behind that fence, the Third Iowa, an Illinois and a Michigan. What a victory! Out in the open ground! Not firing a single gun from the line until we had received their fire! Rushing breastworks with men lying coolly and calmly on the ground taking dead aim! Firing a deliberate volley at the word of command in broken doses: "Make ready! Take aim! Fire!" at seventy-five yards, and then for one regiment, the old 7th Tennessee (Confederate) not more than 350 men in line, to utterly rout and place *hors de combat* three regiments, at least three to one if not more.

It has been my good fortune, in our reunions, to meet with several Federals who were in the same fight and fought "vis-a-vis." When I say good fortune, I mean it. I really enjoyed it. I have nothing but the utmost respect for one who has shouldered his musket through conviction and duty. At one of our reunions, just after eating my dinner and lighting my pipe, I strolled to a bench, took my seat by a gentleman dressed in citizen's garb, I with my uniform of gray. He noticed it and said, "I see you have once been a soldier, what command did you belong to?" I answered, "Forrest's." "Were you at the Guntown fight?" I looked him in the face and said, "You are a Yankee?" "No, not a Yankee, but a Westerner. How did you know that I was on the other side?" "That fight is called Guntown by the Federals, Bryce's Cross Roads or Tishomingo Creek by the Confederates." I asked if he was there. He replied, "Yes, in the 3rd Iowa Cavalry." "In that fight you were behind a fence doubled down with logs and brush piled on top?" "Yes." "You were armed with Spencer seven-shooting rifles?" "Yes. How is it," he asked, "you know all this?" "I was one of the boys in that field, in your front, and after driving you from the fence and we had taken possession, in front of me on the opposite of the fence was a dead Yank with a 3rd Iowa cartridge box belted around him and the noted 7-shooting Spencer rifle in his hand. I found his cartridge box full, exchanged my Sharp's carbine (which only shot one time) for his and went through that fight with a 3rd Iowa Cartridge box belted around me and a Spencer rifle. But in the next engagement discarded the much-lauded Spencer and went back to the old reliable Sharp's carbine. The Spencer had too much trigger works, getting out of fix, in battle with men, was not like a gun becoming cranky in a squirrel or duck hunt. Forty-five Federals were reported killed at that fence." "My brother," said the 3rd Iowan, "was killed there."

We had a good talk over the fight. I asked the question, "How was it that 350 Rebs did whip three regiments of Yanks (not Yanks, as he termed them Westerners) well armed as they were, from that fence?"

He said, "Sturgiss was drunk that day."

"Ah, no," I remarked, "that won't do for Sturgiss was not there with you and probably not in a mile of that place."

"Well, you are right," he said. "I will now tell you. There are three circumstances that helped you in your victory. First, while lying behind that fence, quietly and calmly (if a fellow can be said to be quiet and calm in battle, for you remember you were coming on us in a walk and not firing) we were ordered to hold our fire until command was given. We talked to each other with our guns pointed through the fence, taking good aim on your advancing line. We will kill every man in that line. At the word fire, we poured a deadly volley into you, and as we expected, you all fell and we were sure that we had completely wiped you from the face of the earth, but to our surprise and astonishment, it seemed that the dead line had bounded to their feet, with double their number, yelling and shooting like mad devils. Second, you were so close, it enabled you to get over the fence behind us before we could recover from our surprise. Third, you Rebs had, besides your carbines, two navy sixes, instead we had sabres. You saw and we both know the difference in close quarters between the sabre and navy sixes."

Now, this attack was by our center on the center of the Federals, General Lyon on our right and General Bell on our left. Apparently all firing had ceased to see how that charge would result.

When it was over and success assured, the firing became general on both sides of us. Lieutenant Colonel W. F. Taylor (now a cotton merchant of Memphis, Tenn.) was in command of the 7th Tennessee that day. A purer, braver, or better man never commanded a body of men than W. F. Taylor. As we could hear the Yanks talking in the dense black-jack woods, not far in our front, we got back over the fence, anticipating the Yanks would probably attempt to retake the position.

In a short while, an exclamation from Colonel Taylor, "Look, boys," and pointing to our left we saw that General Bell was falling back and the Yankee flags were passing down in our rear. Colonel Taylor said, "Boys, this looks like Fort Alton for some, Johnson's Island for others, but we will stick to this fence and do the best we can." Privates were sent to the former, officers to the latter.

About that time there was a crashing of limbs and brush, and a voice rang out, "Where is the 7th Tennessee?" We all knew that voice. It was General Forrest on his noble, dapple iron-gray.

Colonel Taylor answered, "Here we are, General, what is left of us; we suffered severely in that charge and I have only about seventy-five men left."

Now, to understand our position, the field, a narrow strip, extended farther up on our left where the fence barricade was, seemed to be an offset or rather a corner in the field. General Forrest rode out in the edge of the opening and ordered us to charge (By the way, I don't think General Forrest ever mastered Hardee's tactics any further or had any use for it, than the single command, "Charge!" He often said he could whip any man if he could get in the first blow.) the d—d Yankees in the rear. I notice some writers on Forrest say he seldom cursed; well, the fellow that writes that way was not where the 7th Tennessee was that day. In camp he did not swear, but in battle his acts and words were the first, superhuman, and the later, old Nick himself would have been dismounted.

Colonel Taylor replied to General Forrest, in his quiet way, "General, I have not more than seventy-five men."

Colonel Taylor had seen too many Yankee flags passing in our rear for seventy-five men to handle. And we boys thought the Colonel was looking at the situation about right, but not so with Forrest. We were ordered into line to make the charge. Our movement was too slow to suit Forrest, he would curse, then praise, and then threaten to shoot us himself, if we were so afraid the Yanks might hit us. All this time he was sitting on his horse in the open field; the Yanks espied him, and then what a deluge of grapeshot, cannister, bomb shells, ricochet shots plowed up the ground to the front, to the rear, to the sides, above and under old Dapple Gray, but Forrest and old Dapple Gray did not seem to care. It looked fearful to that meagre, thin line of seventy-five men. I expected every moment to see Forrest and horse torn into fragments, but good fortune favored him. As I have before stated, he would praise in one breath, then in the next would curse us and finally said, "I will lead you."

Colonel Taylor replied to us, "Boys, if he leads, we will have to follow."

Forrest ordered us to give the yell and follow. We did so after getting out into the opening, where bombshells were bursting and ricochet shots coming along like winding blades. We hustled and across that narrow field was a race—double quick nowhere in it. But Forrest fooled us, he did not lead; instead, he went down the way we had advanced like a bolt of lightning by the side of the Yanks and got to Bell's men, who were falling back and urged them to rally; told them he had the d—d Yankees whipped, was charging them in the rear and one more rally and he would have them. Now, all of Forrest's men had such confidence in him they were easy to believe, whatever he said, and the rally was made.

Now, what was the situation of the apparently victorious Yanks? They heard that Rebel yell and firing in their rear, they did not know it was only a handful of men. They halted, and it was then that Bell's men rallied and with a yell, charged. Just as we got across the field and about to get over in the woods, here came the Yanks back in a long, sweeping trot; we got down to the fence and it was then we had our fun shooting through the cracks of a fence. It was now between 3 and 4 o'clock p.m., and the bulk of the fight that day over with.

You can not speak of this fight without telling of Captain John Morton (Forrest's chief of artillery) and his renowned four "Bull Pups" (not that they were sure enough bull pups of the dog species, but what we boys called Morton's artillery). It would be like acting Hamlet with Hamlet left out. I met with Captain Morton at Jackson, Tennessee, shortly after the publication in Harper's Magazine of Dr. Wyeth's History of Forrest and His Men on the Tishomingo Creek battle. As we were participants in the fight, we talked about Dr. Wyeth's version of it. Captain Morton asked me to give him my idea.

I said to him, "We opened that fight about 9 o'clock a.m., with not more than 3,200 men, all cavalry, against the Federal forces, consisting of 9000 infantry, 3000 cavalry and twenty-two pieces of artillery, and we had no artillery in the fight until past 12 o'clock (noon) and by 4 o'clock p.m. we had the Yanks completely routed and had captured more men and guns than we had in the engagement that day."

He said, "You and I agree in all except I can be definite as to the time and amount of artillery. I (Captain Morton) looked at my watch the first gun I fired, it was exactly 1:30 p.m. and I did not lose any time in opening with the Bull Pups after getting on the battle ground. I went up in a run, General Forrest ordered me to get up close and give them (the Yanks) grape and cannister double-shotted. I remarked to the General I had no support, he (Forrest) said, 'Go, I would like to see the Yanks capture you, Morton,' and go I did. You boys had driven them to the cross roads and they were massed forty deep, and you bet it was terrible execution."

"Dr. Wyeth gives you nine pieces of artillery and we boys did not see but the Bull Pups."

"The four Bull Pups were all I had, and what is strange to me, I got a letter from Dr. Wyeth stating that he was writing a history of that fight, and as I (Captain Morton) was Forrest's chief of artillery, give him what the artillery did in that engagement. I wrote to him just what I have told you. I am surprised at his version. Now, I can't think Dr. Wyeth would not wish to give Forrest and his men all the credit due them. He must have thought after getting the view of the participants, it looked to him like 'there were too many squirrels up that tree,' it would be better to moderate it a little for his readers would look upon his book as a romance or fiction."

And as he makes it, it was a superb victory with the numbers engaged, the results accomplished. It has not been excelled or even equaled in ancient or modern times.

Dr. Wyeth's version: "Confederates, 4875 men and 12 pieces artillery; Federals, 8000 men and 22 pieces of artillery."

At the Louisville reunion, 1905, I met with General Lyons, of Kentucky, the same General Lyons who opened the fight. His version: "We (Confederates) did not have exceeding 2800 men, and Morton's four Bull Pups. I (Lyons) know what I say to be true for I was in a position to get the official facts, and did so. Sturgiss (Federal) had 13,000 men and twenty-two pieces of artillery."

We fought dismounted, consequently every fourth man was a horse-holder, 3200 (my version) minus (one-fourth) 800, gives 2800, who whipped and all but extirpated a picked command of more than four and one-half times their strength.

Read the histories of Grant and Sherman, written by themselves, and they will tell you that force under Sturgiss and Grierson was selected for the express purpose of capturing or killing that Hell-hound, as General Sherman so often termed General N. B. Forrest.

I am again digressing from the fight, but what old Vet can help it, when he is writing about such things. He forgets the present and is living over again those stormy days.

When Sturgiss left Memphis, Tennessee, in his command

were two full regiments (900 each) of negroes. Before starting on the march they knelt upon the ground, swearing eternal vengeance on Forrest and his men, and revenge for Fort Pillow, with black flags having inscribed thereon "Remember Fort Pillow." From Memphis to Ripley, Mississippi, Sturgiss and his officers were boasting and telling the citizens living along the route they were carrying the negroes along to guard Forrest and his men back to Memphis, and that they would fare as did the negroes at Fort Pillow. All this and whatever else was said or done by them was reported to us by our faithful scouts. Can you wonder now that we fought not like common mortals, but like incarnate fiends of hell itself? We will now get back to the fight where I wandered off about 4 o'clock p.m.

We boys knew there were negroes somewhere, but up to that time they were not "come-at-able." We kept asking each other where were the d—d negroes? Most of us did, not all, we had some good boys, who did not use cuss words. Just about that time, shortly after the terrible havoc by Morton's Bull Pups, a cry rang out not far off, "Here are the d—d negroes!" We had been fighting from 9 a.m. to 4 p.m. constant; although we fought like fiends, we were tired like mortals and were feeling pretty well fagged out, but when the cry rang out, "Here are the d—d negroes," new life, energy and action coursed through our bodies and we bounded forward with the fleetness and agility of Old Leather Stockings, of Fennimore Cooper fame. The negroes were in line on a slight ridge and when they heard that yell, coupled with "Here are the d—d negroes" repeated, here and there, all over the woods, and then saw the maddening rush of the infuriated Rebs, they did as mortal men will do under like circumstances—threw down their guns, without firing a shot, and bounded off with the fleetness of a deer.

Sturgiss, in his report, says he brought up the negroes as the last resort to check the enemy. Who can blame the poor deluded negro? After listening, for ten days past, to the boasting of the Yanks how easily with their superior force they would whip Forrest and turn all prisoners over to them (negroes). The whites (Yanks) were to do all the fighting and the negroes the guarding. Keeping the negroes in the rear and as the last resort shows this to be the plan, but as Burns says, "The best laid plans of mice and men aft gang a-glee."

One can imagine the 1800 negroes lying upon the ground in some sequestered spot, listening to the sharp crackle of their many rifles, and to the roar of their many pieces of artillery. It would not be long before they (negroes) would have the men who did such havoc on their race at Fort Pillow. How, in their almost savage imagination, did they exult how they would dispose of Forrest. Some would say, shoot him; others, no, we will play Indian, and burn him. No punishment that the most savage mind of the wilds of Africa could concoct would not have been meted out to General Forrest, and his men would have come in for their share, if the battle had been reversed, and the Yanks would have stood quietly by, notwithstanding their boasted civilization, and rejoiced.

The Fort Pillow affair is not, by long odds, what it is reported to be by the Yankee side of the house, and our own (Southern) make too many apologies. It needs none. The negroes had blue buckets (the common water bucket at that time) filled with whiskey and tin dippers (to drink with) passed around on their line on the breastworks, and were drinking and making sport and contumely remarks of our boys lying in line and in front and near them, while the first flag of truce was pending. The fact (about the whiskey) was reported to General Forrest; he said, "I will give them time to get drunk," and sent the second flag.

The object was accomplished—the negroes got drunk. Major Booth, the commander, the only *soldier and gentleman* in the fort, was killed at the first of the fight, left the negroes without a head. The white element were all Tennessee home-made Yanks—who had joined the Federals not through any sense of patriotism, but for booty and plunder, and as bad as the worst Yank could do in their line, and they were pretty adept, the home-made Yank could beat him two to one. Enough of this, now back to Tishomingo.

After the rout of the Federals, about 5 p.m., we mounted our horses and began the pursuit. The 7th Tennessee (Forrest) was now in front. Early in the night we overtook a part of their wagon train, filled with provisions for both man and beast. We were ordered to dismount and be our own commissary sergeant, but not to unsaddle. A queer order, we thought, as tired and hungry as both ourselves and horses were. We believed that Forrest had just followed on after Sturgiss, knowing he would soon overtake a part of the wagon train, and his tired, wornout, hungry boys would enjoy a feast from Uncle Sam's larder—and we did. Our haversacks were soon emptied of the corn bread and beef, what to fill them with was hard to decide. Hard-tack, Ham, breakfast bacon, coffee, sugar, cheese and the Lord only knows all the good things they did have; would fill our haversacks, see something we liked better than what we had, another emptying; but you can bet we were eating all the time, and so were our good horses—they, too, had their white cake—shelled oats, hay and corn. Had not more than finished eating, in fact, had not quit, were ordered to mount and fall into line. My company (L) was in front of the regiment and consequently next to the Yanks. About midnight came upon more of the wagon train (Federals), about half dozen, they were burning. We halted and sent word down the line to General Forrest, "Enemy in front and burning their wagon train." Came back the order:

"Move up in front!"

"Enemy in front burning their wagon train," was sent back, would soon be followed by an order from Forrest, "Move up in front!" These orders passed several times down and up the line. Finally one and the last, a little more emphatic: "General Forrest says, G—d d—n it, move up in front!" Forrest was getting hot under the collar. Had started our word, "Enemy," etc., down the line, when a rustle and snapping of bushes and limbs (we were in the woods), was heard coming up the line. Looking around, there were Iron Gray and Forrest; and you can bet again, safely, *we moved up.*

"Don't you see the d—d Yanks are burning my wagons? Get off your horses and throw the burning beds off!"

In a jiffy every wagon was surrounded by men as close as they could stand and off the burning beds went. One of our Lieutenants, a gallant and good soldier, did not dismount. General Forrest espied him and yelled at him why he did not help? The Lieutenant remarked he was an officer. Forrest made at him with his sabre drawn, "I'll officer you," and no acrobat ever was quicker in a movement than our brave lieutenant in getting to the ground; and a full hand he made in upsetting the wagon beds. Now, our Lieutenant was one who would not shirk any duty, was one of our bravest men. Like a great many officers he felt that kind of duty was not in an officer's line, and they (officers) generally acted so if "Marse Bedford" was not around.

We moved on and somewhere between midnight and day came to a wide slough or creek bottom; it was miry and truly the slough of despair and despond to the Yanks. Their artillery and wagons which had heretofore escaped capture were now bogged down and had to be abandoned. This slough was near knee deep in mud and water, with logs lying here and there. On top of every log were Yanks perched, as close as they could be, for there were more Yanks than logs—reminded me of chickens at roost, except each Yank had a lighted candle holding above his head saying, "Don't shoot, don't shoot." Two hundred and seventy-five men and eighteen pieces of artillery captured there. We, who were in front, were ordered to pay no attention to prisoners, those in the rear would look after that.

After passing the slough we came to a creek, Forrest in front. He noticed some obstruction in the creek and asked what it was, some one answered, "I think it is a piece of artillery, but can't see well." Hold on, Forrest said, until I light this candle (he was carrying a candle in his pocket). The light developed a piece of artillery and two dead horses. We turned up the creek a short distance and crossed over. Lieutenant Livingston remarked to General Forrest, "all of the enemy's force are over here and we have but a small force, not exceeding ten men." "That is enough," he replied, "ten good men can whip 1000 in the fix we have them."

We were very close to the rear of the Federals. In fact, they thought we were a part of their force. It was pretty dark and some of them would drop back and ride with us, talk about the fight. One fell in with me and remarked: "Old Forrest gave us hell today."

"Yes," I said, "we were fooled about old Forrest's strength. He (Forrest) certainly had 50,000 men in that fight."

"Yes, you have that about right, the woods were full of them and they were everywhere. I don't know how many of my regiment got away, but I am safe and will take care of

Number One from now on. I have a good horse and can do so."

I thought the joke had been humored long enough, with the click of my navy six and it pointing dangerously near him, I said, "You are now with Forrest's men, hand over your arms and roll off that horse."

"No, you can't fool me." But a better inspection than he had at first given us, convinced him that he was in the wrong pew, and off he tumbled. This happened not once but often the latter part of the night with us in front.

Daylight, the rear of the Federals not more than one hundred yards in the front. General Forrest, as always with him when seeing the blue coats, yelled out "Charge."

Colonel Taylor said to him, "We have not over twenty men in sight."

Half a dozen men ordered back to hurry up the boys. We did straggle a little that night; just think of what we had gone through the day before. Up at daylight getting breakfast, sunrise in the saddle, fighting from 9 a.m. till 5 p.m. with no intervals of any moment at rest; with no slow movement, no sound of dinner horn or bell that day; instead, the rattle of spurs, the sharp zip, zip, and singing minnie, the roar of cannon, bombshells bursting, ricochet shots skipping along with plenty of grape and cannister. Such a feast the sons of Mars might enjoy, but sons of Mother Earth had as soon be excused. Half an hour at supper at the expense of Uncle Sam's warm invitation, in the saddle all night long. Yes, we straggled a little, but Forrest did not get mad. Looking back now, I can not see how we did endure the hardships. I just guess Forrest had gotten us *used* to it.

By sunrise we had about 200 boys up and to charging we went. The Federal cavalry were in the rear of their infantry, we would rush the cavalry over the infantry (the infantry had thown away their arms) and consequently the infantry were prisoners. On the next hill the cavalry would make a faint stand, a yell with a charge and they were gone again. This charging was on tap all day up to their last stand, four miles north of Ripley, Mississippi, on the road to Salem, Mississippi. Forrest was raised near Salem and knew of an old road that went there. He divided his command and went with all the speed he could make on that route with part, but we boys that were behind the Yanks had them on the run and kept them running. When Forrest had reached Salem not more than twenty-five Yanks, as the citizens reported, had passed through Salem. Forrest felt sure he had bagged his game, but lo and behold! We met and not a Yank betwixt us. It was then, as Dr. Wyeth says in his history: "Forrest laid down upon the ground completely exhausted." Well, Forrest was not by himself in that condition, his boys were in it also.

We all felt bad about that handful of Yanks getting away, like the greedy boy—we wanted all. The fight and race was now over seventy-five miles from where we started. This may not be the exact distance, but I'm writing just as we boys called it at that time.

In this long fight, long in distance and time—seventy-five miles distance and two days and night in time—many acts of the heroic and *unheroic* happened. I shall speak of one of each that occurred within my knowledge. Of the first relates to Tanner, the M. and O. engineer I spoke of in the first of this article, a brave, gallant soldier, now dead, I think.

At the last stand by the Federals, four miles north of Ripley, Mississippi, when charged, they gave more resistance than they had been doing, but finally all ran except one, a fine looking, manly fellow, well mounted and well armed. He was sitting quietly upon his horse, about seventy-five yards from us in the woods, whence "all but him had fled," he could truly say. Tanner saw him, said to the boys, "Yonder's my meat," started towards him in a gallop, not expecting any resistance from one who was all but surrounded. When near, the Yank out with his pistol and about to fire, Tanner drove his spurs into his horse, at a bound was on the Yank, knocked him from his horse, jumped down a-straddle of the Yank as he was endeavoring to get up, wrenched the pistol from his hand and made him a prisoner. We asked the Yank why he had resisted? He said he was d—d tired of running, and had made up his mind to sell himself as dear as possible, that he let Johnny get too close. Fortunately for him, and probably fortunate for Tanner—both brave men—the death of both or either would not have made any change in the result.

The unheroic—if such a word, I hate to say the other meaning for the party made a good *camp soldier* and stayed with us throughout the war and was surrendered at Gainesville, Alabama. Previous to the war he was a fighter, at least made folks think so; he so maneuvered that he was never in battle from the first of the war until this fight. He had heard Forrest say, as he (Forrest) was passing by our command the morning previous to the battle, "You boys had your fun the other day, I am going to put you in the rear." As we were not to do any fighting that day, our fighter was not particular of his number. In forming our company line we count off by fours, now No. 4, when dismounted, and we fought near all the time dismounted, holds the horses of his set (1, 2, 3, 4). That morning, not being particular, his number was odd, either 1 or 3. My position was in the rear of my company to see that every man kept his place. To my surprise, and I am certain to his, when the order to load, trot, gallop and to the run came, we had probably gone a mile, my fighter was sitting on his horse by the roadside, with his saddle-blanket on the ground. I ordered him to his place; he went. Did not go far before he stopped with his saddle bags, containing all his clothes, on the ground. I ordered him again to his place, he went; had not gone far, there he was again on the roadside, pointing down to the ground, saying, "Lieutenant, I have dropped my carbine, pistols and cartridge box." He felt sure I would let him stop for these if I did not for his clothes and blanket, but I ordered one of the best men in the company to carry him to his place, which he did. In forming the line of battle at the cornfield I noticed he was holding a horse, I ordered him to his place. He replied he had neither gun, pistol or cartridge. I made No. 4, who was a brave soldier, hand up his arms to our fighter. I went to him when in line, the minnie balls were singing lively over our heads, told him he was not any more afraid than we were, and now was the trying time and just as soon as we commenced shooting the fright was all over, be a man. He went with us and through that charge. Having occasion to fill my canteen with water about 2 o'clock, passing near a log I heard a groan; thinking it might be one of our boys I went to it and there lay my fighter. I was knocked all to pieces. I promised myself I would never force another man in a fight. Of course, I expected to find him shot. I ran to him, lifted up his head in my arms.

"Don't you want water?"

"Yes."

"Where are you hurt?"

"Cannon ball struck, hit my leg."

One of the boys was with me, I had him to examine his leg while I was giving him water. All at once my comrade dropped his leg and remarked, "He is not hurt." I let go his head, jumped to my feet, when I said, "it is time we were

getting away from here, as the Yankees would soon be here."
He sprang from the ground and bounded off like a deer.

I did not see him again until the second day after, when
going into Ripley with a good squad of prisoners picked up in
the woods between Salem and Ripley. He was standing near
the Court House (Ripley) surrounded by a good group of
ladies—a hero. He had the day before been trailing in the rear
north of Ripley alone, twenty Yankees stepped out into the
road, he said to them, "I surrender." "No, you don't. You turn
around and take us back to Ripley," which he did. After getting
into Ripley, where were several hundred of Forrest's men, my
fighter made the Yanks get in his front and he marched in that
way to the Court House. One Reb bringing in twenty Yanks
alone made him the hero for the time. The ladies could not do
enough for him. As I got in with my prisoners he saw me and
came to me telling me how much better he had done. Of course
we boys laughed, not believing his story. The ladies soon spoke
up—said it was true—and that I should be proud of him. I
carried my prisoners to the Court House. He, unfortunately for
him, followed and when in the Court House one of his twenty
Yanks espied him, saying, "Here is our man, boys, that we
captured yesterday." After that our fighter had played; told me
he could not fight—put him on all duty. I did so, and he
surrendered with us at Gainesville, a good *camp soldier*.

After meeting Forrest near Salem, and no Yanks ahead
but that handful, we knew they had to be somewhere. It is a
ridgey, broken country, between Salem and Ripley, and we
scattered in small bodies on both sides of the road, just exactly
as we would have done had we been hunting rabbits in deep
snow time, feeling there was no more danger of a Yank
shooting than a rabbit's biting. It was fun—big sport; up and
down the hollows we would ride; come on them in squads

ranging from a half a dozen to twenty and more. Up would go their hands, exclaiming, "We surrender!" No sign of resistance, really unarmed, most of them had thrown away not only their arms but their haver-sacks, clothing and blankets; foot-sore, tired and hungry. But all that were not, what they considered their worst discomfort was having those negroes along with them. Conscience was now putting in its sharp and stinging work. They, the whites, knew how they had boasted and acted on that same road a few days before. The negroes of the oath, on bended knee at Memphis, and the black flags, their insults to the mothers and sisters probably of some of the men now after them. When found in mixed squads, Yanks and negroes, often they would be fighting, whites endeavoring to force the negroes away and the negroes equally determined on staying with the Yanks. The Yank afraid to be caught with the negro and the negro afraid to be caught without the Yank.

On their (Federals) way down South several negro soldiers entered a house in which a mother and several small children were living—the youngest, a baby boy, lying in the cradle. One of the negroes caught it up by the heels and said to the mother he would stop the breed of Forrest men, was about to dash its brains out against the door, when the mother, with the strength and ferocity of a lioness, snatched her child from the brute's hands and saved her baby boy. It was this and its like that rendered Forrest and his men irresistible, and the other (Federal) side quake and tremble when the battle was on. The question may be asked how it was possible Forrest whipped Sturgiss at Tishomingo. It can be attributed to several causes: His unexcelled and unequaled bravery; good common sense and judgment; the unbound confidence of the men in Forrest and whatever he undertook. Forrest was, in truth, a leader. He never said, go ahead boys! but "follow!" He was always in front and where the battle waxed warmest. This style of fighting was the reverse of West Pointism. Every man that could shoot was in the fight from start to finish; not as West Point, one-half to two-thirds held as a reserve, which we found to our cost at Britton Lane and Harrisburgh, where West Point controlled. Forrest went in to win—got in the first blow and won not by holding back men as a reserve to make a graceful or, more properly termed, a shameful retreat, which was generally practiced by West Pointers.

Forrest found Sturgiss as he predicted, stretched seven miles on the road, weather dry and hot. Sturgiss knew Forrest's strength, knew where Lee was, and his strength. West Point tactics said to Sturgiss: Forrest will not dare to fight with his small force (3200) but will fall back and make a junction with Lee and his 3500. West Point would have said (and as it did if Tanner's story is true) to Forrest, fall back. It would be foolhardy to tackle 12,000 with twenty-two pieces of artillery with your force, 3200 and four pieces of artillery. Join Lee's force, he is only thirty-five miles distant, and you may win or at least so cripple Sturgiss he will have to go back to Memphis. But Old Common Sense, Forrest's tactician, said, pitch into Sturgiss as you commanded General Lyon to do, with all your might, whip him as fast as he can get his men up, you are 200 stronger than his cavalry. Whip that before the infantry can be gotten to its support; you can handle the infantry as fast as it can get up; true, your men will have no rest, still their condition will be as good as the infantry that has already double-quicked from two to seven miles. Thus Forrest planned and fought, gaining a victory that almost annihilated Sturgiss' army. So it resolves itself into this: Forrest, with his alertness, bravery and good judgment, his style of fighting without reserves—with a small force, was vastly superior to a stronger, numerically, one to four and one-half, handled by West Point tactics. What material composed Forrest's cavalry? The best type of the young manhood of Kentucky, Tennessee, Alabama, Missouri and Mississippi. The equal of the earth. Furnished their own in everything—horses, accoutrements, arms and service—no expense to the Confederate government but for corn and beef —that not too plentiful or good. But we grumbled not; were not fighting for grub. The principles that actuated our grandsires in 1776 actuated us in 1861.

It is said history repeats itself. My grandfather, John Witherspoon, of North Carolina, fought with Marion, the great cavalry leader of the Revolutionary War, 1776, for the defense of his home against the aggression of England. He furnished his horse and squirrel rifle and was called by so doing a rebel against the best government on earth. I, his grandson, William Witherspoon, Jackson, Tennessee, followed the "Wizard of the Saddle," N. B. Forrest, the greatest cavalry leader the world has ever produced, throughout the Civil War; fighting for the defense of home and property, against the aggressions of the North. I, too, furnished my horse and the double-barrel shotgun I formerly shot squirrels with, and by doing so am called a rebel against the best government on earth. My grandfather was proud of the term "Rebel." I may have the love for the term "Rebel" by inheritance, yet I love it and will so teach my children. I simply look at it that grandfather in 1776 and myself in 1861 were standing in the same shoes.

CHAPTER FOUR

Private Hubbard's Notes

John Milton Hubbard was "of the conservatives who had voted steadily against secession," including a vote for Stephen A. Douglas for President. He had few illusions, moreover, about the prospects of success for secession. But when secession came, and the youngsters who had been his pupils in the "male academy" which he conducted at Bolivar, Tennessee, began to enlist, he felt that duty and loyalty called him to the same course.

In May, 1861, therefore, he rode away from Bolivar with the "Hardeman Avengers," who were to become Company E of the Seventh Tennessee Cavalry. Four years later, at Gainesville, Alabama, still Private Hubbard, he made out the paroles for the men of his company at the surrender.

The author of these "Notes" was born in Anson County, North Carolina, and was taken to Mississippi, a six weeks' journey by wagon, in 1850. He was educated at Centenary College in Louisiana and at the Florence Wesleyan University at Florence, Alabama, where he graduated in 1858. In the same year he married Miss Lucy Hawkins of Florence, who died before the outbreak of the war, leaving the young school teacher a widower with an infant son. The child remained with

137

his mother's family through the war, as is touchingly told in the "Notes."

Mr. Hubbard was a teacher in the old classical tradition— Latin, Greek and mathematics. When his fighting days were done he returned to Bolivar and re-opened his school in the railroad station which was not in use because no trains were running yet. In more than forty years of varied experience, he was president of the Female College at Stanford, Kentucky, and later of Howard Female College at Gallatin, Tennessee. He was twice married after the war—in 1868 to Miss Sallie Pybass of Bolivar, who became the mother of two sons, and two years after her death in 1887 to Miss Mary MacAnally, principal of the Marion Female Seminary in Alabama.

His notes are those of a thoughtful and observant soldier who seems to have enjoyed the confidence of fellow soldiers and officers alike. One of his fellow soldiers in the early days of the Seventh Tennessee was "Bedford Forrest, only a private like myself, whom I had known ten years before down in Mississippi." Hubbard and Forrest were not fellow privates for long but, as Hubbard remarks, he "had occasion afterward to see a good deal of him."

What Private Hubbard saw, and his reflections upon those things, throw light on the causes and the course of the rise of Private Forrest to Lieutenant-General Forrest.

Private Hubbard's observations were first printed for the author, in Memphis, in 1909. The success of this edition led to a reprinting in St. Louis in 1911, and a third edition, also printed in St. Louis, in 1913. The printing and sale of the book, says the retired school head turned author in the preface to the last edition "resulted in giving me congenial employment in my old age." Reading what he set down, it is believed, will give both pleasure and some insight into the ways and the minds of the men who fought with Forrest.

Note: In this reprinting of the Notes *Chapters II, III, IV and V have been omitted since they deal with the life and career of the regiment in what might be called the "non-Forrest" period.*

Chapter 1

MUSTERING IN—"GOOD-BYE, SWEETHEARTS"

I am to write here of men with whom I was associated in a great war, and of things in which I was a participant. To do even and exact justice shall be my aim, and there shall be no motive other than to give truthful accounts of men and events as they came under my personal observation.

When we mounted our horses at the Bills Corner, in Bolivar, Tennessee, and started for the war, there were one hundred and one of us. This company was composed largely of a jolly, rollicking set of young men from the farms of Hardeman County, who knew little of restraint and less of discipline. Like any other hundred and one men, promiscuously enlisted, some of these in time became fine soldiers, others fairly so, while still others dropped out of the ranks and abandoned the cause. One hundred and eighty-nine names were finally carried on the rolls, but from these a large company could have been taken which added nothing to the renown acquired by our regiment before the close of the war. Considering the fierce political contest through which the country had just passed and the thorough discussion of the questions at issue, the rapid enlistment of volunteers was surprising. It was evident that the election of a President by a party entirely sectional, and the open threats of a radical press in regard to slavery, had aroused an exuberance of Southern sentiment which the conservative element could not withstand. There was a strong feeling for preserving the Union in our community, but on that bright morning in May, 1861, the sentiment for war seemed to be in the ascendant. There were the usual extravagant talk and nonsense, but all were patriotic and meant well. I was of the conservatives who had voted steadily against secession and was prepared to maintain my mental equilibrium in almost any kind of political revulsion. Some of the more enthusiastic women threatened to put petticoats on the young fellows who did not enter the ranks promptly. These same women worked till their fingers were sore in getting the soldiers ready for service. We knew nothing about war and had a problem in deciding just what to carry along. No page in the old school histories had told us how little a soldier must get along on, and there was no experienced campaigner present to tell us. Some of us thought that a white shirt or two would be essential. Razors, combs, brushes and hand glasses were in our outfits. It bothered us to reduce these things to a small package that we could handle easily. We had many details to settle. Saddle-bags? They had all been appropriated by the "early birds"—the fellows who were afraid the war would be over before they could get to it. We resorted to the use of the old-fashioned wallet, an article fashioned after the similitude of a pillow-slip, closed at both ends and with a slit in the middle. Made of stout osnaburgs, it proved to be a sufficient receptacle. But the "wallet" was not tidy enough for the "trim soldier," and in case of rain the contents were drenched. All this was remedied afterward by experience in packing, necessity for economy, and by spoils captured on the field. We, too, got to using McClellan saddles with large pockets, rubber cloths and regulation blankets. Indeed, later on, if Grant had met one of us, he would have pronounced us "correct" from halter to spur, if only he could have been blinded to the suit of gray or butternut. There came a time when we had new Yankee guns and were constantly on the lookout for cartridges of the right caliber. You see, we "paid some attention to details," if we did sometimes leave in a hurry.

But we are off for Jackson to be mustered in. At Medon the good people who had that day given a farewell dinner to their home company had a bountiful spread for us. As Company E of the Seventh Cavalry we advanced in line of battle over this very spot at the old brick church on the "Armstrong raid," and here we had the first real taste of heavy firing. Our gallant young Captain Tate here used his favorite word, "Steady," which we had heard so often on drill, and reproached us for trying to dodge the balls.

Our mustering officer was A. W. Campbell, who rose to the rank of Brigadier-General, and it was another coincidence that Company E was in his brigade at the surrender. Like Chalmers, he carried his good breeding into camp, and even in the woods there was an air of refinement in all his ways. We had six weeks of hot weather and strenuous drill on the Jackson Fair Grounds. Plentiful rations and boxes from home, but in these fifty years I haven't forgotten the Jackson flies. I remember that a Bolivar girl said they were "the laziest flies she had ever seen." This depended upon the point of view. They came on with a rush, but were a little slow in getting out of the way.

Orders came to march to Randolph by way of Bolivar. We were all happy in the prospect of spending a few days at home. We were now soldiers sure enough—in the estimation of our friends. Hadn't we been in camp six long, hot weeks? Pleasures incident to such occasions are sufficiently sweet to last a long time. Alas! they never do.

"Boots and saddles" for Randolph. At the "old factory" on Clear Creek the people of the Whiteville country prepared a dinner for us that was simply above criticism, except to say that it was perfect in every particular. We had our first bivouac at Stanton. Moving under a July sun and along miles and miles of dusty road, we reached the vicinity of Randolph tired and hungry. We reverted to the "flesh pots" and dreamed of Medon and Whiteville, and other good things that we had seen. The hills and valleys were covered with the tents of the Provisional Army of Tennessee, under General John L. T. Sneed. We certainly got the impression here that the war was a fixed fact. Preparations went forward day and night. It was time for serious reflection. Some of us, though young men, had been thinking over the grave questions for some time, particularly during the exciting political canvass of the previous year. Many who admitted the abstract right of secession but had voted against it as wrong under the circumstances, if not impracticable, were yet hoping that a wicked war would somehow be averted. All the elements of opposition to the Republicans had a popular majority in the election of 1860 of over one million votes, and a majority of eight in the Senate and twenty-one in the House. They could have contested Republican measures or even blocked legislation for two more years. Lincoln had always protested against the policy of interfering with slavery in the States. Was there not here food for reflection on the part of the thoughtful soldier, who was about to stake everything, even life itself, upon the result of a war in which he knew the chances of success were against him? He could reason that wise and patriotic statesmanship could change the whole policy of government in less than two years.

But here comes the battle of Bull Run, in which the Federal Army was scattered to the four winds. Oh, yes, we just knew *now* that we could whip three or four to one! How easy it was to conclude that the very best thing to do was to present a united front and, if not our independence, we could at least get liberal concessions in regard to slavery in the territories. But this is merely a reminiscence, and I am not an Herodotus.

We called the place, assigned us near Randolph, Camp Yellow Jacket. There was good reason for this, for thousands of yellow jackets were in the ground on which we proposed to make our beds and stake our horses. In a day or two we cleared the camp of these pests so that it was habitable. Two cavalry companies from Memphis were in camp near us—Logwood's and White's. In riding near these one day I met a soldier speeding a magnificent black horse along a country road as if for exercise, and the pleasure of being astride of so fine an animal. On closer inspection I saw it was Bedford Forrest, only a private like myself, whom I had known ten years before down in Mississippi. I had occasion afterward to see a good deal of him.

We were to be a part of Pillow's Army of Occupation, and to that end, we went aboard the steamer Ohio with orders to debark at New Madrid, Mo. Soon there came a great victory to McCulloch and Price at Oak Hill, and some folks said that we would march straight to St. Louis. We reported to General M. Jeff Thompson of the Missouri State troops, forty miles in the interior. Though Missouri was a Southern State, we soon began to feel that we were bordering on the enemy's country. We had hurriedly gone forward without our wagon train and were somewhat dependent upon the Missourians for rations. When our Captain spoke to the General in regard to our needs, he blurted out these words: "By God, Captain Neely, my men can soon furnish your men with as much beef as they want and a pile of bread as high as a tree." *We got the rations.*

Thompson's men were armed mostly with shotguns and old-fashioned squirrel rifles. Trained to the use of firearms and largely destitute of fear, they were dangerous antagonists. The General, as I remember him, was a wiry little fellow, active as the traditional cat and a fine horseman. He was mounted on a milk-white stallion with black spots. He dashed around among his men like a boy on his first pony, and was invariably followed by his big Indian orderly, dressed largely in the garb of his tribe. These men told us much about their little combats with the "home guards," and made us feel that we were getting still nearer to real war. False alarms were frequent and afforded us plenty of material to excite our risibles when the imaginary danger had passed. Still further out we encamped on the farm of General Watkins, who was a half brother of Henry Clay. Rations were not at hand in abundance for a day or two, but the owner of the farm donated to us a twenty-acre field in the roasting ear. Some of the boys said that Alf. Coleman ate thirty ears a day while it lasted—the same he took out for his horse. Green corn, roasted in the shuck, or baked before a hot fire, is very palatable. I had learned this "down on the old plantation" in the Pee Dee country. We really enjoyed camp life here, as it was not so full of dull routine. A lively little scout or an amusing picket incident made our daily duties a little more spicy than usual, while scarcely a man escaped being the butt of a ridiculous joke or a little "white lie." A funny little story got into camp which concerned a young man of the company, who had been enjoying a short furlough at home. The ladies there, ever mindful of the welfare of the soldiers, had made up a lot of small red flannel aprons, which were said to be good for warding off disease, if worn next to the person. The young fellow had been presented with one and instructed as to its benefit, but not as to the manner of wearing it. He wore it on the outside and strutted about the town to the great amusement of many good people.

It was on this expedition that the now famous story was started on R. U. Brown. It was told by the reserve picket that Private Brown, while on post at midnight in the great swamp near Sikeston, called Nigger Head, imagined that a big old owl in the distance was saying "Who, who, who are you?" Taking it for a human voice, Brown tremblingly replied "R. U. Brown, sir, a friend of yours." Dick never heard the last of this story while the war lasted, and at the Reunion in Memphis many a one of the "old boys" greeted him with the same old words that rang in his ears just forty years before. He and Coleman, afterwards sutler of the regiment, I am happy to know, are still alive in Texas. Like others, who sickened and died or met death on the firing line, they were gloriously good fellows to have in camp.

It was during our stay in Missouri that we made an expedition to Charleston, situated in that vast flat prairie just west of the mouth of the Ohio, which we always reverted to with the keenest pleasure. The Federal Cavalry from Bird's Point had been making almost daily visits to the town, which was strongly Southern in sentiment. This was thought to be a fine opportunity to show them "a taste of our quality," or perhaps to capture the visiting detachment. But all was quiet in the village, as the enemy had made their visit and departed. Night was at hand and we were dirty, tired and hungry. It seemed to me that the whole population went to cooking for and feeding the soldiers. This was another one of those "big eating times" that we never did forget. When we were ready to depart, even the pretty maidens would say to us, "Which will you have in your canteen, whisky, water or milk?" It was thought best not to take any risk as to snake bites in the great swamp, which we had to recross, and I think the command took whisky to a man. The inhabitants must have enjoyed a freedom from intoxicants for a season, for their town "had gone dry" by an immense majority. We learned afterwards that there was a "whisky famine." We never saw Charleston again, as we very soon received orders to advance into Kentucky and take post at Columbus. We were among the first troops to reach that point. The Kentuckians seemed to be pleased with our coming and recruiting went forward encouragingly. We pitched our tents out on the Clinton road and near the camp of the Haywood Rangers, commanded by Captain Haywood of Brownsville. This company, whose members seemed to have been reared in the saddle, had been with us from the beginning of our service, and, I may say here, that it stood by us till the end. The history of Company E is largely the history of Company D. The men of the two companies were brothers-in-arms, who could confidently rely upon the valor of each other, and those now living are loving friends to this day. Through the long hard winter, or till the evacuation of Columbus, the two companies guarded the Clinton and Milburn roads. For a while we reported directly to Albert Sydney Johnston. His noble personality and soldierly bearing were impressive and stamped him as a man born to command.

The portions of Hubbard's account here omitted (Chapters II-V inclusive) treat of the period September 1861-December 1863. During the early part of this period Hubbard and his comrades of the Seventh Tennessee Cavalry Regiment participated in numerous raids and skirmishes in West Tennessee and Kentucky. In October, 1862, they took part in the battle of Corinth and on December 20, 1862, they were with Van Dorn when he made his spectacular attack on Grant's supply depot at Holly Springs. During the first eleven months of 1863 the regiment took part in no major engagements but performed many minor scouting and raiding missions in the country between Grenada and Memphis.

Chapter 6

ORGANIZATION OF "FORREST'S CAVALRY CORPS" THE SOOY SMITH RAID—FORT PILLOW.

When the snow began to fly, Company E was comfortably quartered in the vacant storehouses at Coldwater, thirty-one miles from Memphis. The men provided themselves with heavier clothing, some articles of which were brought through the lines from home, while others were secured through block-ade runners, as those citizens were called who carried cotton to Memphis and brought out supplies on a Federal permit. The service was light, with no picket duty, for the winter was so cold and the roads so bad that a Federal raid could hardly be expected. But the hours must be whiled away. So, when the boys were not rubbing up their arms and grooming their horses, they were cutting firewood, playing poker or dancing. The dancing was a feature. Boots were heavy, but the dancers were muscular and strong. They could thread the Virginia reel or tread through the mazes of a quartet, but the eight-couple cotillion, in which a greater number could participate, thus giving more spirit to the amusement, was the favorite. In this the most intricate figures were practiced to give zest to the performances. These included the "grand cutshort," which, as I recall it, after nearly half a century, was a combination of "swing corners," "ladies' grand chain" and "set to your part-ner." In the parlance of that day, it was "immense," for I feel it in my old bones as I tell you about it. The said figure was learned from a blue-eyed fiddler of Company H of Weakley County, who, like many others, after a short experience in

-1862, concluded he couldn't kill them all anyhow, and would, therefore, engage in more peaceful pursuits beyond the range of the conscript officers. James H. Grove and I, both of whom knew how to draw the bow, furnished the music, and the boys declared, of course, that it was good. Grove was the father of E. W. Grove, the famous manufacturer of medicines of St. Louis, whose remedies are sold in every civilized country on the globe. The father and I were fellow private soldiers in the army. The son and I, for some time after the war, sustained the relation of teacher and pupil.

One day, while on a short scout to Hernando, I met a body of Federals, under a flag of truce, who were negotiating an exchange of prisoners, the details of which were soon arranged with a Confederate officer. Very soon the Yanks and Johnny Rebs were mingling as if they expected never to shoot at one another again. I had the unusual experience that day of dining with the Federal officers at the house of Judge Vance, a well-known citizen.

On the 4th of December, Company E, leaving all impediments in camp, made a demonstration along the Memphis & Charleston Railroad, between Rossville and Moscow. While tearing up some railroad track we heard the noise of battle at Moscow, where Stephen D. Lee, with Ross' and McCulloch's Brigades, met with a hot resistance and considerable loss, while trying to destroy the railroad bridge over Wolf river. It was understood at the time that these demonstrations were made mostly for the purpose of covering Forrest's advance north. He crossed the railroad that day at Saulsbury, and, proceeding north, received a cordial welcome on the next day at Bolivar. It was known that he came across from Rome, Ga., to Okolona, Miss., with not more than three hundred men, including Mortons' Battery, around which small command as a nucleus he was to form Forrest's Cavalry Corps. His resources consisted of Ross', McCulloch's and Richardson's Brigades, all very much depleted, with a few petty commands scattered here and there over the country. The weather was so cold and the roads so bad that we thought Company E was safely immune from an attack on its camp at Coldwater, yet Forrest was making a raid within the enemy's lines, where he was to stay twenty-one days, defeat superior forces in five considerable battles, and day and night display such energy and military genius as would keep him out of the hands of the enemy, who were moving from many directions to entrap him. He set about collecting the absentees and other recruits, many of whom were without arms and poorly mounted. He acted upon the principle that an unarmed man was better for the occasion than no man at all, for, if a recruit had nothing at hand but the "rebel yell," he could at least help to intimidate an adversary.

Bad roads and swollen streams had no terrors for our General, who, at the critical moment, turned his face south with his command greatly augmented, and with a convoy of wagons laden with supplies, besides about two hundred beef cattle and three hundred hogs.

The Seventh Tennessee did not participate in this campaign, the history of which is only slightly sketched here in order to give a clear view of the military situation at the time Company E was ordered to rejoin the regiment at Como, Miss. Great attention was now given to organization and equipment. Very many of the recruits had to be armed, and even clothed, before they could become effective soldiers. The work had to be done with dispatch, as we were now having more sunshine, and the roads were drying up. The enemy might soon be on the move. Forrest, having been promoted to the rank of Major-General, assumed command of all the cavalry in North Mississippi and West Tennessee. Within a few days the organizations were perfected, the Seventh Tennessee being assigned to the Fourth Brigade, commanded by Colonel Jeffry Forrest, the youngest of the Forrest brothers. The entire command was greatly elated by the success of the recent raid, the addition of so many new men, and the prospect of serving under a man who knew nothing but success.

Rumors came in thick and fast that the Federals were preparing to advance both from Memphis and Vicksburg. The Fourth Brigade dropped down to Grenada, in order to watch and frustrate any movement from the south. We had frequently camped at Grenada, and the scenes were familiar. As for myself, I had known the country and many of the people ten years before—yes, indeed, before old college days. We occupied the very ground whence we started on the Holly Springs raid, about one year before. Who could tell but that we should start on one just as remarkable from the same place?

Strong columns of Federals were reported moving from Memphis. From his headquarters at Oxford, the Confederate commander made such dispositions of his four brigades as would most likely defeat the plans of the enemy, so far as they were developed. During the first days of February, it was discovered that about seven thousand well-appointed cavalry were on the road to the rich prairie lands of East Mississippi. Gen. Sooy Smith, their commander, moved with so much dispatch that Forrest, though moving with celerity eastward, found it impossible to head him off till the Federal forces had reached West Point. It was the morning of the 20th of February, 1864. The Federals, going down through Pontotoc and Okolona, had marked their advance by burning houses, barns and fences, and plundering larders and hen roosts. Up to that date, nothing like this had been seen in our part of the country. Our soldiers were aroused by the reports brought in. Of course, there was a firm-set resolution not only to give the ruthless enemy blow for blow, but to avenge the wrongs done to old men, women and children. It looked as if a great battle was impending, and the Confederates were never more ready. We did not know it then, but Forrest was merely trying to hold the enemy in check until reinforcements, under Stephen D. Lee, could arrive from some point below. Jeffry Forrest's brigade had already come in contact with Smith's cavalry between West Point and Aberdeen, and was being pressed back upon West Point. General Forrest, attacking the enemy with a small force on their extreme right wing, discovered, to his chagrin, that they were retreating. There was nothing to do but to press them with energy, so as to inflict as great a loss as possible upon them. Soon it was a lively chase, and the men of Company E were, for the first time, to see Forrest in battle. He was soon right up with the Seventh Regiment, as the men urged their horses through that black prairie mud. Four miles north of West Point the enemy made a stubborn resistance, in the edge of a small woods, but the pursuers, dismounting quickly, drove them away in confusion. Again it was a rattling pace through the mud till the enemy made another stand, five miles further on, where they sought to protect themselves at a rude bridge over a miry little creek, by tearing down fences and making barricades with the rails. Here the Confederates again pressed them in front and on the flanks till they gave way. This running fight, with intervals of resistance, was kept up till nightfall. It was an all-day fight, and we had many sad things to remember. Our dead and wounded were behind us, even if victory was in front of us. Weary and worn, our men and horses were given a few hours of rest. Fortunately, the men found plenty of subsistence and forage in the camp abandoned by the Federals, which helped wonderfully in the work to be done next day.

By 4 o'clock on the morning of the 22d of February, McCulloch's and Jeffrey Forrest's brigades, led by Forrest himself, were moving toward Okolona, and driving the enemy before them. The distance was fourteen miles, over a road almost impassable.

When the Confederates arrived at Okolona, they found a strong line of the enemy drawn up in such a position that they could have made a stubborn resistance, but Barteau, commanding Bell's Brigade, and McCullough with his own, promptly drove them from the position and rushed them in some confusion along the road towards Pontotoc. The Federals adopted the tactics of the previous day by forming heavy lines in favorable positions and resisting stubbornly till attacked front and flank, in many instances with Forrest in the forefront, they were compelled to retreat. The last stand made was at Prairie Mound, seven miles from Okolona and some thirty miles from West Point, where the fighting began on the morning of the previous day. The Sooy Smith raid was at an end with heavy loss to the invaders and a proportionate loss to the victors, for during the two days Forrest fought the 7,000 well equipped cavalry with a force only about half as large and made up largely of raw recruits. In one of the last encounters Jeffrey Forrest was killed at the head of his brigade, and died in the arms of his famous brother. No more pathetic scene was ever witnessed on any battlefield.

To look upon the ghastly dead or to hear the groans of the wounded lessens the sweets of victory and emphasizes the horrors of war.

After so strenuous a campaign, both men and horses needed recuperation, and so the Seventh Tennessee went into camp in that bountiful section of country about Mayhew, west of Columbus. It was easy to see that the military situation, now at the opening of spring, was such that if the Federals did not come after Forrest, he would certainly go after them. Therefore, preparations for a campaign were active and men and horses were put in the best possible condition. On the 15th of March Forrest with only part of his command was moving north for the purpose of crossing the railroad at Corinth and marching into Tennessee. By the 23rd we had passed Trenton and were still moving north without any resistance. We were now satisfied that either Union City or Paducah was Forrest's objective point.

On the morning of the 24th Colonel William L. Duckworth of the Seventh Tennessee, in command of a temporary brigade, consisting of his own regiment, McDonald's battalion and Faulkner's Kentucky regiment, was ordered to attack the Federal works at Union City, while Forrest with the main force was hastening towards Paducah. Duckworth with his 500 men completely invested the Federal fort at Union City in the early morning and after a brisk firing, participated in by both sides, under a flag of truce demanded a surrender of the place. Lieutenant Henry J. Livingston of Brownsville, with a detail of three or four men of which I happened to be one, had charge of the flag of truce. When the firing ceased we rode up close to the fort, where an officer met us. Livingston requested to communicate directly with Colonel Isaac R. Hawkins, the commander of the post. This was granted and a short parley ensued in which Livingston, acting under orders of his superior, demanded a surrender. Hawkins demurred and asked for an interview with Forrest. Colonel Duckworth, being now called in and acting with an adroitness and finesse that were altogether creditable, insisted that he was acting under the direct orders of Forrest, who was near at hand with his artillery (sic) and who was not in the habit of meeting officers of inferior rank to himself. That most gentlemanly Federal officer, Colonel Hawkins, who was now about to surrender to some part of Forrest's cavalry for the second time, wishing to avoid the effusion of blood, which might be caused by Duckworth's imaginary artillery, concluded to make an unconditional surrender. When the facts came out and there was slight jeering on the part of our men, these men of the Seventh Tennessee, Federal, bore up manfully and turned out to be jolly good fellows, molded much after the pattern of the men of our own Seventh Tennessee, Confederate. Talking with many of the officers and men I concluded that their chagrin would have been amusing, if it had not been pathetic. Four hundred and seventy-five prisoners with all their supplies and camp equipage and three hundred horses with accoutrements were surrendered. There was not at that time an effective Confederate cannon in West Tennessee, and Forrest was well on his way to Paducah.

When the Confederates reached the objective point led by Forrest in person, they took possession of the town, but met with a bloody resistance when they charged the fort in which the Federals had taken refuge. They drew off with large spoils of war, consisting of horses and equipments. The whole force now turned south, having accomplished the object of the expedition. Company E was ordered to Bolivar, where the men, subject to order, dispersed to their homes to enjoy a furlough. The good old town "put her best foot foremost" and gave us a quiet but hearty welcome. Some of the boys "shucked their army duds," and appeared in other vestments as beaux, for there was a bevy of pretty girls in Bolivar. In the round of dances and other social gatherings, there was many a sweet word spoken upon which, it was hoped, something might be realized "after the ratification of a treaty of peace," as the Confederate bills all said. Doubtless, some of my friends found, when peace did come to the land, that love, even the platonic kind, which is sporadic only, is somewhat like Mr. Finnegin's train, which was "off agin, on agin, gone agin." In other words, the grand passion does not always stick like Spalding's Prepared Glue or Aunt Jemimy's Plaster, which the more you try to take it off, the more it sticks the faster.

But there was a bugle call and all good things must end. The men came rushing in to report. In the little excitement incident to the occasion, Sol Phillips, while romping with some of his fellow soldiers, jumped into what he took to be a large box, which turned out to be an old well. Sol soon found bottom and set up a yell to which there was a quick response by his friends, who drew Sol up greatly frightened but only slightly bruised. He still makes his home in the hills of Hardeman.

At the end of about three weeks, or more precisely on the 2nd of May, 1864, there was hurrying and scurrying among the soldiers. Company E was present in force for duty and McDonald's Battalion was on the ground under Major Crews. General Sturgis, with a large force of cavalry and artillery, was in such close proximity that he would reach Bolivar late in the day. Forrest had already been properly informed and had given orders for our little force to check the Federal advance in order that everything on wheels moving south might have a better chance to escape. When the Confederates had been properly placed behind the old Federal earthworks, west of the town and the battle had begun, General Forrest with his escort came unexpectedly upon the field at a gallop and took charge. Knowing that he was fighting at great odds, at an opportune moment he drew off, but not until several men and horses had been wounded. Here D. Hill and John McClammer, temporarily

attached to Company E, were wounded so severely that they
were left in the hands of the Federals. Major Strange of
Forrest's staff had his right arm broken, but rode off the field.
The enemy numbering two thousand sustained a heavy loss,
forty or fifty killed and wounded, as they fought at a dis-
advantage, the Confederates being fairly protected by the old
works constructed by Grant two years before.

The Confederates necessarily retreated in some confusion,
as the Federals making a flank movement had the advantage
when our men started to leave their partial shelter. Bringing
forward their artillery they threw several shots into the town.
One struck the residence of Mrs. Brooks, another went through
the roof of the stable on the Harkins place, and I saw one cut
off the top of a cedar tree in front of the Dr. Peters place, now
the residence of Dr. Hugh Tate. Just think of it. Here was
Company E, being chased through its home town. It threw a
damper over every tender sentiment and all thoughts of love
vanished into thin air, for we were thanking our stars that we
had escaped death at the hands of the Federals. Just as we were
procuring forage at the Dave McKinney place south of Bolivar,
I heard the report of the gun in the hands of Robert Galloway
that killed Major Sol Street, a somewhat famous partisan
fighter or guerrilla. On the 44th anniversary of this tragedy
I met Mr. Galloway in Memphis. In reply to my request to
give me a statement in regard to the killing of Street, he said,
in substance, that he killed him because Street had killed his
father for the purpose of robbery. That a younger brother of
Galloway's was with his father at the time of the murder, and
was able to give full particulars. The boy remembered the exact
dying words of his father. Street and his companions did not
secure the elder Galloway's money as something, unknown to
the boy, caused them to hastily leave the locality. This was when

Robert Galloway was about sixteen years old. When in about two years he reached the military age, he joined the army and was in the fight at Bolivar where Street was pointed out to him by a friend. He shot Street before they had dismounted at the bivouac, and in the confusion made his escape, but was arrested by Lieutenant Statler of Company E. He offered Statler a thousand dollars to release him, but the offer was declined. Galloway and others state that General Forrest was in a towering rage when Galloway was brought before him, and said that a drumhead courtmartial would sentence Galloway to be shot at sun up. He tells me that he knows just how it feels to be condemned to death, but was not present at the contemplated tragedy, as he made his escape at daylight, and within a few days was safe within the Federal lines at Memphis. Mr. Galloway resided in Illinois till after the surrender when he returned to Hardeman county. He has reared a large family and is an excellent citizen.

There was much talk when we got quietly settled in camp at Verona, Miss., about the capture of Fort Pillow, an affair in which the Seventh Tennessee, being on detached duty near Randolph, did not participate. Most of this was in regard to what seemed to be the senseless conduct of the garrison after they must have seen that the place was doomed. After the officer in command had refused to comply with the demand to surrender and the whole Confederate force moved on their works, the entire garrison, having left their flag flying, fell back to a safer place under the bank of the river. Much has since been said by Northern writers concerning what they term an unnecessary slaughter. It should be remembered that this same garrison of both whites and negroes had committed numerous outrages upon the people of the surrounding country. These things had come to the ears of the Confederates and many of the victims had petitioned Forrest to avenge their wrongs by breaking up what appeared to be a den of thieves and marauders. Howbeit, part of them were Tennesseans. Add to all this, that the garrison had been lavishly stimulated with whisky, as was evident from the fact that a number of barrels of whisky and beer with tin dippers attached were found by the Confederates, and it is not hard to see why there was unnecessary slaughter. The incident could be dismissed by saying that those within the fort knew that they deserved condign punishment because of the outrages committed on innocent people, and being somewhat in a state of intoxication, were incited to resist to the last extremity, while the Confederates were incited to victory by every instinct that impels a manly soldier to resent an insult and to protect the innocent. If General Forrest had no other victory to his credit, his fame would be secure.

Belated soldiers coming down from Tennessee soon brought to us the information that Sturgis took possession of Bolivar as soon as we had retreated on the evening of the 2nd of May, and burned the courthouse, the Baptist church, one of the hotels and several other buildings. Bad news for Company E.

Chapter 7

BRICE'S CROSS ROADS

In the beautiful month of May, and it is a lovely season away down in Mississippi, the Seventh Tennessee was moved around so much and camped at so many places, that it is difficult to remember which places came first. The service was not especially irksome and the weather was fine. A half dozen men of Company E were sent on a tour of observation up through Holly Springs and in the direction of Memphis, which I remember to have greatly enjoyed. The danger of the service was sufficiently great to make us alert while enjoying the hospitality of the people who were not only ready, day and night, to give us of their scanty stores, but to help us with such information as they had in regard to the movements of the enemy. We rejoined the regiment at Abbeville, feeling as if we had had a vacation.

About this time the Seventh Tennessee was brigaded with Duff's Regiment and A. H. Chalmers' Battalion, about as good a body of fighting men as could have been gotten together. This organization was known as Rucker's Brigade that won distinction at Brice's Cross Roads and Harrisburg. We had only known Rucker as the gallant commander of the upper batteries at Island No. 10. We had seen men there, carrying ammunition to his guns, wade in water up to their waists, when it looked from a distance like the outflow from the river might carry away every man that stood to his post. At our first sight of him the boys said he had "a sort of bulldog look." We soon discovered that tenacity was one of his characteristics.

It was now about the first of June, 1864, and General Sturgis moving out from Memphis was north of Ripley with an army reported to be about 10,000 of all arms. Rucker was ordered to cross the Tallahatchie at New Albany and fall upon the right flank of the enemy, as they advanced south, in the vicinity of Ripley. After some brisk fighting just south of Ripley with very little loss to either side Rucker, seeing that the enemy was in great force, prudently drew off and took post at Baldwyn. In the meantime, Lee and Forrest were concentrating their forces to deliver battle somewhere further south.

In the little affair south of Ripley, when ordered with one or two men to a position on our extreme left until relieved, I saw approaching along a country pathway a fine ambulance drawn by two splendid mules. A Federal outfit, perhaps, which would inevitably fall into our hands. It came up at a sweeping trot. The face of the man in charge was familiar. It was that of the late William H. Wood of Memphis. Strange position in which to find so steadfast a Union man—moving rapidly ahead of the Federal army and seeking refuge within the Confederate lines. This he would accomplish in a few minutes, but there was no time to ask questions, for the firing was heavy on the main road. The gentleman must be on an important mission, at least to him. He *was,* for at a time, when thousands of negroes had taken refuge within the Federal lines and the day for buying and selling this species of property had passed, Mr. Wood had conceived the idea of running his negroes south, converting them into cotton, and eventually into gold. This incident is chiefly worth mentioning, in a reminiscent way, first because it illustrates a thing that sometimes occurs in real life, but more frequently in fiction, namely, that acquaintances occasionally come face to face under strange conditions and peculiar circumstances; and, secondly, because it shows that there was a singular state of affairs existing when the slaves of one man, amid all the demoralization, were subject to his will and did that which seemed like leaving freedom behind. I am not fully informed as to how the scheme worked, but have always understood that it turned out profitably to the projector. There was nothing wrong about it, at least, from a Southern standpoint, but very many good people, even some descendants of slaveholders, are, at this day, squemish about what they are pleased to term "traffick in human flesh."

It must not be concluded that the negroes spoken of were in that vicinity, for they were, at that very moment, under a prudent guide, safe within the Southern lines.

It is not untimely to remark, right here, that the

descendants of slave-holders will, possibly, have some difficulty in justifying them for consenting to the existence of an institution, which existed in this country more than two hundred years, but which has been condemned by the laws of every civilized country on the globe. This difficulty will arise chiefly from the fact that the true history concerning slavery, its existence in all the original States, its abolition by some, its retention by others and, above all, the motives controlling those who dealt with it, is not now, nor is likely to be, persistently taught in the family or school. It is one of those questions of which it may be said the further we get from it, the less we say or know about it.

We went into camp at Baldwyn drenched by the continuous rains and fatigued by the exigencies of an arduous service. The Federals had moved steadily southeast from Ripley, and were in close proximity to a part of our forces. Everything at Baldwyn gave evidence of an impending struggle. In the midst of the acute feeling in the minds of the soldiers, it was announced that three men had been tried by court-martial and condemned to be shot for desertion. This was a phase of war with which we were not familiar. The poor fellows, confined in a box car, gave forth the most pitiful wailings. The cries of one of the condemned, a mere stripling, were particularly distressing. The whole brigade was mustered to witness the execution. Guilty or not guilty, I somehow wished these victims of their own acts would escape the impending doom. Each man was placed by his grave and coffin. A file of eight men appeared with bristling guns. The suspense was terrible. Death on the battlefield was nothing compared to that which we were to witness. The sentence of the court-martial was read. The boy was released and, still weeping, left the field. At the firm command of the officer in charge, the shots rang out and one man fell dead. The same thing was repeated and another went to his death. Though the justice of the court-martial was never questioned, there was a profound sensation among the soldiers, which it took a battle to shake off.

Know ye, that the very next morning, June 10th, 1864, we were galloping to Brice's Cross Roads. Acting under the orders of Lee, Forrest was trying to keep his forces between the Federal vanguard and Tupelo, so as to finally turn upon them when a more open country was reached. To do this with dispatch, he must reach the cross roads, by a road leading southwest, ahead of the Federals, who were moving towards the same point by a road leading southeast. The Federal cavalry advance, moving rapidly, passed the point and even went some distance beyond in the direction of Guntown. When the Confederate advance came up, the enemy was ready to block their way on the road from Baldwyn and had the advantage of position. Johnson's Alabamians in advance fell upon them furiously while Rucker's Brigade was coming to the rescue. At this critical juncture, Forrest seems to have abandoned all intention of merely holding the enemy in check and deferring a battle to a more convenient season. He had his own little army well in hand, though it was having a hard time to reach the desired point promptly on account of the muddy roads. A man of wonderful military instinct and surpassing genius for war, he saw at a glance that, although the cavalry of the Federals, at that moment, held the advantage of position, their main body was strung along a narrow road, and their general would assuredly have trouble in protecting his left flank, crossing Tishomingo creek, and throwing his infantry and artillery into line of battle. It was indeed the psychological moment and the faith of the general spread to the men. Rucker was turned to the left and into the woods, where his men were quickly dismounted and gotten ready for battle. At the word they sprung over a fence and into a muddy cornfield. Will I ever forget it? The enemy posted in a dense wood and behind a heavy fence poured a galling fire into our ranks. It looked like death to go to the fence, but many of the men reached it. Four of Company E were killed in this charge. Men could not stay there and live. The Seventh Tennessee with Chalmers' Battalion on the left was driven back in confusion. With the steadiness of veterans, they re-formed for another onset. As I remember it, this time we went over the fence. Reinforcements were evidently at hand for the Federals, for on they came like a resistless tide. It was death not to give back. Another readjustment of lines, and we were at them again. I cannot now say how many times this was repeated, for men in the very presence of death take no note of time. The roar of artillery and the fusillade of small arms were deafening. Sheets of flame were along both lines while dense clouds of smoke arose above the heavily wooded field. No language is adequate to paint the verities of the moment. High tide of battle had come, and one side or the other must quail very soon. Which side should it be? The answer came when apparently by common consent both drew back just far enough for the intervening trees and dense undergrowth to obscure the vision. Our men still in line of battle lay on the ground for a much needed rest.

Here we had a bountiful supply of water from the rills, which had been fed by the recent rains. I never tasted better. The cessation of battle was as grateful as the water, but there was intense anxiety to know the final result. An order to retire from the field would have brought no surprise. But Forrest and his brigade commanders were better informed. Mounted on his big sorrel horse, sabre in hand, sleeves rolled up, his coat lying on the pommel of his saddle, looking the very God of War, the General rode down our line as far as we could see him. I remember his words, which I heard more than once: "Get up, men. I have ordered Bell to charge on the left. When you hear his guns, and the bugle sounds, every man must charge, and we will give them hell." That was enough. We heard Bell's guns and the bugle. Advancing over the dead bodies of Federals and Confederates and regaining the ground lost in the last repulse, Rucker's Brigade in one grand last charge moved to the assault of the enemy's position. Small bushes, cut off near the ground and falling in our front, meant that the Federals had been reinforced by veteran infantry and were firing low. So close were we now to their line and the fighting so nearly hand to hand that our navy sixes were used with deadly effect. The Federals bravely withstood our onslaught for a time, but soon gave way in confusion and broke to the rear. Rucker's men, greatly encouraged, moved rapidly to the front and, with no regard for formation, came out into the open at the Brice residence, which stands in the angle formed by the Guntown and Pontotoc roads. The men of the various commands, concentrating upon this point, became intermingled as they charged up to where all could see the grand scamper of the Federals running down towards Tishomingo creek. Six pieces of their own artillery had been turned upon them and these were quickly reinforced by Morton's and Rice's batteries. These, double shotted with canister, added to the confusion of the entangled mass of infantry, cavalry, ambulances and wagons. The Federal dead and wounded lay on every hand about the cross roads, showing the deadly aim of our men in the last charge, while our loss at this point was inconsiderable, though the rain of bullets from the Federal line appeared sufficient to destroy the whole brigade. The negro brigade under Boulton came in for its full share of the calamity, the deluded creatures, in many instances, having ceased their war cry of "Remember Fort Pillow," and throwing away their badges, took to the woods.

When hundreds of our men had crossed the creek and conditions had become a little more quiet, they began to realize that they were very tired and very hungry. No time was lost in helping themselves to the subsistence in the abandoned wagons where there was an abundance for both man and horse.

A reflection or two. General Forrest, in fighting this battle at his own discretion, had shown that he very well knew just when a commander, acting on the defensive-active, should fall upon an invading army. He had, not for the first time, particularly emphasized the fact that Southern cavalrymen, dismounted and well handled, could cope with trained infantry, and even put them to rout when fighting at odds of two to one against themselves. On this eventful day he had put into practice his favorite tactics, which had uniformly brought him success, that of launching his entire command, as soon as he could get it into action, against his adversary. Forrest's Cavalry never looked around for reserves, but confidently expected to do the work themselves and to do it quickly. Hence, at Brice's Cross Roads they fought with the intrepidity of veteran infantry and exhibited the dash of the best type of Southern cavalry. In other words, they fought when Forrest said so, and every charge was like the first one in which they expected to break the lines of the enemy. The man behind the gun was in evidence at Tishomingo, and it was a glorious victory. May his tribe increase.

A consideration of the comparative forces is interesting. According to information, which is fairly authentic, Forrest had 3,200 men, including two four-gun batteries. Federal official report gives them 3,300 cavalry and 5,400 infantry, or 8,700 men. In addition, they had, according to the best information, 24 pieces of artillery and men to man them. Notice the respective losses. Forrest loss about 140 officers and men killed, and about 500 wounded and none taken prisoners. Sturgis lost, according to official report, 23 officers and 594 men killed and 52 officers and 1,571 men captured, or a total of 2,240 men. Forrest says he captured 1,571 men and 52 officers, an ordnance train with a large supply of fixed ammunition, ten days' rations for the whole Federal army, over two hundred wagons and parts of their teams, and large quantities of supplies, thirty ambulances and twenty-one caissons. Clearly then, we fought them at an odds of nearly three to one in their favor.

Now, a few incidents of the battle. When riding to the battle-field that morning, and at a place where we were passing over a rough causeway on which many a horse cast a shoe, Isaac H. Pipkin (Doc.), riding by my side, remarked that if he should be killed that day, all he asked was to be put away decently. He was in the first charge, through the muddy cornfield. Imagine my feelings, when driven back in one of the repulses, I came upon his body still in death. Doc was a typical rustic, a good fellow in camp, a true soldier in action, a man you might lean on. The people of Bolivar have long ago graven his name in marble. Tom Boucher was a plain and unassuming citizen of the Whiteville neighborhood, who was always at his post, took life easy and never fretted. He died on the field.

In the first charge, I noticed William C. Hardy, of Bolivar, handling his gun as if something was the matter with the lock. I never saw him again, for he never got to the second fence. Billy was a pupil of mine, a fiery young fellow and a perfectly reliable soldier.

Another schoolboy of mine who fell in this first charge was Charles R. Neely of Bolivar. He was a boy of gentle birth and noble instincts. He was a loving friend, a soldier tried and true, who poured out his young life's blood upon the field. Could higher eulogy be spoken?

In connection with young Neely's death I mention the faithful conduct of James F. Dunlap, his mess mate and true friend. As soon as practicable Dunlap placed the corpse of his young friend in their small mess wagon and carrying it through the country delivered it to his mother in Bolivar, Tenn. This was an exhibition of fidelity hard to surpass.

Suffering from an old wound, Captain Tate, early in the action turned over the command of the company to Lieutenant J. P. Satler, with whom I had already agreed to remain through whatever might come to us that day. Thank heaven, we both came through unscathed.

Do you remember where I left off the main narrative? It was at Tishomingo creek where we had halted to partake of the bountiful refreshments, which the Federals had rather unwillingly left in our hands. When the horse-holders brought forward our mounts, my little black seemed as glad to see me as I was to see him. I stripped him for a rubbing and a rest and gorged him on Federal forage.

Instead of an undisturbed night of repose, as we had fondly hoped for, the Seventh Tennessee was aroused from its slumbers at 2 o'clock in the morning with the information that Forrest himself was to lead it in pursuit of the enemy. With Company E in front I, happening to be in the front file, could very well see everything that was likely to come up on this memorable advance. Much of our way was lighted up by wagons and other abandoned property burning. In one place the forewheel of a gun carriage had been locked by a tree and this and several other handsome brass pieces in its rear had been abandoned. Many Federal soldiers, now thoroughly exhausted, were sleeping by the roadside, while others, armed and unarmed, willingly surrendered. They were invariably told to go to the rear. Further along, I counted ninety-five wagons laden with supplies strung along the narrow road. The wheels of some had been locked by trees and evidently abandoned in hot haste by those who had ridden the teams away. I saw much of General Forrest that night, who was in great good humor in regard to the results of the previous day's battle. When approaching Ripley, early in the day, which town is about twenty miles from the battle-field, we were relieved by other troops going forward to press the enemy, who were making a stand just north of the town. Buford and Bell were there, and we knew what that meant.

We rode leisurely through the town and to the outskirts. A battle was going on, but the enemy was believed to be retreating. The command to form fours and prepare to charge was given. Company E, in front was soon going at a lively pace and it soon became a question of speed as to who should reach the enemy first. My little black horse responded in fine style. At a flying gallop we went straight up the road and, though hearing guns on every hand, could see no enemy to charge. Instantly we saw in the woods to our left a whole regiment of Federal cavalry aiming to reach the road at an angle and speed that would throw them into it just ahead of us. Over the hill they went as fast as their horses would carry them. Tom Nelson of Company L, coming up, he and I found ourselves in uncomfortable proximity to the enemy, for as we too went over the hill, there they were with their rear huddled together in the valley, with something, apparently blocking their front. Nelson and I had not intended to fight a whole regiment, but we shot out everything we had at them. Pressing towards the front and turning in their saddles, as they went up the hill, they gave us a few shots from their carbines which,

I remember well, they held in one hand. At a cooler moment, I inquired with some interest how it was that such a thing as I have related could happen. No one attempted an explanation. Nelson and I were present in the flesh and had occasion to remember well all that took place, though events were passing with lightning celerity. Perhaps, perchance and maybe, it was a case of horseflesh. It was the Third Iowa Cavalry we were charging. Colonel C. A. Stanton, not so very long ago a citizen of Memphis, was an officer in this regiment and has a clear recollection of the incident. I was somewhat surprised a few years ago when Billy Elkins, a member of Company E, reminded me of the occasion and rehearsed what took place about as I remember it myself.

The regiment came up in much less time than it has taken me to tell it, and advanced to the top of the hill where there was firing by some Federals posted in an old house and a plum orchard. At this moment, Captain William J. Tate of Company E, who, sick and suffering was forced to go to the rear the previous day, came up with the company in pursuit. Standing for a moment in a protected position, I reminded Tate that if he forced his horse to mount an embankment by the roadside, he would be a fair target for bullets, they flying thick about us. He disregarded my admonition, mounted the embankment and rode forward for a better view. I quickly changed my position, as many others had come forward. Very soon I saw Tate supported by two men who were taking him to a less exposed place. He was asking some one to catch his horse, which was moving off towards the enemy. At this moment Tommy Elcan, of Company B, standing by my side, was struck in the head by a minnie ball and fell from his horse dead. The gallant Lieutenant-Colonel A. H. Chalmers came riding forward and asked about the position of the enemy. He advanced down the hill at the head of his battalion, but soon returned afoot. His fine brown mare had been killed. A word more concerning Captain Tate. It appears that smarting under an absence enforced by a threatened attack of erysipelas in an old wound, this gallant gentleman had concluded that he could not forego the pleasure of seeing the Federal army in full retreat and his own regiment participating in the pursuit. Mounting Billy Hardy's white horse he rode to the front at a gallop. Joining the regiment in time for the charge, he had his horse almost instantly shot under him. Determined to go forward he mounted James E. Wood's horse, which was kindly offered, and appeared on the firing line, as I have related. He was a young man of gentle demeanor from the mountains of North Carolina, who shortly before the war had engaged in farming near Bolivar. He affected few of the refinements of cultivated society, but was a young countryman of courage, who made friends and kept them. When we were organizing a company, he attended the meetings and showed an aptitude for learning and teaching the cavalry drill. Never did a man more effectually advance himself in the confidence of a company than he did by perfectly fair dealing and sheer force of character. Serving as fourth sergeant the first year, he developed rapidly as a drill master and officer. Physically, Captain Tate was a man of medium weight and erect and well knit frame. He was a pronounced blonde with clear blue eyes and very light hair. Active on foot and tireless when there was stress of work, he always seemed most at home on horseback. The manner of his death was, perhaps, such as he would have desired it to be, had he known it was to come so soon. When I heard that he had succumbed to his wounds, I hastened to give him decent burial in the cemetery at Ripley, Miss. He sleeps among the people in whose defense he died.

Forty-four years have come and gone since the scenes of which I write passed before the vision, but they were so indelibly impressed upon the tablet of the memory that it is easy to recall them. The slightest incident often recalls the fiercest battle scene, and for the moment I live in the past. I am recording events while there are yet living witnesses to bear me out. As such I mention with pleasure the names of Lieutenant-Colonel W. F. Taylor, who always bore himself proudly on the field; A. H. D. Perkins, whom I have seen flaunt the colors of the regiment in the faces of the enemy, and Captain H. A. Tyler, who with his squadron of two small companies gallantly bore the brunt of battle on the extreme left at Tishomingo, and was ready with his Kentuckians to join in the pursuit of the broken battalions of the enemy.

Chapter 8

HARRISBURG

That the great victory at Brice's Cross Roads had revived the spirits and brightened the hopes of Forrest's men there could be no doubt. Flushed with victory, they believed that what had been done on the 10th of June could be done again. In a word, they concluded that Forrest now knew better how to defeat a superior force than ever before. Their confidence was so implicit that, even if conditions should not improve in other parts of the Confederacy, Forrest would continue to defeat superior forces whenever he went against them. It is well to make a note of this sentiment, for it served somewhat to explain the seemingly reckless bravery of the men in the next battle.

When we settled down to camp life at Aberdeen and Verona, I could but notice the smallness of the companies, and when on the march the regiment did not string out as it formerly did. This was significant. Here again was food for thought. Though one man could not do the work of two, preparations for another battle went forward. We were stirred by the reports brought in as to the strength of the next army that would meet us. It was said to be at Ripley and coming toward Pontotoc. Their objective point was Okolona and points further south, if practicable. Stephen D. Lee and Forrest occupied a strong natural position south of Pontotoc, and set about strengthening it. It was thought that General A. J. Smith, confident of his ability to envelope the Confederates, would assail the position in force. He had acquired a reputation as a tactician and fighter on other fields. Finding that the road to Okolona was blocked he withdrew from the Confederate front, and moving by the left flank took the road to Tupelo. A tactician thoroughly acquainted with the topography of the country could not have made a more judicious move, or taken more proper steps to select his own position for battle, and thus have his adversary assail him on his own ground, or not at all, while he was so posted. The quick eye of Forrest having detected, in a personal reconnaissance, the movement made, he made such disposition of his own forces that he could attack the enemy in the rear and on their right flank.

General Smith and General Forrest had approximately and respectively 14,000 and 10,000 men of all arms. Smith kept his army in such compact column movement and so well protected by guards and flankers that Forrest had strenuous work in trying to break into it. The Federals were always ready. This manner of fighting was kept up for about fourteen miles and under a July sun. Men and horses suffered greatly for want of water. Each side lost heavily. The Confederates confidently expected that victory would come to them much as it did in their last great contest. Therefore they fought desperately. The Federals adhering strictly to the tactics laid down by their General declined a general engagement till they could reach a strong natural position. In this respect, Smith acted just as if he knew exactly where he would find an advantageous position in which to deliver battle. And this he found at Harrisburg, a deserted village, which had been absorbed by Tupelo, when the railroad was built. They literally tore up the town by tearing down the houses and using the lumber for breast-works. They brought into requisition every conceivable solid object they could find and, in many places, threw on dirt. They had ample time during the night to make proper dispositions of their troops, so as to be ready for an assault. The Federal line was about a mile and a half in length, and much in the form of a semi-circle. Their twenty-four pieces of artillery were advantageously placed and there was a cavalry brigade on each flank. Their improvised works were garnished with a heavy line of infantry. Certainly the morale of the whole army must have been perfect because of its skillful handling and its success in repulsing the Confederates several times the previous day.

But what of the Southern soldiers, who were to be sent against this formidable array on this memorable morning of the 14th of July, 1864? Having bivouacked in the vicinity they were in line at 7 o'clock. General Forrest, at great risk and with a single individual, that gallant gentleman, Sam Donelson of his staff, having made a careful reconnaissance during the night, was advising with General Lee, who was now in chief command. That these two parties, distinguished in war, capable in command and trusted by their country, felt a heavy weight of responsibility is unquestionable. No element of selfishness was involved in this conference of two men who held in their hands the fate of thousands. They expected to share that day the dangers on the firing line, as was their habit, and therefore might very soon be in the presence of their Maker. Lee generously offered to waive his rank and tender the command for the day to Forrest. This the latter declined, giving as his chief reason the condition of his health. Neither was a man to shirk a responsibility. Lee said that they would move on the enemy's lines at once. That Forrest did not acquiesce in this determination of Lee, though consenting to lead the right wing in the fight, I am prepared to believe from an incident that occurred the following day and of which I will write further along. Lee urged in support of his position the threatening attitude of the Federals at Mobile, Vicksburg and in North Alabama. Forrest knew that, after deducting horse-holders and other details incident to a battle, the effective fighting force of the Confederates did not exceed seven thousand and five hundred men, the casualties of battle and the large number of men rendered unfit for duty by the excessive heat the previous day being considered in the estimate. The Confederates must move to the assault on the right and center through an open space of two hundred yards or more and on their left for fully a mile through an open old field. In the formation, Roddy's Alabamians, led by Forrest, held the right; Buford's Kentuckians and Tennesseeans, the center, and Mabry's Mississippians the left, with the four batteries of artillery properly placed. From the moment the signal gun was heard the fighting was fast and furious, the officers and men struggling to reach the works notwithstanding the withering fire from the protected Federals. Rucker's Brigade of Chalmers' division, which had been held in reserve only for a short while, was ordered to the support of Mabry's Brigade, which, though fighting to the death, was sorely pressed. This movement was on foot, through the open field and facing a broiling sun. This proud little brigade, composed of the Seventh Tennessee, Duff's Regiment and A. H. Chalmers' Battalion,

rushed to its work with the rebel yell, and was soon intermingled with Mabry's men near the Federal works. Rucker's
men, as did others, unmindful of their already depleted ranks
and seemingly regardless of the issues of life and death, fought
as if they expected some supreme moment was near when they
would repeat the work of Brice's Cross Roads. Rucker himself,
when within fifty yards of the works, was wounded twice and
carried from the field. Captain Statler, of Company E and
three of his men were killed here and others wounded. The
ground at this point was covered with the dead and wounded
while the living were famished because of the intense heat and
the lack of water. Human endurance had reached a limit. The
Confederates, leaving their dead and wounded on the field,
retreated with no attention to order. To save individual life
was now all that could be expected of the living.

The battle had been lost, but not for the lack of courage,
devotion to duty or gallant leadership. Both sides can't win, but
it is interesting, even at this distant day, especially to old soldiers, to consider the reasons of our defeat. A careful review
of the campaign is fairly convincing that Forrest with the whole
army, perhaps with less, could have defeated Smith on the hills
just south of Pontotoc and, may be, would have turned the
defeat into the usual Federal disaster. A like result might have
been brought about anywhere on the road to Harrisburg, if
Smith had turned upon Forrest for a pitched battle in the open
field. But Smith, as I have heretofore shown, declined all offers
of battle except such little engagements as were essential to
protect his rear and right flank. He moved rapidly and in close
order till he reached a choice natural position.

The great disparity of forces in actual battle, the fortified
position of the enemy, the intense heat in a rapid charge and
the long distance through an open field were all elements in

the defeat of the Confederates. If, as some writers assert, our army was fought too much in detail, of which I know nothing, that of itself would have contributed to our defeat. Judging Forrest by his former and subsequent performances, it is safe to say that, if he had been in chief command and had concluded to make an assault at all, which is doubtful, he would have had every available man in the charge and made the work short, sharp and decisive.

But why assault at all? Here was an army in a strong position for defense, it is true, but in the best possible position to be held by an opposing force till starvation threatened. It was over a hundred miles from Memphis and in an enemy's country, which had been devastated by two other raids. It was reasonable to suppose that this army, so far from its base, was running short of rations. It had expected to live off the rich country just below, which it never reached. Nothing demoralizes an army more than a prospect of impending hunger. Then why not wait one day or two days or a little longer, even in the face of threatening movements of the Federals at Mobile and other points? It is in the histories that they did not make any such move just then. Again, our commissary at Okolona, twenty miles distant, was furnishing us with supplies by wagon train. Within two days our army would have been in fine condition to pursue a hungry army in retreat. It is shown in General Smith's official report that he had only one day's rations when he left Tupelo, just as might have been reasonably expected. He abandoned his position fifteen hours after the repulse of the Confederates. He moved on the retreat much as he had on the march from Pontotoc to Harrisburg. Lee and Forrest having gathered up their shattered remnants attacked him at Old Town creek, where he made a stubborn resistance but only till his troops and trains could get well on the road. Clearly our men were in no condition to make anything more than a spiritless pursuit.

It is hardly worth while to speculate as to what would have been the result, if Smith had pressed his advantage, when he had driven the Confederates from his front. Undoubtedly it would have resulted disastrously to the Confederates. If he made a tactical error in the whole campaign, it was in this regard. True, he did not reach his objective, but neither did Sooy Smith and Sturgis. He saved his army intact, all of his artillery, and most of his wagons. The comparison is easily drawn. Having experienced the soothing influences of forty-four years, we can be just, liberal and fair. Then, A. J. Smith was a capable commander, and in the Harrisburg campaign did not lessen the prestige acquired on other fields.

As soon as the Federals abandoned their position and it had been occupied by the Confederates, I took advantage of the movement and hastened to the spot occupied by Company E, the previous day. The ground was literally strewn with the bodies of our precious slain, which had been lying where they fell for twenty-four hours. It was impossible to identify them except by their clothing and other articles. Captain J. P. Statler, William Wood, Jehu Field and David McKinney, another schoolboy of mine, must have been killed about the same time, as their bodies lay close together. First Wood, then Statler a few feet in advance and a still shorter space forward Field and McKinney at the foot of a post-oak that did not protect them from the enfilading fire of the enemy. In this group was Colonel Isham Harrison of the Sixth Mississippi with many of his own dead men about him. It was a most sorrowful sight to see Statler and his men wrapped in their blankets and buried where they fell. They appropriately sleep on the field of honor. The earth lay fresh on the grave of Captain Tate when Captain

Statler was killed. Besides the four named, Robert D. Durrett of Bolivar, and Sam Gibson were mortally wounded earlier in the action and carried to the rear. Company E could ill afford to lose the men who fell at Harrisburg. Statler had shown himself to be a worthy successor to Tate. He was a faithful friend, a dashing gallant soldier and a fine horseman. I yet hold dear the friendship knitted closely by our association at Brice's Cross Roads and on other fields.

In riding over the field at the time of which I write I heard of the deaths of others whom I knew. Among these was that of that fine young soldier, Tom Nelson of Company L, of whom I have had occasion to speak in connection with an incident at Ripley. Killed on the 13th at Barrow's shop.

I found the breastworks of the Federals all that I have heretofore described. That part in front of which Company E fought was built like a Virginia worm fence, but with heavy house logs and other weighty objects. Thus their fire was enfilading upon all points of their front. The few trees standing there afforded little protection to our men. A grape shot and twenty-one minnie balls struck the tree at the foot of which Field and McKinney lay dead.

I passed over to where the Kentuckians had fought under Crossland. Oh, the ghastly dead, and so many of them! Lieutenant-Colonel Sherrill of the Seventh Kentucky, killed near the works, was among them. The officer in charge of the burial squad quoted the lines:

Man's inhumanity to man
Makes countless thousands mourn.

I agreed with him. This was near the old Harrisburg church. I rode down the slope with others and stopped by the roadside. Along came General Forrest, wounded and riding in an open buggy. Just from the battle-field and suffering with

a wound, he was somewhat excited. I remember well the sentiment he uttered. It was that expressed by the words: "Boys,
this is not my fight, and I take no responsibility for it," or
words tantamount to these. I knew what he meant.

Now, I had known General Forrest for thirteen years
Why, the first creosote I ever saw he put into an aching tooth
of mine, when on one of his trading expeditions he was camping in front of my father's house on the road from Grenada
to Greensboro. He was a man to impress even a stripling, as I
was then. I should have carried his image in my mind to this
day even if there had never been a war. A stalwart, who habi-
tually went in his shirt sleeves. A man of commanding, but
pleasing personality, with grayish-blue eyes who spoke kindly
to children. A broad felt hat, turned up at the sides and sur-
mounting a shock of black hair about completes the picture.
I contrast this with this same figure, clothed in the resplendent
uniform of a major-general, mounted on King Philip, at the
head of his escort and with hat in hand in recognition of the
plaudits extended, with hearty good will, by the people of
Florence, Ala.

I insert here two extracts from the utterances of
Lieutenant-Colonel David C. Kelley, at once the "Fighting
Parson" and the Marshal Ney of Forrest's Cavalry, but in
peace the eminent citizen and eloquent divine: "Every individual private was trained to an unbounded belief in Forrest's
power to succeed."

"The practical suggestions of the natural warrior were
the safeguard of Hood's army."

Forrest's last words: *"I trust not in what I have done, but
in the Captain of my salvation."*

Chapter 9

THE MEMPHIS RAID

The rest of the month of July, 1864, was spent by the Confederates in the rich prairie country below Okolona. About Gunn's church we found the fields full of green corn, some in the roasting ear and much of it in that state of maturity when it is best to make jaded horses thrifty. Watermelons were cheap and abundant. There was no talk of scant rations. The farmers had been raising corn and hogs for war times. These conditions wonderfully revived the spirits of the men. Cornbread now and no biscuit. Plenty of greasy bacon and some with a streak of lean and a streak of fat. This held on a sharp stick and over the fire, and with the gravy dripping on the bread, was some- thing good to look at. Some managed to always have a little sugar and coffee which they had secured with other captured spoils. As a rule, Confederate soldiers did not tolerate rye or other substitutes for coffee. They wanted the "pure stuff" or nothing. The weather was warm, and sleeping in the open air was refreshing. Company E had not stretched a tent for more than a year. Occasionally quartered in unoccupied houses, the men were generally protected against the elements by rude structures of such materials as was at hand, but mostly by cap- tured rubber cloths, stretched over a pole resting in two forks stuck in the ground. If only one was to be accommodated, a convenient sapling was bent down till it assumed the shape of a bow and its top secured to the ground. Then the rubber cloth was stretched over this so that a soldier could crawl under. In both cases, the shelter was called a "shebang." A good rest and full stomachs went far towards getting those of us who had been spared ready for the next campaign. We left the goodly land where "if you tickle the soil with a hoe, it will laugh with a harvest." We went to Oxford to meet our late antagonist,

General A. J. Smith, who was moving south with another fine army. Forrest with a greatly reduced force was compelled to meet him. It might be remembered as the wet August, for it rained almost incessantly. It would require every available man now. We stretched out our thin line along Hurricane creek, six miles north of Oxford. The Federals were crossing the Tallahatchie at Abbeville a few miles north of our position. Skirmishing began at once with the advance of the superior force of the Federals. By the 10th of August, 1864, Forrest had all his forces in line except Buford's division, which was posted at Pontotoc to watch any movement east by the Federals. Before the main body of the Confederates arrived Smith had driven Chalmers' division to the south side of the Yokona, several miles below Oxford. On the approach of reinforcements the Federals fell back across Hurricane creek to their former position. The heavy rains continued to fall and added greatly to the discomforts of our men. It was impossible to keep even moderately dry under the best *"shebangs"* that could be constructed, because the ground was saturated. We continued to strengthen our works with such poor material as we could get. At best, they would have given us poor protection in case of attack.

Rucker's Brigade was now a thing of the past and the Seventh Tennessee was attached to Richardson's Brigade, commanded by Colonel J. J. Neely. At his instance I had been temporarily detailed to attend to some clerical and other work in the ordnance department. For the time being I stopped at the quarters of Lieutenant-Colonel White, commanding the Fourteenth Tennessee, where we spent most of the time in trying to keep dry. Rations were in plenty, but we could scarcely get dry wood enough to cook them. Much of our ammunition was ruined and in our skirmishes many of the cartridges would not explode. All efforts to induce the Federals to cross to our side of the shallow creek failed, though our men frequently crossed to their side and, having engaged their advance, fell back hurriedly with the design of drawing them into a disadvantageous place. Colonel Neely one day, between showers, concluded to make an effort to lead the Federal cavalry into a well planned ambuscade by offering them superior inducements. The Fourteenth Regiment under White was ordered to cross the creek, dismount and get in a well-chosen place in the thick bushes and parallel with the road. A detachment of Neely's escort, with which I crossed over, was to ride forward, engage the Federal advance briskly, and retreat in some confusion. The enemy took the bait and came on at a canter. Luckily for them, their flankers struck the right of the dismounted regiment and gave the alarm. However, part of their pursuing force came up to where the escort was posted. The dense growth of timber on this spot so obscured the view that the Federal cavalry soon found themselves face to face with, and in short range of, our reserve, and those who had rallied. It was a most exciting contest for only a minute or two, and chiefly with pistols, on our side, but both parties seemed to have lost the knack of hitting anything, for I saw no dead or wounded, though we quickly drove the enemy upon their reserve and kept up a spirited gunplay until it was our time to fall back. Everybody realized the inability of the Confederates to cope with the greatly superior force of the Federals, and we were liable to be driven from our position by a heavy flank movement at any time. A knowledge of this, of course, was possessed by the rank and file, and the suspense concerning coming results was great. In the midst of our anxiety, Colonel White received orders to prepare rations for an expedition. That something radical was on the tapis was evident. Only picked men and horses were wanted. It got abroad in camp that we were going to Memphis. That looked radical, but pleased us. There was a weeding out of sick men, sore back and lame horses. The camp took on new life. As the duties of my special assignment were about discharged, I could have asked to be relieved and to be returned to my own company, which was not under orders, but I preferred to take part in whatever excitement was in store for us, so I said nothing and went to Memphis with Colonel White. We left camp on the night of the 18th of August, 1864, in a downpour and in darkness so great that we could scarcely see the road. I had hard work that night with the help of a small detachment in having a quantity of cornbread baked by the good women along our way; keeping it dry, and promptly joining the regiment next morning on the road to Panola. At this old town there was a short delay to get the column well up, and to have another culling of disabled men and horses, for the night march had been a severe one on both man and beast. Having crossed the Tallahatchie, we turned our faces toward Memphis. The sun was now shining, and everybody was in jolly, good spirits. Our clothing was drying rapidly by evaporation. Reaching Senatobia, twenty-three miles from Panola, we rested till next morning. In the meantime, a competent detail was building a bridge over the Hickahala, a creek just north of the town, and swollen by the heavy rains. And such a bridge! An old flatboat placed in midstream for a central pontoon, and strengthened by floats made of dry cedar telegraph poles, which were bound together by grapevines, constituted the body of the structure. Other poles were used as beams to piece out the bridge, and over the whole was laid a floor of planks brought by hand from the ginhouses in the neighborhood. Finally, a twisted cable of grapevines was placed on the side down stream, and lashed to trees on either bank. The men dismounted and led their horses over in column of twos. The two pieces of artillery with their caissons were wheeled across by hand. At Coldwater river, seven miles further north, a longer bridge was required. The men assigned to the work of building one were not long in completing it, and the command crossed over as they did over the first bridge. Twice that morning I was reminded of the aphorism that "necessity is the mother of invention."

At the Coldwater bridge there was a wagon heavily loaded with corn in the shuck, which was thought to be too heavy for the bridge. General Forrest ordered the corn thrown out and the wagon and corn carried over by hand. He was the first man to carry an armful across. There was hardly need of his setting the example for the men, for everybody was for leaving nothing undone that would hasten the expedition to a glorious conclusion. I never saw a command look more like it was out for a holiday. At Hernando we were twenty-five miles from our objective. From there on we had no rain, the road was better, and we moved along at a pace like that of Van Dorn, when on his way to Holly Springs. We were fondly expecting to write *ditto* under his performance, but in much larger letters, the very next morning. Forrest left Oxford with about fifteen hundred men, and every one of them thought that, if he "sought the bubble reputation at the cannon's mouth," he would likely draw a prize package into the bargain. The latter might be in the shape of a pair of boots or a horse, a suit of clothes or a small quantity of "store coffee." A buttermilk and soda biscuit would not be "turned down," if we took the town. Hilarity was hilarious and that's the truth about it.

To water and to rest the horses a little were imperative. Every man carried a small quantity of shelled corn. The utmost quiet was now insisted upon. When within a few miles of the city Forrest had a consultation with his field officers, and these with their company officers, who gave quiet and explicit instructions to the men. The most drastic order was that if any officer or soldier saw one plundering he should shoot him on the spot. The different regiments were assigned to particular duties in certain localities in the city. More information was imparted to subordinate officers and private soldiers than is usual on such occasions. I think that it was intended that every man in the command should, as nearly as possible, understand just what his own regiment was to do in taking the city. Everybody about the head of the Fourteenth Tennessee understood that Captain Bill Forrest and his company would surprise and capture the vidette and outpost. While we believed that General Forrest was acting upon reliable information from spies and scouts as to the situation of affairs in Memphis, we knew that there was always a chance for an enemy to be fully informed. In that case, we did not know but that deadly ambuscades would be set for us. As we moved at a walk, the report of a single gun was heard. It was likely that some poor fellow had gone to his death. Day was breaking, but there was a dense fog. The column, moving by fours, struck a lively pace. The Fourteenth Regiment, turning into Mississippi avenue at Kerr soon plunged into a mudhole, which, in the dim light, looked interminable. Another command ahead of us was struggling to get through it. The men in the rear crowded upon those retarded in front, and the confusion was likely to defeat the whole plan of attack, which was to be executed promptly and rapidly. It added to the excitement that Captain Forrest's company, pushing on into the city, had encountered a Federal battery near Trigg avenue, and we could hear the firing. The delay was unfortunate, but we soon got upon firmer ground. The men, by this time, had broken into a shout. As the Fourteenth Regiment was one of those designated for that purpose, Colonel White quickly dashed into the large Federal encampment to the right, and in a large grove, a part of which is yet standing. The tents stood in long white rows, but their occupants, recovering somewhat from their surprise, had rallied a little further north, and were delivering a brisk fire in the darkness, caused by the fog, but to very little purpose. In large, bold letters, I could see on the tents inscribed the words "One Hundred and Thirty-seventh Illinois Infantry." The smoke from the guns of both sides intensified the foggy darkness. As we pushed through the encampment, I espied a man lying in one of the bunks with which the tents were supplied. The poor fellow had been left alone and sick. I advised him to lie still, as I did not care to see a non-resistant increase his chances of death by rising up. A splendid pair of army shoes was sitting on a shelf in front of a tent. Somehow, in the excitement, I reached down for the shoes and tied them to my saddle. I thought of the strict orders given in regard to appropriating anything prematurely, but I was practically barefoot. The shoes were new and a perfect fit. They supplied the place of the boots secured at Union City, and were good shoes at the surrender. I was fully repaid for my part in the raid.

Forrest's movement on Memphis was now a success or a failure, for we understood that in a surprise orders were to be executed rapidly.

Colonel Neely, with the Fourteenth Tennessee, Second Missouri, and Chalmers' Battalion, drove the infantry force in his front rapidly back to a position about the State Female College, in and around which there was some stubborn fighting. The Confederate loss here was light.

As we were all anxious to hear what our men in the city had done, I rode to the intersection of Mississippi avenue and

McLemore to seek information. This was scant, but to the effect that our men were carrying everything before them; in fact, that Forrest had complete possession of the city, notwithstanding the Federals had an effective force of five thousand men of all arms, including that part of it fighting around the college. The fog had lifted, and we were having a bright day. By 9 o'clock the object of the raid had been fairly accomplished, and the Confederates in the city began to come out in disorganized squads. Two of our men were reported killed on Main street. A son of Dr. J. S. Robinson, of Whiteville, was killed in the fight about the college. As the superior Federal force rapidly recovered from its surprise, it became dangerous for those who had lingered to depart from the city. At one point, Forrest himself, with the Second Missouri, attacked an advancing Federal detachment of cavalry, and with his own hands killed Colonel Starr, a Federal officer. It only remained to secure the spoils which had been gathered, up and a large number of horses besides about six hundred prisoners. If, as a result of the raid, a retrograde movement of Smith's army at Oxford was at hand, it could be written down as a big success, for that was its main purpose. It is true that Forrest had planned to capture the three Federal Generals, who escaped the clutches of the Confederates by the merest chance. In connection with what our men did really accomplish, I have heard some interesting stories, but I have always regarded these as largely fanciful. Many believe to this day that Forrest, booted and spurred, rode into the Gayoso Hotel, but in his lifetime, he never lent encouragement to this belief. However, it is authentically stated that Captain Forrest, with some of his company, did what has been attributed to his brother, the General. I have it from a reliable witness that the Captain did kill a Federal officer, who did not promptly realize that he had fallen into the hands of his enemies. I remark that this account is not intended to be a history of all things that transpired on that memorable morning of August 21, 1864, but rather a reminiscence of those things that fell under my personal observation, or of which I had authentic information on the spot.

We retired at our leisure to Mississippi, where news soon reached us that the Federals had driven Chalmers, with his inferior force, to the south side of the Yokona, and were committing depredations in and around Oxford. They had burnt the courthouse and many other buildings, including the fine residence of Jacob Thompson, with its hundred thousand dollars worth of furnishings. It was said, and it turned out to be true, that Mrs. Thompson was robbed of such valuable articles as she could hastily carry out. In giving his men such license, General Edward Hatch had revealed his true character as a man. He had won renown on the battle-field, and shown himself to be an able commander and skillful tactician, but had disgraced himself in the eyes of all advocates of civilized warfare.

Just as Forrest had anticipated, the Federals began to fall back from Oxford, as soon as their commander heard the news from Memphis. General James R. Chalmers was entitled to great praise for the skillful manner in which he had handled his troops and concealed from the enemy the absence of Forrest. He held a position that required tact, discretion and courage, and met the expectations of his chief. I remember him well, and can recall his character as that of a man who, as occasion required, could move an audience by his eloquence, charm the fastidious with his felicity of diction, and gallantly lead his men in battle. Personally, "Little un" was popular with the rank and file, as he was one of the most approachable of men.

Scrupulously uniformed and finely mounted, he presented an attractive figure on review. A man of literary taste, he sometimes courted the muses. He was the reputed author of some words I heard sung in war times to the air of Bonnie Doone. These words might well be brought to light again and take their place in popular esteem by the side of "Dixie" and "The Bonnie Blue Flag." Perhaps some one of those who used to be called "the pretty girls of Bolivar," but who, alas, are now wearing frosted crowns, could find in her old portfolios the words which might serve to keep green the memory of a gallant Confederate.

To rest in shady groves, to sleep by lulling waters, to hear the songs of birds, the hum of bees, the tinkling bells of lowing kine, bring more pleasing thoughts to mind than those of war and deadly strife. To things like these we turned after the Memphis raid, but not for long. The people praised the deeds of Forrest's Cavalry, the marvel of horseback fighting, and the worthy rival of trained infantry, but the soldiers' pæans of victory always had a minor note of sorrow for our desolate land, the tears of widows and orphans, and our increasing casualties in battle. Our poor fellows were falling, and our line becoming shorter, as the living pressed their shoulders together.

We camped on the Yokona, at Oakland and Grenada, and I returned to Company E.

Chapter 10

INCIDENTS OF THE MIDDLE TENNESSEE RAID

An entire reorganization of Forrest's Cavalry Corps was effected just after the Memphis raid, by which a new brigade, composed exclusively of Tennesseans, was formed for Colonel

Rucker, who was absent on account of a wound received at Harrisburg. The regiments in this were the Seventh, Twelfth, Fourteenth, Fifteenth and Forrest's old regiment, commanded respectively by Duckworth, Green, Neely, Stewart and Kelly. The other brigade of Chalmers' division was that of McCulloch, composed of men from Missouri, Texas and Mississippi. Rumors were rife, as usual, that we were on the eve of some important move, but those only in whose hands the duty of projecting campaigns had been placed knew what that move would be. Uncertainty brought no suspense to the minds of the men, as we had become accustomed to go with alacrity to the discharge of any duty assigned. To one who has studied closely the military situation at the time, it is plain that the affairs of the Confederacy had reached the desperate stage, though Forrest had subverted the plans of the Federals on the Memphis lines. The humblest of us could reflect that the territory to which we had been assigned was only a small part of the country, and that our movements on the military chessboard were scarcely noticed, except when Forrest had gained another brilliant victory. Think of it. The Confederacy had been cut in twain for more than a year by the opening of the Mississippi river; Sherman had driven Joe Johnston from Dalton to Atlanta, and a hundred days of fighting had not barred the way of the Federals toward the sea. The first trial of arms between Lee and Grant had been made at the Wilderness, and Lee had failed, even by grand tactics, to permanently stay the flank movement of the overwhelming legions of Grant at Spottsylvania, who was now moving steadily on the bloody road to Richmond. In the light which a knowledge of these conditions afforded, our immediate part of the war appeared comparatively insignificant. The reader well might ask how Forrest, or any other commander, could, under given conditions, keep up the fighting spirits of his men. We well know that he did this as long as he had occasion to lead his men in battle, but how he did it, or whence this power, I leave to the consideration of those philosophers who revel in the discussion of abstract questions of metaphysics. And I give them a thousand years to settle it.

During the first days of September we were taking a long ride over to the Mobile & Ohio Railroad. Cui bono? We reasoned, of course, that as we had gotten rid of our immediate enemies, who had so long been troubling us, we should probably be sent to other fields of action. It finally came to light that affairs at Mobile were thought to be in such critical condition that Chalmers' division must be sent to that city at once. McCulloch's brigade was actually sent forward, while Rucker's was at West Point, ready to take the cars. Before this information reached the men, the order was countermanded. So we did not go to Mobile, but our enterprising General was not idle. It was soon openly talked that he was projecting a raid into Middle Tennessee, where he proposed to so damage the railroad between Nashville and Stephenson as to cut off Sherman's army at Atlanta from its base of supplies. Rucker had not yet assumed command of his new brigade, but it was thought he would do so before we started on the projected expedition. The four Colonels of the brigade and the officer temporarily in command of Forrest's old regiment, evidently considering it a reflection on them for an outsider, and only a Colonel, to take precedence over them, flatly refused to consent to the new arrangement. There was a great stir in camp at Sook-a-toncha bridge, near West Point. For a whole day nothing else was discussed and little else thought of. As might be supposed, there were two factions in the contest as to who should command the brigade. The humblest private was in evidence, and had something to say in the spirited, though friendly, discussion. General Chalmers, with his staff, rode out to the camp and made an earnest address to officers and soldiers as to the necessity of obeying orders and disregarding personal ambition. The character and efficiency of the officers involved were favorably alluded to, but not an offensive word spoken. While speaking in rather a persuasive tone, he did not hesitate to make an earnest and honest declaration of his sentiments. The address made a good impression, and, so far as I could see, the excitement was much less intense the following day, and, by the time the movement began, the rank and file looked upon the whole thing as a closed incident. The officers refusing to recognize the assignment of Rucker were placed in arrest upon the charge of insubordination, and sent to a distant post to await orders. I never heard of any action being taken by a court-martial in these cases, but I do know that they saw little more of the war, as they returned to the command only a few days before the surrender. The whole affair was unpleasant to me because of my friendly attitude toward two of them— Colonel Duckworth, formerly a Lieutenant in the Haywood Rangers (Company D), and Colonel Neely, the first Captain of Company E. I knew the others by their reputations as true men and efficient commanders. The whole trouble might have been avoided, or at least deferred, for as it turned out, Colonel Rucker, still suffering with his wound, did not go on the raid at all, and Lieutenant-Colonel Kelly, the senior officer present, took charge of the brigade. It could not have falled into better hands. No aspersion was cast on the character of Rucker as a man, or adverse criticism made of his capability as a commander. A man of great physical force and a fine horseman, he impressed men with his prowess in battle. Recklessly brave, he did not mind riding down an enemy, or engaging him in single combat. He helped to make the reputation of his old brigade as a body of fast and furious fighters.

With Lieutenant-Colonel W. F. Taylor in command, the Seventh Tennessee moved up to Verona, and then to Tupelo. Here final preparations were made. And here General Forrest, from a platform made for the purpose, delivered a lively address to our brigade, a part of which was a scathing criticism of the action of the officers whom he had recently placed in arrest. He was full of his subject, and had language at hand to express his thoughts.

September 16th, 1864. On this day 3,542 men reported for duty, to which number Roddys' division was to be added, making in all a force of about 4,500 cavalry, artillery and dismounted men. The cavalry was to traverse the hypotenuse of a right triangle, reaching from Tupelo, Miss., to Cherokee, Ala., while General Forrest, his escort, dismounted men and every thing on wheels, were to traverse the other two sides by way of Corinth and over railroads, which had been recently repaired. I never saw men in better spirits as the several commands took their places in line. I had good reason to feel glad in anticipation, as will be shown further along. When the Fourteenth Regiment, passing the Seventh in line, was moving to its place in column, Colonel Raleigh White, seeing me lined up in my company, insisted that I go with him on the raid, just as I had on the Memphis raid. Knowing that I could discharge my full duty, and that White would grant me any reasonable request when we reached North Alabama, I joined him as soon as the matter was arranged. As there was no necessity for rushing, we moved leisurely to Cherokee. There was need that the command should be in good trim when it should reach the north side of the Tennessee river. Seeing from the orders that the command was likely to remain at rest for a day or two, I determined to reach Florence, if possible, at least one day in advance. But I could not cross the river without a pass from General Forrest. Nothing daunted, I went straight to his headquarters, as soon as I could get my plans mentally arranged, which, I now remember, was done with some degree of fear and trembling. He was absent. It might be fortunate, thought I, for I would lay my case before Major Strange, and get his opinion as to the merits of my plea. My desire to see my child must have touched a tender chord in his heart, as he said that the General would return by a certain hour, and that, if I would call again, I would likely get the pass. I was promptly on hand. Again the General was absent. My feelings were now intense, for it was growing late in the day. Seeing this, Major Strange graciously and kindly said that he would furnish me with a document that would take me across the river and through all picket lines. I mounted my horse and made for the river, which I hoped to reach before night. It was seven miles away, and I had no information as to where I might find a means of crossing. Somewhere in a long lane I happily met an old school fellow— Charlie Trimble of Tuscumbia—who could give me the necessary information. When I finished the last mile, it was growing so dark that the soldiers in charge would not venture to go on the river in the rickety old boat. The prospect was now so good that I made myself content. At daylight next morning Little Black and I were on the bosom of the Tennessee, and nearing the northern shore. Poor fellow, he could go over with a dry skin now, but within a few days he must swim the same stream over a hundred miles below, where it was much larger and at floodtide. Now for the nearest road to Florence. At Dr. McAlexander's, just as the family were sitting down to breakfast. Good coffee and hot biscuits. Lucky hit, thought I. A thousand thoughts of happy days come trooping in. For the nonce, I have forgotten the war and scenes of peace pass in review.

" 'Tis sweet to hear the watchdog's honest bark
  Bay deep-mouthed welcome as we draw near home;
'Tis sweet to know there is an eye will mark
  Our coming, and look brighter when we come.
'Tis sweet to be awaken'd by the lark,
  Or lull'd by falling waters; sweet the hum
Of bees, the voice of girls, the song of birds,
  The lisp of children, and their earliest words."

Was ever picture more divinely drawn? The last line—"the lisp of children and their earliest words"—arouses the tenderest emotions of the soul.

I stopped at the Smith cottage, a well-known landmark, just across from the Methodist Church. I gazed up at the old steeple in respectful silence, and felt glad to stand in its shadow once more. But I am now at the door of the cottage, which was closed. I step along the veranda to an open window. Unobserved, I gaze for some moments on the picture within. To me, at least, "the prettiest and loveliest boy" in all the land, engaged in childish pranks with his colored nurse. I hesitated to break the spell, for it seemed to me that happiness had reached its full fruition. Ernest was a happy little boy in a happy home, for war times, as his aunt, the late Mrs. Henry W. Sample, was devoted to him as she had been devoted to his mother. I never could repay her for all her kindness to me and mine, but I place here in print a sincere tribute to her memory as that of a noble woman, who was altogether unselfish, whose religion was a daily affair, who cultivated a charitable spirit, who reached out her hand to those in trouble, and who went to her grave with the love and respect of the people among whom she had lived seventy-two years.

On the 21st of September, 1864, Forrest's whole command crossed the Tennessee river. The artillery, wagon train and dismounted men were taken across in boats at Colbert's Ferry, while the whole mounted force passed the river at Ross' Ford, a short distance below. The latter is said to have furnished one of the most picturesque scenes of the war. The river at this point is seldom fordable and always dangerous. A careful guide led the long column, marching by twos, along the winding shallows for over two miles, in order to avoid the dangerous places in the bed of the river, which at this point was scarcely a mile wide. There were no casualties, but many men lost their hats and other articles when their horses slipped on the rocks. On the morning of the 22d Florence was all agog to see Forrest and his men, and pretty well filled up with Confederate soldiers, who, like myself, were making friendly or family calls. There were many small reunions of old friends, who never met again, on this seeming holiday in war times. In the early forenoon of a perfect day, Forrest, mounted on King Philip, and riding at the head of his escort, came in from the west, turned into Court street and then into Tennessee street, running east. The streets were lined with men, women and children, whose shouts were ably supplemented by the yells of the visiting soldiers. To have stood on Mitchell's corner that day, as I did, would mark an event in a life otherwise filled with adventures.

Conditions at Florence had changed somewhat for the worse since my last visit, nearly two years before. The country had been occupied alternately by the Federals and Confederates, and thousands of acres had gone to waste for the want of labor. There was hardly a worse overrun country in the South. Clothing and food were hard to get with any kind of money. Of course, what might be termed Confederate devices were put into practice, and very plain living was the order of the day.

Tarrying to the limit with loved ones whom I might never see again, I left Florence late at night to overtake the command the next day before it reached Athens. As I rode out towards the suburbs, the silence was so pronounced that Florence seemed to be a town of houses without inhabitants. I approached the cemetery—to me a sacred spot—where the waters of the Tennessee, bounding over the rocks of Mussel Shoals, sing an eternal requiem to our dead. The monuments stood like sentinels at the graves of many whom I had known. Out on the hillside was one erected by myself. I paused to ponder. Stillness reigned supreme, for it was midnight's solemn hour. No voice of man nor chirp of bird was on the air. No painful loneliness disturbed my soul, for silent friends were there. She, a mother for a short month only, about whom I was thinking, having died at the age of nineteen years, escaped the sorrow, trials and experiences of a cruel war. Perhaps it were well.

General Forrest invested the Federal works at Athens, about forty miles from Florence, late in the afternoon of the 23rd of September. There was no concerted attack then, but careful dispositions were made for the next morning. An assault meant a dreadful slaughter of our men, as the works were strong, and held by about fourteen hundred well-drilled negro troops, officered by white men. At 7 o'clock the fire of all the artillery was concentrated upon the fort, and the cavalry, dismounted, moved up as if for assault. Forrest ordered his artillery to cease firing, and sent a flag of truce to the Federal commander, demanding a surrender. There was a parley and a refusal. Forrest then adopted his favorite plan of magnifying his own forces and intimidating his adversary. In a personal interview outside the fort, Forrest proposed to the Federal commander that he should take a ride around the lines, and see for himself how well the Confederates were prepared for an assault. The proposition was accepted, but Forrest so manipulated his troops by dismounting and remounting and changing the position of his artillery, that the Federal commander was soon convinced that the Confederates were sufficiently strong to make a successful assault. While the terms of the surrender were being arranged, a reinforcement of white troops arrived from Decatur, and made a determined effort to cut their way through to the fort. This was met by the Seventh Tennessee and other regiments, and a bloody battle was fought before the Federals were captured. To complete the victory, the artillery was brought up to capture two blockhouses, which were held by about one hundred men. In the fight along the railroad, Lieutenant V. F. Ruffin of Company E, a promising young man and a splendid soldier, was killed. He was the only brother of two orphan sisters. Their loss was grievous. Our loss at Athens was five killed and twenty-five wounded. We captured two trains, two locomotives, a large quantity of stores, two pieces of artillery, a number of wagons and ambulances, and three hundred horses. The Federal loss in killed and wounded was considerable, including the death of the Colonel commanding the detachment from the direction of Decatur. Their loss in prisoners was about 1,900.

As Colonel White had been ordered to tear up portions of the railroad toward Decatur, I found it impracticable to join him. Falling in with Captain John Overton, of Rucker's staff, we rode along our lines to view the situation. As Forrest was having an interview with the Federals, we concluded it would be perfectly safe for us to accept an invitation to breakfast at a nearby house. We had not more than dispatched that breakfast when firing was heard down the railroad. Overton mounted and rode rapidly to the position where part of our brigade was engaged. There he had his fine blooded mare killed under him. Thirty-two years after that he walked into the station at Tullahoma carrying what he said was a box of rattlesnakes. Oh, horrors! thought I. As he evidently did not fully recognize me, and only knew I was someone whom he had seen before, I said to him: "Captain, don't you remember something about a good breakfast you and I had together down in Athens when we were younger men than we are now?" Brightening up, he replied: "Yes, but don't you remember about my losing my fine mare that morning?" John Overton's immediate or prospective wealth never puffed him up, or made any difference with him in his intercourse with all classes of men in the army. He had none of the graces of horseback riding, and moved about the camp much after the manner of some plain farmer, when looking after the crop of crabgrass or considering the advisability of planting his potatoes in the dark of the moon. He was "a chip off the old block"—his grand old father, whom we sometimes saw in camp.

Four miles north of Athens, a blockhouse, with thirty-two men was surrendered. We bivouacked for the night, thinking that we had made a fine beginning. Eleven miles from Athens, there was a strong fort, which protected what was known as Sulphur Branch trestle, a structure three hundred feet long and seventy-two feet high. In order to destroy this, it was necessary to capture the fort and two large blockhouses. On the morning of the 25th of September, the Confederate artillery was concentrated on the fort, in which were several rude cabins covered with oak boards. At the same time, Forrest ordered a heavy force to advance on foot against the position. There was severe fighting for only a little while, as our artillery quickly scattered the lighter timbers and roofs of the cabins in every direction, and killed many of the garrison. The Federals ceased firing, but did not display the white flag. Their commander had already been killed, and there seemed to be great consternation in the fort. They surrendered as soon as a demand was made on them. This surrender included the two blockhouses. I saw no more horrid spectacle during the war than the one which the interior of that fort presented. If a cyclone had struck the place, the damage could hardly have been much worse. Here, again, the spoils were great, including three hundred cavalry horses and their equipments, a large number of wagons and ambulances, two pieces of artillery, all kinds of army stores, with nearly a thousand prisoners. Forrest was compelled now to send south a second installment of prisoners and captured property under a strong guard, the first having been sent from Athens. Sulphur Branch trestle being demolished, we moved towards Pulaski. The lame and disabled horses were now replaced by captured ones, and all the dismounted men, who had been crowded to the limit to keep up on the march, were furnished with horses. Some of our men were engaged in tearing up railroad track, while others were driving the enemy back towards Pulaski. Within six miles of the town we had heavy fighting, and again within three miles. At the former place, I saw the dead body of Stratton Jones, another schoolboy of mine, and the eldest son of Judge Henry C. Jones of Florence, now, perhaps, the oldest citizen of his city, and one of less than half a dozen of the surviving members of the Confederate Congress.

At the Brown farm, still nearer to Pulaski, we captured a corral containing about 2,000 negroes, who were being supported by the Federal commissary. They were a dirty and ragged lot, who were content to grasp at the mere shadow of freedom. Forrest ordered them to remove their filthy belongings from the miserable hovels, and set about two hundred of the latter on fire. Here was the richest depot of supplies I had seen since the capture of Holly Springs by Van Dorn. A bountiful supply of sugar and coffee was distributed to the men. Our horses were put in fine condition here by many hours of rest and good feed. Our loss for the day was about 100 in killed and wounded. That of the Federals was very much greater.

The Federals, under General Rousseau, took lodgment within their works, which were very strong. Having made a spirited demonstration on the enemy's front, Forrest, after nightfall, leaving numerous campfires burning, just as Washington did the night before the battle of Princeton, drew off and took the road to Fayetteville. Having bivouacked a few miles out, we started at daylight for a ride of forty miles, which put us several miles east of that town. The country was fearfully rough and rocky, but the men and horses held up well. Some time during the following day, September 29th, we reached the village of Mulberry. It was pleasant to see a large school in session and the boys and girls climbing upon the fence to see the soldiers. It was more like peace than war. But here was a pause, for Forrest concluded that it was impracticable to reach the Nashville & Chattanooga Railroad, because of the concentration of thousands of Federals along that line, for it was all-important to them to protect Sherman's communication with his base of supplies. The plan now was that Buford should take 1,500 men, including Rucker's brigade, under Kelley, and the artillery and wagons, march to Huntsville, capture the place, if possible, but, by all means, to push his trains toward some available crossing on the Tennessee river, while Forrest was to take the rest of the command, swing around by Lewisburg, strike the railroad above Columbia, do all the damage possible, and hurry on to Florence.

We kept up the march towards Huntsville till after nightfall, as it was necessary to make a bold feint, at least, against the position commanded by General Granger. I noticed Buford, who was a notably large man, making his way that night on a very fine mule. He was one type of ye jolly Kentuckian, popular with his men, and perfectly reliable in a fight. Our fifteen hundred men were so placed about the town as to make as big a show of force as possible. Before this could be done, it was so dark that a lantern was procured from some citizen, so that the usual flag of truce and demand for surrender could be sent in. There was the expected refusal, and a consequent delay till morning. In the meantime, our trains were moving rapidly toward Florence. After daylight, the best possible demonstration without too much exposure of our men was made, and was succeeded by another demand and another refusal to surrender. As General Granger expected to be attacked by the whole of Forrest's command, as had been intimated to him under the last flag of truce, he order women and children to be removed from the city, so as to avoid a bombardment by all of Forrest's artillery. There was great commotion and distress among the non-combatants, who had no means of finding out that they were really in no danger. The Federal artillery was sending an occasional shot, perhaps for the purpose of getting the range of our lines. One of these went straight down the pike leading west, along which a few people were moving. I saw two ladies and a boy abandon their carriage and advance rapidly through the open field in which I was standing, leaving the colored driver to get out of harm's way by rapid driving. Riding forward, I noticed that they were greatly excited and badly frightened. The party turned out to be old friends of mine, the wife of Professor Mayhew and son and Miss Sue Murphy, who became, after the war, the plaintiff in an historical lawsuit against the government for damage and loss of property at Decatur, in which she sustained her plea. I directed them how to get to the rear, and around to where their carriage had probably gone. When the command drew off and took the road to Athens, I came upon this same party, who informed me that their trunks had been ransacked and their horses taken by some of our own men. I soon found the horses, and fastened the outrage upon men whom I knew. I lost no time in reporting the matter to Colonel Kelley, who ordered the horses to be turned over to a friend of the ladies.

It was found, when we reached Athens, that the fort, which had been surrendered to us only a few days before, was held by the Federals. There was some exchange of shots, and we had one man wounded. He caught in his mouth an ounce ball which had passed through the fleshy part of his jaw. He kept it as a nice little souvenir of a painful incident. Our part of Forrest's command reached Florence on the 3d of October, and General Buford set about the task of getting to the south side of the river. The rains had been heavy in the mountains. The river was already high for the season, and still rising. There were only three ferryboats with which to do all the work in hand. Reports came in that overwhelming numbers of the enemy were on the move to encompass the capture or defeat of Forrest, who arrived on the 5th of October. I knew that the situation would be critical, if they pressed us before we accomplished the passage of the river, but I concluded to remain in Florence till the Seventh Regiment came in, when I could join my own company. It came in on the 7th, closely followed by the enemy. The Seventh, Second and Sixteenth Regiments stoutly resisted the advance of the Federals at Martin's factory, on Cypress creek, just west of town. This was a strong position from which to resist a front attack, but a Federal brigade, crossing three miles above, came near taking us in reverse and capturing the three regiments. Our command had an exciting experience from there to old Newport, where Forrest, in person, was trying to get as many men and horses as possible across to an island thickly set with timber and cane. From the shore to the island was fully two hundred feet. The horses were made to swim this place. In the absence of Lieutenant-Colonel Taylor, who was wounded and sick, the regiment was commanded by Captain H. C. McCutchen of Company H, who received orders from Forrest to save his men, if possible, in any practicable way. The Federals were then right on us in great numbers, and still another column was reported to be advancing east from Waterloo. We did not know but that we were practically in the clutches of the enemy. The anxiety of the men had reached a high pitch. There was a determination to ride out of the situation at almost any risk. I was glad that I knew the country well enough to guide the six companies present to safety, if immediate danger could be passed. I moved right off from the river, through woods and fields, with the command following at a lively gait. My purpose was to cross the Florence and Waterloo road before the two columns of the enemy could form a junction, in which case we should have to cut our way out or surrender. I knew that body of men would ride through or over any ordinary resistance in our front. When we crossed the Colbert's Ferry road, I felt that one danger was passed, but not the main one. Sometimes we took advantage of country roads leading our way, but our course was north, regardless of roads. Our horses were smoking when we reached the desired highway, and we felt relieved when we saw the way clear. We halted to take a survey of the situation, and to perfect plans for getting into West Tennessee. It was decided to be best for the regiment to disperse, and the commander of each company to lead his men out of danger by whatever means he should think proper to adopt. Company D and Company E had gone into the service together, and it was natural that they should stand by each other in trouble. When these two companies got over into the hills of Wayne County, we hired a guerrilla guide, whom his followers called "Captain" Miller, to show us a place on the river where we could cross. His remuneration was a thousand dollars in Confederate money, which was likely more money of any kind than he had ever seen in one lump. The people along the route cheerfully furnished us with supplies. I remember, we went down Trace creek and across the head-waters of Buffalo, and reached the river at the mouth of Morgan's creek, in Decatur County. Here was a booming river about a half mile wide, and no means of transportation but a large "dugout" some eighteen or twenty feet in length. We had grown about reckless enough now to try the impracticable and test the impossible. Three men with their horses and trappings were to make the first trip, two to bring back the boat, then three more men with their horses, to go with the two who had brought the boat back, and so on till all had crossed. Everybody worked. Two men took their places at the oars, while I sat in the stern, where I was to hold each horse by the bridle as he was pushed from the bank, which was four or five feet sheer down to the water. Little Black was the first to make the plunge. He made one futile effort to touch bottom, and sank up to his ears. I pulled him up by the reins, and slipped my right hand up close to the bits, so as to keep his nose above the water. He floated up on one side and became perfectly quiet. I soon had the noses of the other two close up to the boat. The men at the oars pulled for dear life against the booming tide, the swellings of which we could feel under the boat. Our object was to make an old ferry landing several hundred yards below. We had no fear for the horses now, for they were behaving admirably. Though the men at the oars exerted themselves to the limit, we missed the landing, and were carried some distance below it. When we did pull into shallow water, I turned the horses loose. My own horse was the first to mount a steep, slippery bank, where he shook himself, and, looking back, gave me a friendly nicker. The first trip was a success, and the men took on fresh courage. The work began at sunrise, and ended with darkness. It added greatly to our critical situation that the Federal gunboats were liable to pass up or down at any moment.

Forrest did not accomplish the chief object of the Middle Tennessee raid, as heretofore stated, which was the destruction of portions of the Nashville & Chattanooga Railroad, which connected Sherman's army, at Atlanta, with its base of supplies. He said afterward that he killed and captured, upon an average, one man for every man he had in the fights. He tore up about one hundred miles of railroad, destroyed ten block-houses, captured more supplies than his men could carry off and 800 horses, gathered up more than a thousand recruits, and marched five hundred miles in twenty-three days. He lost about three hundred men in killed and wounded.

That a little fun can be mixed up with the horrors of war was illustrated on this trip somewhere over in the hills of Wayne. James E. Wood's little chestnut sorrel, the horse which had been tendered by his owner to Captain Tate, as related in the account of the fight at Ripley, and from which that gallant officer was shot, struck the frog of one foot against a stone and was rendered unserviceable. Austin Statler and Tom Joyner set about the task of helping their fellow-soldier to a remount. This was difficult to do in a country which had been stripped of all the good stock. The only animal available appeared to be a three-year-old, standing in an enclosure near an humble cottage. Statler, in his blandest manner, explained the situation to the mistress of the cottage, and alluded in earnest words to the fine points of the lame horse, which needed only a few days' rest to restore him to his former condition of usefulness. No, no; the old lady couldn't see it in the light in which it had been so earnestly presented. There were seven stout daughters standing by ready to assist their mother, who averred that the animal was "Sal's colt," and he couldn't have it upon any terms whatever. Statler persisted until high words resulted, and the soldiers advanced towards "Sal's colt." Thoroughly aroused, and reinforced by her mother and sisters, Sal herself, a buxom lassie, now came to the rescue, cleared the fence at a bound, and sat astride of the bridleless colt. Victory now seemed to perch upon the banner of the females, but the soldiers, who had no idea of seeing their comrade hotfoot it along the roads of Wayne, moved to the assault, determined to capture the colt, but anxious to inflict no bruises upon their adversaries, who fought like wildcats. The contest was fast and furious, but in a class entirely by itself. There was blood and hair in evidence, but no mortal casualties. There was pinching and twisting, wrenching and wringing, clutching and hugging, yes, hugging, till the female side had mostly lost its wind and Sal, grasping the mane of the colt with the grip of despair, while she planted her heels in its sides, was gently lifted from her position by the gallant trio. "It was all over but the shouting." The bit was forced and the girth was buckled. "Sal's colt" had changed its politics and been mustered into the service of the Confederacy. The old lady intimated that "men folks" were at hand and ready to avenge all her wrongs. Statler, as a precautionary measure, rode out in the direction indicated by her and saw three armed citizens approaching. With cocked gun and ready pistol he commanded them, with assumed bravado, to lead the way to the cottage, while he assured them that he, too, had "a whole gang in reach." Tableau vivant: An elderly man "breathing out threatening and slaughter" and declaring that he would have have satisfaction before the sun went down; two lusty young men with guns and in the poise of interested spectators; six bouncing young girls well distributed in the ensemble and joining in a chorus of abuse; an elderly woman standing in the kitchen door and wiping the sweat from her neck and ears with her checked apron, beaten but not conquered; Sal perched upon the top rail of the front fence in the attitude of a show girl about to dance a hornpipe, and gazing at three vanishing cavaliers just then turning a corner and making time to overtake the command; lastly, the abandoned warhorse, which had heard the guns at Tishomingo, stripped of his trappings and "turned out to grass," was standing meekly by and looking as if he might be thinking he had no friends at all.

Chapter 11

HOOD'S EXPEDITION—THE WILSON RAID TO SELMA.

We had not more than gotten the last three men with their horses and accoutrements across the Tennessee river, as related in the preceding chapter, than two gunboats and two transports came puffing along. It was easy to conjecture what would have happened to five men and three horses, if our little craft with its burden had been met in midstream by the gunboats. And yet we had been taking the risk of being sunk or captured all that day. We rode leisurely to Bolivar and the men dispersed to their homes for a much needed rest.

Just as I was congratulating myself that I would have a few days for recuperation, several carbuncles developed on my body as a result of poor food and exposure. This affliction virtually placed me on furlough from the middle of October till the middle of January. In the meantime, Forrest's Cavalry had assembled at Corinth and gone on an expedition to the Tennessee river, which finally culminated in the movement with Hood to Nashville. Others have written graphic accounts of how Forrest with a force of three thousand men, cavalry and artillery, boldly attacked transports and gunboats and concluded his operations in that quarter by the total destruction of an immense depot of supplies at Johnsonville. He said himself that he captured and destroyed in two or three days four gunboats, fourteen transports, twenty barges, twenty-six pieces of artillery which, with stores destroyed, amounted to a money value of over six million dollars. He captured 150 prisoners, while his own loss was two killed and nine wounded. Altogether this was one of the most remarkable campaigns of the whole war, and I have always somewhat regretted that I could not participate in its operations. As for the expedition to Nashville which followed, I have always considered myself fortunate in having missed it. The history of it is a pitiful story and well worth reading, particularly by those who did not hear it from the lips of hundreds of brave men who gave vivid accounts of personal experiences. I began to hear these pitiful accounts early in January from soldiers returning to their homes in an utter state of demoralization. I began to consider whether or not I could recover my health and join Company E ere there was a collapse of the Confederacy. However, as the men of our regiment had been permitted to go to their homes for a few days, there was time for consideration.

When I reported for duty at Verona, Miss., late in January, 1865, Colonel Richardson was in command of Rucker's Brigade, the ranks of which were filling up surprisingly well, considering the heavy blow we had received in the disastrous repulse of our army in front of Nashville. Most of our men had spent some time at home and came in with new clothes and fresh horses. The rations were good but we had no tents. We constructed rude shelters with whatever timber was at hand, principally fence rails, and over this spread our rubber cloths. Then a good layer of corn stalks was placed for a floor and on this our army blankets. With a roaring log fire in front, we were measurably comfortable. We really had little to do for some time. It was in this camp that it got to the ears of Colonel Richardson that A. S. Coleman, our sutler, who kept a variety of articles in store, was dealing out to the boys a poor article of Confederate whisky. Richardson determined to confiscate the sutler's whole stock of goods, and sent an officer to seize them. The members of Company E went to the rescue and, it being dark, succeeded, while Coleman was parleying with the officer, in "purloining" all the goods on hand, which they carried out through the back of the tent and kept concealed till the trouble blew over. Coleman was soon doing business at the old stand.

In February, 1865, Forrest was raised to the rank of Lieutenant-General and given the command of about ten thousand cavalry widely dispersed in Alabama, Mississippi and Louisiana. Joe Johnston had superseded Hood and had transferred the remnant of our army further east to place it in the path of Sherman who was marching north from Savannah through South Carolina. So far as our part of the country was concerned, it seemed to me then that the Federals would have had little trouble in sending in a large force and taking possession. With Forrest it was a case of gathering up the fragments, but man never went about anything more earnestly. His work had a telling effect. By a complete reorganization of the cavalry, the troops from each State were thrown into brigades and divisions of their own. This may have added somewhat to the morale of the command, but I do not know that it improved the fighting qualities of the men to any great extent. Certainly there was no better fighting body of men than Rucker's Old Brigade, composed of Tennesseeans and Mississippians. By the new arrangement, the Tennessee Division was commanded by W. H. Jackson. His two brigade commanders were A. W. Campbell and T. H. Bell. This division now had fat horses, good clothes and good rations. But every man there knew that our quasi holiday would be of short duration. Though the Confederacy seemed tottering to its fall, Jackson's Division was ready for a campaign. It did not have long to wait. Twelve thousand cavalry were assembled in North Alabama under General James H. Wilson, one of the most capable and enterprising commanders in the Federal army. Accompanied by an immense supply train and a commensurate amount of artillery, this best equipped of all Federal commands set out about the 22nd of March for Selma, Ala., which was a depot for Confederate stores and the location of large factories of arms and ammunition. Being provided with a pontoon train it had little trouble in crossing the swollen streams. It moved rapidly in a southeasterly direction. It was the task of Forrest to move east from Columbus, Miss., fall upon Wilson's right flank, defeat such detachments as he could cope with, destroy his trains, if possible, and finally beat him to Selma. Forrest's plans involved the possibility of throwing his whole force against that of Wilson in some favorable position east of Tuskaloosa and to risk the consequences of the greatest cavalry battle ever fought on the continent. How near we subordinates were to witnessing a great event impending and yet how ignorant we were of it! Unforeseen difficulties lay in Forrest's path while he was apparently making superhuman efforts to concentrate his forces for a great battle in which his enemy would number fully two to one. It is painful even to conjecture what the consequences of such a battle might have been. But I anticipate. Prior to the movement towards Selma I had been detailed for duty with the provost guard of Campbell's Brigade, which was agreeable to me because of the fact that I had not entirely recovered my health, and would have more privileges on the road, though no less responsible service. Our chief duty was to move in the rear and to prevent straggling. It turned out on this expedition to be a position of great danger.

We passed through Columbus, Miss., and took the road to Tuskaloosa. We moved all day and much of the night over muddy roads, miry swamps and rugged hills. Our great commander had the details all in his mind, but we had only a vague idea that we would have to fight at almost any turn in the road. This was an army of veterans, who had been tried in the fire. Jackson's Division was a long way from home, but was ready for a last desperate struggle in a strange land. It looked like a forlorn hope, for Lee was falling back upon Appomattox and Johnston was in a death struggle with Sherman. But the defeat of Wilson's cavalry would mean its destruction and the capture of his trains. Such a victory here might change the face of things within a few hours, as we had no idea that any one of our armies would so soon surrender. Anyhow, the men were there to obey orders and to do their whole duty. We were at Sipsey river and the column was moving slowly through its slashy bottom. A weird looking place where the foliage of the heavy timber largely shut out the light of day. A rumor came down the line that two soldiers, at the instance of a drum-head court-martial, had been shot to death for desertion. As the provost guard closed up the column it passed the dead men lying one on each side of the road with their heads against trees. Their hats had been placed over their faces, but labels written in large letters told the story: *Shot for Desertion.* It was said at the time that this was intended as a deterrent to desertion. It may have had the effect intended. It would be passing over it most kindly to state that the affair caused a profound sensation. It would be nearer the truth to say that, with the rank and file, it met with pronounced condemnation. Only one other writer has touched upon this incident, and he was not on the ground as I was. Therefore, he could not speak personally concerning what might be called the popular verdict of the soldiers. He does say, in substance, that the execution was extremely unfortunate, though coming within the province of military law, in that the declarations of the victims that the older was above the military age and the younger was under it turned out to be true in every particular. It was a matter of common talk that the men were Kentuckians, who had nothing on their persons by which they could be identified, and that there was no proof adduced to show that they belonged to our cavalry. They were possibly deserters from some arm of the Confederate service, but the prevailing sentiment, which is a force to be reckoned with in a volunteer army, was that a drumhead court-martial, instituted on the march and when the command was practically in the presence of the enemy, could not exercise that calm consideration and quiet deliberation required in a case where human life was involved. While, as a general proposition, it were well not to tear open old wounds, yet it were also well to state exact facts in history, in order that the mistakes of the past may enable those who come after us to avoid errors in the future. The power of all Confederate courts-martial was flitting fast, and the bloody hand, under all the circumstances in this case, might well have been stayed. Everybody was glad to change the scene and the subject of thought, for death has no attractive form. Tuskaloosa was a fine old Southern town, with palatial homes, wide streets, shaded by three rows of water oaks, well kept yards, extensive flower gardens, and a large complement of pretty women. The gates were open and the city was ours for the asking. They had never seen a Southern army, and more than that, they had never imagined the like of Forrest's cavalry as, brimful of fight, it moved along their lovely streets. Alas! all this, within three days, was to be in the grasp of men who did not hesitate to apply the torch even to the State University.

As we entered the extensive piney woods section east of Tuskaloosa, we were critically near the right flank of the enemy, pushing on towards Selma. Croxton's Federal Brigade had been detached to destroy the Confederate supplies at Tuskaloosa and burn the university. It so happened that this brigade dropped into the road between the rear of Jackson's Cavalry and the front of his artillery and wagon train. If the Federals had continued to move west, they inevitably would have captured the trains. They turned east to follow the cavalry, and Jackson being apprised of this made the proper disposition to fall upon them in camp in the early morning. In the meantime, Croxton had changed his mind and had turned again to march, as luck would have it, by another road to Tuskaloosa, without knowing that he had our trains so nearly within his grasp. As it was, Jackson ran on his rear company in camp and captured men, horses, and ambulances. Croxton fled north with his command, crossed the Warrior forty miles above, turned south and reached Tuskaloosa, where he carried out his orders. This was the 3rd day of April, and he was now so far separated from his chief that he did not join him at Macon, Ga., till the 20th of May When Jackson turned to pursue Croxton, unfortunately another detachment under one of the Fighting McCooks, took possession of the bridge over the Cahawba, where Forrest, with his escort, had already crossed, and where we were expected to cross. They boldly came to the west side and put themselves across our path at the village of Scottsville. That night the woods seemed to be full of them. Some of our men, getting out to do the usual little "buttermilk foraging" met some Yanks at a farm house where Johnny Reb thought he had the exclusive privilege. There was a tacit consent to a truce while they shared such good things as the farmer had to contribute. The next morning, April 2nd, Bell's Brigade of Jackson's Division collided with a part of McCook's men and rapidly pushed them back to Centerville. They completely blocked our way by burning the bridge over the Cahawba. It was now impossible for Jackson to join Forrest on the road from Montevallo to Selma, where with Roddy's Cavalry and Crossland's small brigade of Kentuckians, he and escort were fighting to the death to hold Wilson in check till the Confederate divisions could be concentrated and hurled against those of the Federals in one grand conflict. The Federals, having intercepted certain dispatches of Forrest and Jackson, knew just how to subvert their plans. Wilson, seeing that there was now no chance for Jackson to fall upon his rear, according to the original plan of Forrest, pushed his forces with all his energy in the direction of Selma. Forrest, being reinforced by some militia and two hundred picked men of Armstrong's Brigade of Chalmers' Division, on the first day of April, did some of the fiercest fighting of the war, much of it hand to hand. At Bogler's creek near Plantersville, it was at close quarters with two thousand against nine thousand, but the Confederates had the advantage of position. The Federal advance was a regiment of veteran cavalry who charged with drawn sabers. The Confederates received them at first with rifles and closed in with six-shooters, most of the men having two each. The Confederates being forced back by a flank movement, there was a bloody running fight for several miles. From the desperate character of the fighting here, it might be inferred that the great contest, planned to take place along these lines, would have been terrific, if Forrest, Jackson, Chalmers and Roddy could have joined their forces.

If all the forces named had been concentrated, as Forrest had intended, somewhere between Montevallo and Selma, Ala., would have been fought the cavalry battle of the ages. Who is not glad the whole plan miscarried?

When the Confederates were crowded into Selma the next day, their lines were so attenuated that the Federals, with overwhelming numbers, assailed the works and carried them, though with very heavy loss. Night was coming on as the contest ended and the streets were filled with Federals and Confederates in the greatest possible confusion. This enabled Forrest and Armstrong, with hundreds of their men, to find an opening through which they rode out and escaped in the darkness. In doing this, Forrest cut down his thirtieth man in the war, which closed his fighting career.

I had more than ordinary anxiety in regard to the fighting in front of Selma, as I had a brother with Armstrong and a brother-in-law with Roddy. The former escaped with Armstrong, but the latter, Wiley Hawkins of Florence, a mere youth, the last of four brothers to die during the war, was killed at Bogler's creek.

With Forrest's Cavalry the war was over. His command had fired its last gun at Selma. At Marion, Greensboro, Eutaw, and finally at Sumterville, where Jackson's Division had its last camp, we found the very best type of Southern people. They had really seen very little of the war, though sorrow had been brought to many a home by the casualties of battle. Here was a lovely country in which a war-worn soldier could sit down to commune with nature, where she was never more beautifully and bountifully manifested in birds, flowers and fertile fields. It was so restful to the soul to know that we were done with guns and bloody work. The present was the present, the future was the future. We were taking care of the present. We would take care of the future when we got to it. Whipped or not, we had loved ones at home and were going to them; whipped or not, we felt assured that we had done our duty to our prostrate country, which never had more than the shadow of a chance for the success of a separate existence; whipped or not, we could face those who had urged us to go to the war, and say that we had fought it to a finish. It perhaps seems strange to many that there was no weeping or wailing, at least about where I was, because of the defeat of Southern hopes. I account for this upon the hypothesis that both officers and privates had been, for nearly two years, contemplating not only the possibility but the probability of defeat, and were therefore mentally prepared for almost anything which fate should decree. Certainly, the consensus of opinion was, that many mistakes had been made by the civil and military authorities during the four years of war, but there was no intense spirit of criticism. Whether a Confederate soldier thought that everything possible had been done, with the limited resources at hand, or not, he was very apt to be of the opinion that some means should have been brought into play to stop the war long before it was. I am of the opinion that the diligent student of history has come to the same conclusion. Why so many held on so tenaciously to a cause that had grown so desperate, I have tried to show on other pages. Duty and honor are the chief elements in a long story, though this statement of the case can hardly be so well appreciated by the present generation as by the active participants in the war.

The following excerpt is taken from *Destruction and Reconstruction,* by Lieutenant-General Dick Taylor, the only son of the last Whig president, and a man whose mental acumen was of the sharper kind, and whose varied learning would have graced any court: "Upon what foundations the civil authorities of the Confederacy rested their hopes of success, after the campaign of 1864 fully opened, I am unable to say; but their commanders in the field, whose rank and position enabled them to estimate the situation, fought simply to afford statesmanship an opportunity to mitigate the sorrows of inevitable defeat."

This comports well with what I heard Confederate State Senator James Phelan of Mississippi, say, more than forty years ago, to the effect that the politicians at Richmond consumed most of their time in discussing abtruse questions of constitutional law and other subjects that might well have been deferred till the armies in the field could settle the question of independence. I took it that he thought there was little use for a constitution in a time of revolution or rebellion, but the chief concern should have been the perfecting of such measures as would strengthen our armies and achieve victories. It was well known that there were jealousies and dissensions among the officers of our armies from the beginning to the close of the war. What was at first war gossip became of record as soon after the surrender as some of these were able to contribute to our current literature. Posterity will be asking why some of the serious accusations made were not, at the proper time, brought to the notice of a court-martial.

When the future historian comes to make up the sum total of the causes which led to the downfall of the Confederacy, he will have only a written record to draw from, and will possibly be perplexed in his endeavor to pronounce an honest judgment in regard to men who, though differing so widely in opinion, were believed to be brave and patriotic.

Chapter 12

CONCLUSION

When I was a boy in Anson County, North Carolina, where I was born "with a full suit of hair" about the time "the stars fell," I had two brothers living in Sumter County, Alabama, which was said to be six hundred miles away. That seemed to me then to be about as much as six thousand miles seem now. It was an inscrutable order of Providence that, after having lived in four other States, attended two colleges, become the father of a family, and served four years in a great civil war, I should lay down my arms in that same Sumter County.

The details of surrender were all arranged without the appearance of a Federal officer in our camp, the same being conducted in the most punctilious manner and without any effort to humiliate. We were pleased to learn that the same terms upon which Lee and Johnston had surrendered would be accorded to us. The officers retained their arms and horses and the men their horses. Blank paroles were furnished by the Federals. Those of Company E were filled out in my handwriting.

The noble address of General Forrest, urging his men to become as good citizens in peace as they had been soldiers in war, was pronounced entirely appropriate and a model in sentiment and expression.

The ceremony of tearing up the flag, fashioned from the bridal dress of an Aberdeen lady, was gone through with and small bits of it distributed among the soldiers and officers of the Seventh Tennessee Regiment. I did not think then that this was exactly the thing to do and have regretted the proceeding since, particularly because of the liberality of the Federal government in restoring the captured flags of the Southern States. Ours was a regular confederate flag and made of such material that it could have been preserved indefinitely.

In our camp it was "pretty well, I thank you; how do you do yourself?" Billy Yank, Johnny Reb, or anybody else—a pleasant abandon in regard to environments and no thought of prolonging the war beyond the Mississippi or helping Maximilian to a throne in Mexico. We were going home. The direct road to Bolivar, Tenn., over two hundred miles in length, was uppermost in our minds. At Macon, Miss., we drew our last rations, which were bountiful, as there was now no need of economy, and we had a long road before us. The men were entirely without official restraint, but those of Company E preserved their organization till we reached Saulsbury, Tenn., where we gave the first friendly salute to Federal soldiers and the men went their several ways. I was riding the last few miles with three of my former pupils. That dear good fellow and gallant little soldier, James E. Wood, the man who rode "Sal's Colt," but has been more recently a well known editor and a distinguished member of the Arkansas senate, turned off at Middleburg and left George Bright, now of Danville, Ky., and Billy Myrick, long since dead, with me to face the folks at home.

The transition from soldier to citizen was easy. By a dive into my ancient wardrobe, I secured several articles of wearing apparel, among them a Prince Albert coat. I was not exactly *a la mode,* or whatever the French say, but with a new blockade hat I felt "mighty fine," and doubtless looked as innocent of war as the Goddess of Peace. "Whatsoever cometh to your hands to do, do it with all your might." I acted upon that. I opened a summer session of the Bolivar Male Academy in the railway station on the 31st of May, 1865. The Academy building had been defaced by the Federal army to such an extent that it was untenable, and we had no cars running for more than three months. So much changed had conditions become that of the sixty-six pupils in school in May, 1861, only four, James J. Neely, Jr., George B. Peters, Jr., James Fentress, Jr., and Charles A. Miller, returned to greet me. Seventeen of the sixty-six entered the army, fourteen as members of Company E and three as members of other commands. Four of the fourteen were killed on the field and all of the others served till the close of the war. Eleven of the seventeen are dead and six are living.

The station was a pleasant place for a summer session and boys were so anxious for instruction that I was soon teaching seven hours a day. They wanted Latin and Greek and mathematics, and we went at them with a will. The roots of the verbs and the rules of syntax had only lain dormant in my own mind during the four years and were easily recalled. The work became so much a part of my life, and the homelike feeling of the schoolroom returned so readily, that an assurance of my forty-odd years of like employment would have come as a pleasing announcement. But so it is, the forty years and more have come and gone, and I am still walking among my fellows, hardly knowing how to put on the ways of an old man, but in good humor with all the world. I have concluded to conclude this book with the following conclusions:

1. That it is an everlasting pity the war was not averted because of the great mortality of good citizens on both sides, the backset given to the morals of the whole country, the sec-

tional feeling engendered and likely to endure for a season, and the loss of wealth and prestige by the Southern people.

2. That the victors in a civil war pay dearly for their success in the demoralization of the people at large by having so numerous an element supported by the government; in the rascally transactions connected with army contracts; and in the enlargment of that class of pestiferous statesmen (?) who have been aptly described as being "invisible in war and invincible in peace."

3. That the most peaceful of Southern men can be readily converted into the most warlike soldiers when convinced that they have a proper grievance; can march further on starvation rations and in all kinds of weather, and will take less note of disparity of numbers in battle than will any other soldiers on earth.

4. That the South, in the war period, was essentially a country of horseback riders, and her young men furnished the material out of which was formed, when properly handled, regiments of cavalry that were practically invincible, even when confronting an adversary of twice or thrice their own strength.

5. That Forrest's men demonstrated the fact that Southern cavalrymen, fighting on foot, can meet, with good chances of victory, a superior number of veteran infantry in the open field.

6. That in cavalry operations, the most essential thing is a bold and dashing leader, who will strike furiously before the enemy has time to consider what is coming, and with every available man in action.

7. That Nathan Bedford Forrest, by his deeds in war, became an exemplar of horseback fighting, whose shining

qualities might well become the measure of other deeds on other fields when war is flagrant.

8. That there is not an instance recorded where so large a body of defeated soldiers returned so contentedly to their former pursuits, "beating their swords into ploughshares and their spears into pruning hooks;" yes, thousands of them going into the fields to plough and plant with the same horses they rode in battle.

9. That the unpreparedness of both sides at the beginning of the war emphasizes the necessity for a thorough preparedness of our united country for any emergency, that is to say, that while Uncle Sam needs not to be strutting around "with a chip on his shoulder," and his hat cocked up on the side of his head, he should be able to say to "the other fellow" that he is rich in men and munitions, and, moreover, has the finest navy that floats.

10. That having taken an humble part in a great war in which I ofttimes looked upon the pale faces of the dead and heard the groans of the wounded, having now had fifty years, from its beginning, to reflect upon its calamities, I am firmly of the opinion that all enlightened nations will finally come to arbitration in the settlement of international questions.

11. That no true picture of war can be drawn, either in words or on canvas, because of the elements so numerous and so complex to be considered. And even if this were possible, it would be a representation of a horrifying spectacle.

12. That the victorious shouts of men in battle bring small remuneration and poor consolation to the bereaved widows and orphans of their dead comrades at home.

13. That Gen. Grant, after a wonderful experience in the bloody work of war, knew himself thoroughly well when he uttered the memorable words: "LET US HAVE PEACE."

CHAPTER FIVE

Notes From The Other Side

No exploits of General Forrest are better known than his pursuit and capture of Colonel Streight and his raiders in April, 1863, and his defeat of General Sturgis at Brice's Cross Roads in June, 1864. To show how these affairs appeared to participants on the Union side, extracts have been selected from a work by Colonel Streight's aide-de-camp, published in 1865,[1] and, for Brice's Cross Roads, from an account by the Adjutant of the Fourth Iowa Veteran Volunteer Cavalry, published in 1893.[2]

As its title indicates, the principal theme of the first narrative, which not only was written by Colonel Streight's aide but was also published by a firm of which the Colonel himself was proprietor, is criticism and complaint about Southern treatment of prisoners of war. The officer prisoners taken in the Streight raid were confined in Libby Prison, Richmond, from which Colonel Streight escaped, with more than 100 other prisoners, through a tunnel on the night of February 9, 1864. At one spot

1. Roach, Lieutenant A. C., A. A. D. C., *The Prisoner of War, and How Treated*, "published by The Railroad City Publishing House, A. D. Streight, Proprietor," Indianapolis, 1865.
2. Scott, Wm. Forse, *The Story of a Cavalry Regiment: The Career of the Fourth Iowa Veteran Volunteers, from Kansas to Georgia, 1861-1865*, New York, The Knickerbocker Press, 1893.

in the tunnel, Colonel Streight, being "somewhat inclined to corpulency, stuck fast, *and was compelled to back out and divest himself of coat, vest and shirt, when he was able to* squeeze *through, pulling the garments aforesaid through with a string after him."*[3]

After his escape from Libby, the Colonel and several of his companions remained in Richmond for a week, hidden in the home of a Union sympathizer, according to arrangements previously made. Having been supplied with money and arms, they made their perilous way northward to the Potomac, reaching Washington on March 1.

Colonel Streight returned to duty and to the command of an infantry brigade in the Army of the Cumberland. In the pursuit after the Battle of Nashville, it was Streight's brigade which laid the pontoon bridge across the flooded Duck River but he did not have the satisfaction of turning the tables on Forrest by overtaking and capturing the commander of the rear guard of the Confederate Army of Tennessee.

Lieutenant Roach has much to say in his 1865 work about Southern barbarities and Confederate atrocities but the extracts given are confined to his story of Forrest's part in the Streight raid from the standpoint of the pursued.

1

This day's march brought us to the base of a range of hills, known as the Sand Mountains. Here it was determined to bivouac for the night. . . . Up to this time we had made slow progress in the direction of the grand object of the expedition, merely marching in that course with our foot soldiers, while our mounted force was engaged, day and night, scouring the country in every direction in search of horses and mules; and

---

3. *The Prisoner of War,* p. 100.

now that a sufficient number had been obtained, we were ready to push forward on the following morning with dispatch and rapidity.

On the morning of April thirtieth, 1863, the sun shone out bright and beautiful, as spring day's sun ever beamed; and from the smouldering camp fires of the previous night the mild blue smoke ascended in graceful curves, and mingled with the gray mist slumbering on the mountain tops above. . . . Scarcely was the column in motion when our rear was attacked by the enemy's advance; sharp skirmishing continued for some time between our rear guard and one of General Roddy's regiments.

It was Colonel Streight's intention to avoid, if possible, a general engagement, as the prosecution of our expedition towards its intended destination was of vastly more importance than a victory in this locality could possibly be to our cause. But the enemy pressing us closely, and bringing up his artillery, throwing shot and shell into our column, a battle was the only alternative; we therefore, soon as a favorable position was obtained, halted and dismounted, and after concealing our animals in a deep ravine in our rear, formed in line of battle for the coming conflict. . . . The hour for action has come, and the battle of Day's Gap soon commences. . . . The cannonading is heavy, and the rattle of musketry is sharp, especially on our left. The enemy fights well, for they are principally General Forrest's trained veterans. A loud and prolonged shout now bursts on the ear. It comes from the Third Ohio and Eightieth Illinois, who have charged and taken the enemy's battery. The enemy feel the loss of their guns and their line wavers! Cheer after cheer bursts from our brave boys, for the enemy are giving way! They are already running in the utmost disorder and con-fusion. Our gallant soldiers still pursue, making the ground quake and the rebels tremble. The rout is complete and the field is ours. But the victory is won by the sacrifice of some of the best and bravest blood in our heroic little brigade.

Those are proud moments for the soldier, when he stands victorious on the bloody field, and sees the columns of the enemy in full retreat before him.

In this fight the enemy received such a severe chastisement that he would not have dared to pursue us further, had he not been reinforced by a large brigade of Forrest's troops, which, unfortunately for us, came to their assistance while his routed and demoralized masses were fleeing from the scene of their late inglorious defeat. . . . After leaving Day's Gap, we proceeded several miles without any evidence of the enemy being in pursuit, but about four o'clock in the evening our rear was again attacked, and as we did not want to lose time by halting to give battle, if it could possibly be avoided, the column was kept in motion, skirmishing fighting going on, however, all the time between Captain Smith's two companies of cavalry and the enemy's advance. Captain Smith, with his little handful of men, kept the enemy at bay for more than two hours. But they were now pressing us so closely that Colonel Streight resolved to halt his command, and again give them battle. In a short time the bloody strife was raging with all the fury of brave and determined men. Charge after charge, made by the enemy, was met and repulsed by our brave boys, who drove back with terrible destruction each successive effort, to dislodge them from the admirable position selected for our line of defense.

This engagement raged with greater desperation for some time than the preceding action in the morning. The report of fire-arms was terrific; the flashes from musketry and artillery lighting up the hills on all sides, rendering the scene, although of death and carnage, one of the grandest sublimity. It was now about ten o'clock, yet by the light of the full moon, which

looked calmly down on the bloody scene, we were able to
discover that the enemy had begun to waver and fall back,
unable to contend longer against the terrible fire our men were
pouring with fearful destruction into their ranks. In a short
time all was quiet, and the still air of night, that but a few
moments before resounded with the roar of artillery and musketry, was only broken by the lonely notes of the whip-poor-
will, as they came from his secluded spot in the surrounding
forest. And the Provisional Brigade was victorious on two
bloody fields in one day. . . . The enemy in this action had their
whole force engaged, yet, by the skillful maneuvering of our
little brigade, we met and repulsed them at every point. To this,
and the bravery and determination of our men, we alone can
ascribe our success in meeting and driving back discomfitted
numbers, so much our superior, and having at their command
several heavy field pieces. Our artillery consisted only of two
small mountain howitzers, and the two pieces taken from
Forrest in the morning; for the latter we had but a small quantity of ammunition, the caissons being nearly empty when
captured; they were, therefore, soon of no service, and were
ordered by the Colonel to be spiked, and the carriages cut down.
. . . Colonel Streight, anticipating an advance of Forrest's forces,
soon as it was known to them that we were moving, directed
Colonel Hathaway, with his regiment, (Seventy-Third Indiana)
to lay concealed in the heavy timber nearby, for the purpose of
ambushing them in case of an immediate advance. But a few
moments elapsed before the enemy's column was discovered
approaching; and soon their advance battalion came up
unsuspectingly within forty yards of our concealed regiment,
which at that instant poured a full volley of musketry into their
ranks, sending them back, pell mell, in the greatest consternation and disorder, with the full conviction, no doubt, that every

tree for miles around concealed a Yankee soldier with a musket charged to the muzzle. But relying on the advantage of being in their own country, consequently acquainted with every road and by-path, also conscious of their superior numbers, they soon rallied, and attacked us again about two o'clock in the morning, when Colonel Streight again resolved to ambush them; which proved so successful, and gave them such a taste of Yankee courage and skill, that we had no further annoyance until about eleven o'clock next day, when our pickets were attacked just as we were leaving Blountsville, where we had halted to feed our animals and refresh the exhausted and fatigued men, who had not had a moment's rest for two days and nights. . . . On the morning of May 2nd we crossed Black Creek, near Gadsden, Alabama, on a fine wooden bridge, which was afterwards burned by our rear guard. This, it was thought, would delay Forrest's forces long enough to enable us to reach Rome, Georgia, before he could again overtake us, as the stream was very deep and seemed to be unfordable. But among a lot of prisoners captured by us in the morning, and paroled, was a young man by the name of Sansom, who, soon as set at liberty, made his way direct to the pursuing force of General Forrest, and piloted that officer and his command to a ford where the whole force soon crossed and started again in pursuit of our brigade. From this incident the rebels manufactured the following bit of romance: "General Forrest had been pursuing the enemy all day, and was close upon their heels, when the pursuit was effectually checked by the destruction by the enemy of a bridge over a deep creek, which, for the time, separated pursuer and pursued. The country was exceedingly wild and rugged, and the banks of the creek too steep for passage on horseback. General Forrest rode up to a modest little farm house on the road side, and seeing a young maiden standing upon the little stoop in front of the dwelling, he accosted her, and inquired if there was any ford or passage for his men across the creek above or below the destroyed bridge. The young girl proceeded to direct him, with animated gesture, and cheeks flushed with excitement, and almost breathless in her eagerness to aid the noble cause of the gallant Confederate General. It was a scene for a painter. The Southern girl, her cheeks glowing and her bright eyes flashing, while her mother, attracted by the colloquy, stood holding the door, and gazing upon the cavalcade over her venerable spectacles, the cavalry chieftain resting his legs carelessly over the saddle-pommel, his staff drawn up around him, and his weather-worn veterans scattered in groups about the road, and some of them actually nodding in their saddles from excessive fatigue. After some further inquiry, General Forrest asked the young lady if she would not mount behind him and show him the way to the ford. She hesitated, and turned to her mother an inquiring look. The mother, with a delicacy becoming a prudent parent, rather seemed to object to her going with the soldiers.

"Mother," she said, "I am not afraid to trust myself with as brave a man as General Forrest."

"But, my dear, folks will talk about you."

"Let them talk," responded the heroic girl, "I must go." And with that she lightly sprang upon the roots of a fallen tree, Forrest drew his mettled charger near her, she grasped the hero fearlessly about the waist and sprung up behind him, and away they went over brake and bramble, through the glade and on towards the ford. The route was a difficult one, even for as experienced a rider as Forrest, but his fair young companion and guide held her seat like an experienced horsewoman, and without the slightest evidence of fear. At length they drew near to the ford. Upon the high ridge above, the quick eye of Forrest descried the Yankee sharpshooters, dodging from tree to tree, and pretty soon an angry minnie whistled by his ear.

" 'What was that, General Forrest?' asked the maiden.

" 'Bullets,' he replied; 'are you afraid?'

"She replied in the negative, and they proceeded on. At length it became necessary, from the density of the undergrowth and snags, to dismount, and Forrest hitched his horse, and the girl preceded him, leading the way herself—remarking that the Yankees would not fire upon her, and they might fire if he went first. To this Forrest objected, not wishing to screen himself behind the brave girl; and, taking the lead himself, the two proceeded on to the ford under the fire of the Yankee rear guard. Having discovered the route he returned, brought up his axemen and cleared out a road, and safely crossed his whole column.

"Upon taking leave of his fair young guide, the General asked if there was anything he might do for her in return for her invaluable services. She told him that the Yankees on ahead had her brother prisoner, and if General Forrest would only release him she should be more than repaid. The General took out his watch, and examined it. It was just five minutes to eleven. 'To-Morrow,' he said, 'at five minutes to eleven o'clock, your brother shall be returned to you.' And so the sequel proved. Streight, with his whole command, was captured at ten the next morning. Young Sansom was released, and dispatched on the fleetest horse in the command to return to his heroic sister, whose courage and presence of mind had contributed so much to the success of one of the most remarkable cavalry pursuits and captures known in the world's history."

The true version of this story is, as near as possible, as follows: whenever we captured any prisoners, they were immediately paroled, and not taken along with the command any distance; especially not forty or fifty miles, as this rebel romance would indicate. And the young Confederate soldier, Sansom was with General Forrest when our command surrendered, and notwithstanding his solemn oath not to aid or comfort in any manner whatever the enemies of the United States, was fully armed and equipped, and boasted that it was the bullet shot from his gun that killed the noble Hathaway.

Soon after crossing Black Creek, we passed through the town of Gadsden, where we destroyed a quantity of rebel stores, and captured some prisoners. We then proceeded on to Blunt's plantation, where we halted for the purpose of giving the men an opportunity of preparing a hasty meal for themselves and to feed their animals. But the anticipated pleasure of a cup of steaming coffee, which the Union soldier considers one of his indispensables, was soon dispelled by the report of musketry in the direction of our picket line. The command was immediately given to prepare for action, and almost instantly every man in the Provisional Brigade seized his gun, and was marching out bravely and defiantly to engage once more the vastly superior force of the enemy, with whom we had contended successfully for three days, and had completely routed and defeated in two regular pitched battles. Colonel Hathaway, with his regiment, was directed to the front and center, to support our two howitzers, which were doing such fearful execution in the ranks of the enemy, that they seemed to have resolved to capture them if possible, regardless of the cost in blood. Their efforts, however, were fruitless, for although nearly every gunner and man connected with the two pieces was either killed or wounded, Colonel Hathaway so determinedly maintained his position that the enemy recoiled in the greatest confusion, our men pouring a perfect hail of lead into his retreating columns. This action lasted for nearly three hours, the enemy charging our lines from right to left repeatedly, but was as often repulsed, with severe loss, by our gallant regiments. When the sun set on that tranquil evening, sinking slowly down behind the forest, unstirred by the least breath of wind, the sharp and bloody struggle was decided. The enemy was retreating badly hurt; his dead men and horses strewing their line of retreat. . . . Affairs are now rapidly approaching a crisis; every one felt that the next twenty-four hours would decide the fate of our expedition. We were now within sixty miles of Rome, the point at which we designed crossing the Coosa river; and if we could reach that place before a force could be thrown in to check our further advance, complete success would be inevitable; for once on the opposite side of the river, and the bridge destroyed after us, the pursuit of Forrest would be effectually checked, and we would then have ample time to recruit the exhausted energies of our men and animals; besides, if necessary we could soon obtain an entire fresh supply of the latter; and could then either fight or decline battle at our own option. On the contrary, should there be a force collected at Rome sufficient to prevent us crossing the bridge, there would be no alternative left us but to surrender, the exhausted condition of our men and animals rendering escape by any route, strategy, or valor in battle, an impossibility. To guard against the above contingency, Captain Russell, of the Fifty-First Indiana, was ordered with two hundred picked men, mounted on our best horses, to proceed with the greatest dispatch to Rome and take possession of the river bridge, railroad stock and telegraph lines, before the forces there could make preparation for defense, or troops be brought from Atlanta and other points on the railroad, in case they were advised by couriers from General Forrest, or otherwise, of the advance of our expedition.

After some active demonstrations, and strategic movements, designed to impress the enemy with the belief that we were preparing for a renewal of the contest at the earliest dawn of day, the balance of the command moved on as fast as the fatigued condition of our animals would permit. Strong hopes were now entertained of success, and would, no doubt, have been realized, had not our guide misled us in regard to the ford by which to cross the Chattogee river. In justice to him, however, it is but proper to remark, that he was a true and faithful man, and this, the only instance in which he seemed at fault; but this irreparable mistake took us at least twelve miles out of our direct course, besides otherwise delaying us.

We marched all this night, making four consecutive days and nights in the saddle, except when fighting or feeding our animals.

It was during this, our last night's march, that one of our scouting parties destroyed the Round Mountain Iron Works, situated in the Cherokee Valley, about thirty miles from Rome. These works were, at the time, largely engaged manufacturing ordnance and material for the rebel army, and employed nearly one thousand hands.

Our vanguard, consisting of two hundred men, under command of Captain Milton Russell, of the Fifty-First Indiana, arrived in the vicinity of Rome about eight o'clock next morning after the battle of Blunt's Farm, at least four hours later than it was expected they would reach that point, but their animals were so completely exhausted that it had been impossible for them to get there sooner, as they had rode all night at the utmost speed of their jaded horses. By this time the city was full of armed men. General Forrest's courier (a citizen of Gadsden) having arrived six hours previous, gave the first intelligence of our near approach, so rapidly and dexterously had our movements been executed. But, in this short time, a large number of troops had been hurried from Atlanta, Kingston and Dalton; besides the citizens and home-guards for miles around, had been collected and put under arms, several pieces of artillery had also been put in position commanding the river bridge and every avenue by which the city could be approached. The floor of the bridge was torn up and piled with straw and turpentine, ready to ignite, in case an attempt was made to force a crossing. . . . Notwithstanding the chastisement we gave the enemy the previous evening, in the engagement at Blunt's Farm, and the intimidation caused by our subsequent demonstrations, the delay occasioned by our guide's mistake, enabled him to overtake us about nine o'clock next morning (Sunday, May 3d,) near Gaylesville, Alabama, where we had halted to feed our animals.

They soon attacked us, and after some slight skirmishing, General Forrest sent a flag of truce to Colonel Streight, demanding a surrender. The Colonel held a consultation with the regimental commanders, in which our situation and chances of success were fully canvassed. We had but a small quantity of artillery ammunition, and the few rounds of rifle and musket cartridges on hand, were unfit for service. The enemy had a brigade on our left endeavoring to flank us, and was, in fact, at this time, nearer Rome than we were. Our men were completely exhausted, having had no rest for four days and nights. While General Forrest, having the advantage of good horses, had been able to rest his command, at least half of each night, his soldiers were, therefore, fresh and vigorous compared with the fatigued and worn-out condition of both our men and animals. Captain Russell, with the advance of two hundred men, as has already been shown, was unable to cross the river at Rome. It was evident that we had now to contend with a superior force, both in front and rear. All circumstances taken

into consideration, our situation seemed hopeless. It was, therefore, decided to surrender on the following terms: Each regiment to retain its colors, and the officers and men their private
property including the side arms of the former. These terms
were agreed to by General Forrest. Our brigade was then drawn
up in line, our arms stacked, and we were prisoners of war.
The same day that we were made prisoners we were marched
under guard to Rome—a considerable change in the programme
we had proposed following, in regard to our entry of that place.
But I trust the preceding chapters are sufficient evidence that
the alteration was no fault of ours. The citizens of the place
gave unmistakable proof of their joy to see us; but had we
entered their town as we expected to have done, I very much
doubt if the ladies would have thronged the streets with gay
dresses, gaudy ribbons, and smiling faces to greet us. At least
I am informed that there was no demonstration of joy, when
the Union troops entered the town a year afterwards, as con-
querors. We remained in Rome until Tuesday morning, May
5th, under orders of General Forrest, who to his credit be it
said, furnished us with sufficient rations for our subsistence,
also with comfortable quarters.

2

*Unlike the work of Lieutenant Roach dealing with the
Streight Raid, which was published almost immediately after
the war, Captain Scott's account of the Battle of Brice's Cross
Roads was not published until almost 30 years after the event.
It has, however, a high degree of freshness and fire perhaps
because the Adjutant was still so resentful of the way in which
General Sturgis treated his regiment and his brigade in his
report of the battle.*

*The regiment whose story is told is the Fourth Iowa
Cavalry, in the brigade of Colonel Edward F. Winslow which,*

with the brigade of Colonel George E. Waring, made up Grierson's Cavalry Division in the Sturgis expedition. The account of the two days of Brice's Cross Roads—the day of battle and the day of pursuit—is from the viewpoint of a member of a brigade which retained its formation and continued to fight. It reflects, however, the completeness of defeat and demoralization of the army which had gone forth with such high hopes of bringing back Forrest's scalp.

The extracts are from Chapter VII of the Scott work.

THE BATTLE OF BRICE'S CROSS ROADS, JUNE 10, 1864.

On the evening of the 9th the cavalry reached Stubbs' plantation, fourteen miles east of Ripley and about ten west of Guntown, a small place on the Mobile & Ohio road. . . . The next morning, Friday, at five o'clock Waring's brigade moved out in advance on the Guntown road, Winslow following closely. The infantry moved later and soon fell behind. It was again dreadfully hot and sultry. At eleven o'clock Waring's brigade encountered the enemy's cavalry at the crossing of Tishomingo Creek.

Half a mile from the creek, at Brice's house, it (the Ripley-Guntown road) crossed the road running from Pontotoc to Baldwyn. The battle takes its name from this place, though it is often called "Guntown" and sometimes "Tishomingo Creek." . . . . The Tishomingo is a stream of important size, and it was then full from recent rains. Its banks were very soft, and impassable for horses in any number. The bridge was narrow and old, and was the only one on the creek within several miles. . . .

It had been Grierson's belief that there were only some six hundred rebels in his front, and he had expected to drive them quickly. . . .

There had been a great mistake. The rebels in front were not a few hundred, but Forrest's whole available force, himself at the head. They were probably six thousand, . . . with . . . twelve guns. Sturgis says the most intelligent officers estimated them at from fifteen to twenty thousand, but this estimate must have sprung from fears or mortification in defeat. If Forrest had had fifteen or twenty thousand, Sturgis would have lost, not the quarter, but the whole of his army. . . .

When Grierson found that the rebels would not be driven, he ordered the whole division into position . . . . dismounted. Sabres and spurs had been left with the horses, which were held in mass in the field east of the creek. It was now twelve o'clock.

[The infantry] were five or six miles in the rear. They were already half-broken from the hardships of the ten days' march and enervated by the great heat. They were now ordered to move at quick time, and finally at double-quick. Their fatigue, the very miry road, and the sultry air, made it impossible to do this in order. Some dropped out, in spite of the efforts of their officers, and the others plunged along in disorder. Long before they reached the battle-field they were exhausted and spiritless. . . .

But the infantry came up, greatly hurried and blown, having lost a large part of their number by straggling and by sheer physical exhaustion, followed by the artillery, and that by the whole wagon train. Everything was rushed over the creek toward the enemy. By some wild order or misunderstanding, even the wagon train was being run over the bridge and parked in the open fields near it, within reach of Forrest's artillery.

Nothing was left undone which could tend to make the disaster complete. . . .

At about two o'clock the infantry appeared and occupied the ground under the immediate direction of Colonel McMillen, and the Iowa cavalry began to retire [under orders to retire and remount as the infantry relieved them] . . . Sturgis said to him [Winslow] that he meant to use the cavalry on the flanks, mounted. . . .

Meantime the noise of the battle was much increased, and the report came back that the infantry were driving the enemy. . . . How vastly different the situation really was from that supposed! The real situation was, that the enemy had advanced in force along his whole line, and had driven back our infantry; that he had successfully pushed his right wing beyond our left; and that he was now almost sure of victory. . . . Their [the infantry] lines were broken at several points, they were thrown into confusion, those who were not taken bravely fighting to the last, fell back in disorder toward the bridge. The whole field was lost and the whole army in danger of capture. Sturgis got the Colored brigade up in time to enable a part of it to take a share in the fighting just before the final rout. But with it appeared all the *impedimenta* of the army. This at least might have been prevented. Pack-animals, wagons, ambulances, the sick, servants, all of those necessary evils which clog an army, came dragging and straggling along in front of the guard. They ought not to have gone over the bridge, but . . . they moved right on . . . .

The broken troops on the Guntown road now began to appear west of the cross-roads, with the enemy pressing after them. The whole field was in a panic. All were disheartened, pride disappeared, and all hurried toward the bridge. Men, horses, wagons, ambulances, guns, and caissons, all in confusion . . . .

It was plain that the infantry had been defeated and broken. Some of the enemy's guns at this time were evidently our own guns turned upon us. . . . Terrible confusion now prevailed at the bridge, which was blocked by the flying troops and by vehicles stuck upon it. . . .

Meantime [after a stand made by McMillen's "brave remnant of an infantry brigade," assisted by the Fourth Iowa cavalry, dismounted] the bridge was cleared, and all of the infantry not already lost crossed over . . . the Fourth Iowa fell back steadily, without haste, and passed the creek the last regiment of all. The whole of the army remaining was now on the road west of the Tishomingo, moving toward Ripley, all in great disorder, except the cavalry and remnants of the infantry brigades. . . .

About three miles west of the Tishomingo, McMillen, with Wilkin, Hoge, and Bouton, formed a new line of the remnants of their [infantry] brigades which still held together, in the hope of preventing any further loss. Sturgis says there were twelve or fifteen hundred men in this line, but that they soon gave way, and that it was impossible to exercise any further control. This line could not have given way under any immediate pressure from the enemy, because Winslow's brigade was between it and the Tishomingo, and still maintained perfect order. It is probable that the cause was the terrible spectacle of their routed and demoralized comrades moving in confusion along the road. The sight of a disorderly retreat causes fear even in good soldiers. And the spectacle then on that road within a few miles west of the creek is beyond any description. The road was filled from side to side with wagons, ambulances, guns and caissons, infantry, afoot and mounted, negroes of both sexes and all ages, all in utter disorder, all struggling to get to the head. The road had been very bad when the columns were moving in the opposite direction a few hours earlier, but now it was far worse. It had been beaten into the deepest mud, and the big army wagons, stuck fast and abandoned here and there, blocked the way and added to the confusion. The screaming of shot and shell flying over or toward the rear of these fugitives increased their terror; and only the coming on of night saved them from destruction or capture.

When Sturgis was overtaken by Winslow, his staff and cavalry escort were in good order, but immediately in his front and rear was seen the dreadful condition of the army. In the conversation which ensued Sturgis remarked, with an injured and disheartened tone, that his army was only a mob of volunteers, worthless in action, becoming demoralized and useless without cause. . . . On hearing that his brigade was unbroken and all in hand, he asked Winslow whether he could forge ahead of the retreating troops and stop them until they could be reorganized and re-formed. Winslow replied that he could, that he thought he could pass all the infantry by the time the first of them reached Stubbs', five miles further, and asked if that place would do. . . . Sturgis said the place would do admirably, and at once ordered Winslow to go there, stop every man and animal, and hold them until he should come up.

Winslow then returned to the rear and moved the brigade forward as fast as possible, through the woods but parallel with and near the road. When Stubbs' plantation was reached, the brigade was ahead of the flying army. . . . all movement was stopped. . . . But when General Sturgis came up he made no attempt to reorganize. Winslow reported his action; the General only replied that "the whole thing had gone to hell," that he did not expect to save any artillery or wagons; and he

directed Winslow to open the road, let the broken troops pass
by, and to exhort them to hurry along. He said, however, that
he intended to reorganize at Ripley, and make a stand there.
Ripley was fourteen miles further on, and it was now dark.
. . . The cavalry then opened the road, and General Sturgis and
a large number of officers with him rode off toward Ripley,
followed by the disordered infantry and the mob of stragglers
on foot. . . .

Meantime the remaining cavalrymen lighted many fires
across the line of march, hoping to deceive the enemy into the
belief that a large force was encamped there. But the intense
darkness of the night would probably alone have saved the
retreating army from attack. . . . At about two in the morning
the road was clear and no more men were found in the
[Hatchie] swamp. All who had so far escaped appeared to be
now safely in front, on the way to Ripley. Half an hour later
the brigade was mounted and marched on the Ripley road.
. . . Shortly after it was again in motion rebel cavalry appeared
and made a dash upon the rear. They had only been waiting for
light enough to enable them to attack. . . .

Forrest pursued closely, with all of his cavalry, confident
of capturing at least the retreating footmen. He pushed the
rear with great daring and persistence, impatient to reach his
expected captives in front. His advanced companies frequently
charged upon the rear with wild yelling; and he lost many men,
not only when these assaults were repulsed, but through the
hardihood of some of his men, who, reckless in the joy of victory, unnecessarily exposed themselves in coming too near. The
Fourth Iowa maintained a formation by companies in echelon,
the rear company always in line facing the enemy. . . . The
enemy were of course, comparatively, in good condition. They
had won a striking victory, and were greatly elated. They knew

that Sturgis had lost a large part of his army, nearly all his artillery, and all of his wagons and supplies. They had, indeed, good occasion for high spirits and high hopes. . . .

As the regiment approached Ripley, Forrest's men became still more truculent, and appeared in increased numbers. They pushed forward on the flanks, now on one and then on the other, attacking there as well as in the rear. . . .

[At Ripley] the rebels pressed their advantage, and produced some disorder. . . . But the disorder was overcome and all fell back to the northwest part of the town. There was nothing to be done but to leave the town while it was yet possible. . . .

The rebels rode immediately through the town, and kept dashing upon the rear-guard. . . . About five miles west of Ripley the road crossed a small creek with steep banks, spanned by a narrow bridge. . . . Scattered about the bridge and the banks of the creek were many infantrymen, sitting and lying down, apparently utterly exhausted. They had stopped there for water or to rest, but they were now so worn out and so dull and hopeless in mind that they could not be moved. The cavalrymen tried to get them to go on, but nothing could stir them. . . . It was a pitiful spectacle of broken spirits. They were no doubt all prisoners within a short time.

But this was not the only instance of the capture of the broken infantry in that terrible retreat. Many hundreds were lost after their escape from the battlefield. They had had little or nothing to eat since the morning of the day before, nor any sleep, and their physical powers had been taxed beyond endurance. Singly and in squads they fell or lay by the roadside or in the woods, all strength and spirit gone, wholly refusing to move. Fear of death or desire to live had no longer any influence. They were stupidly indifferent to fate. The spirit of

the average man in war—the "soul," as old writers call it—
depends upon his stomach and his muscle; it has not an
independent existence.

The passage of the small creek was made by the brigade
at about two o'clock. There Forrest must have given up hope
of success, and probably he there halted the main part of his
forces, because after the creek was crossed the attacks were
light and infrequent. The reason for this respite was, probably,
that his men and horses had become jaded. His horses had,
indeed, on that day done even more than those on the other
side, as they were almost continuously hurrying back and forth
and making circuits over rough country on the flanks of the
Iowa men.

CHAPTER SIX

The Civilian Side

Reports by the civilians among whom war is waged are less frequent and precise than the reports of the military combatants but to every campaign and every conflict there was a civilian side.

This civilian side to the campaign which culminated at Brice's Cross Roads, as seen through the eyes of persons resident at both Ripley, Mississippi, and Brice's, has been preserved through the interest and efforts of Andrew Brown, formerly of Ripley and now of Arlington, Virginia. The selections offered herein are from the diary of Orlando Davis, a prominent attorney of Ripley before and during the war, and of Holly Springs afterward, and from an account of the battle as it appeared to the Reverend Samuel Agnew, the son of Dr. Agnew, whose house was one of the battlefield landmarks. These documents have been made available to present day readers through a series of Historical Sketches by Mr. Brown published in the Southern Sentinel *of Ripley in 1934 and 1935. The Agnew account was earlier published in the same newspaper on March 28, 1895, and the Davis diary in September, 1893.*

Orlando Davis recorded in his diary the details of the 61 times that Ripley was visited by Federal troops. Many, if not most, of the visits were by small patrol parties but the 55th, 56th and 57th visits were different, as appears below:

"55. *Sunday, June 5.* [1864] At midnight one regiment, 2nd New Jersey, under Col. Karge, passed through town, coming in on Salem and leaving on the Rienzi road. They remained only long enough to pass through, searching Dr. Whitlow's house.

"56. *Tuesday, June 7.* At 2 P.M. 10,000 men under Gen. Sturgis and Gen. Grierson arrived on the Saulsbury road. Col. McMillan of the 95th Ohio established headquarters at my house. There were two regiments of negroes in the command. They committed many outrages. They beat Randolph with a wagon whip, struck Mrs. Doxey,[1] robbed all the houses where there was no guard, killed stock, took corn, meat, etc. These were the first negro troops ever seen in Ripley. They had Dick Sexton and John Lindsey as prisoners. The whole crowd remained in town 24 hours, and then left on the Cotton Gin road. They camped at Stricklin's, Ragan's, and Gray's until Thursday morning, when 250 men, with 50 wagons, returned and passed through Ripley going the Salem road."

Further down the road, at the residence of Dr. Agnew and no doubt also at the residence of William Brice and the other homes in and near the little settlement rumors of approaching troop movements were anxiously listened to. But, as appears from the Agnew account, the word was that the Federal forces were moving well to the northeast and that Forrest had shifted his forces in that direction to meet them. On Thursday, June 9, then, the Agnew household slept quietly, "unconscious of the proximity of danger." Indeed, Friday the 10th of June "dawned peacefully" and the household "breakfasted at the usual hour."

---

1. A sister of Major General T. C. Hindman, C.S.A.

Here, in part, is the story of the day as it appeared to young Agnew—or rather, as he recollected it thirty years later:

"While sitting at the table, a negro man came in and reported that the Yankees had camped the night before at Stubbs' farm, seven miles from us in the direction of Ripley. [The Agnew house was three miles northwest of Cross Roads.] . . . The news awakened us from our fancied security. As soon as a few mouthfuls of food were swallowed I took charge of my father's mules and horses and, with negroes to help care for them and a little brother then thirteen years old, went into a dense thicket a mile and a half southwest of our home where we hoped to hide our stock and save it from seizure by the Federal troops if they came our way. . . . We were in a branch bottom back of my father's farm. We heard a roaring northward which we could not explain. Afterward we knew it was the noise made by the advancing Federal army. . . . We did not dare communicate with home, but we did listen intently and anxiously awaited developments. We did not have long to wait. A volley of small arms was heard. . . . The battle began about 10 A.M. and it was after 5 P.M. that the Federals were forced to retreat. . . .

"When the battle was in progress it became evident about 5 o'clock that the firing was nearer, that the Federals were manifestly falling back, and that Forrest was pushing them in this direction. About 6 o'clock, when this long, hot, and anxious day was drawing to a close, to my surprise shells began to fall into the thicket where we were hidden. . . . as the shells passed over my head sputtering and whizzing I couldn't help dodging. . . . We were evidently in an unsafe place and retreated, going south while the shells were flying all around us. . . .

"Next morning as soon as I could see I started out to see what had happened at home. I went cautiously, for I was not certain which force occupied the place. I found that the Yankees had been driven away. Our once pleasant home was a wreck. . . . The fence around the garden and yard had been torn down. Many horses were hitched under every tree in the yard. Soldiers [evidently Confederate] were stalking through the yard and house without ceremony. The public road in both directions was lined with wagons as far as could be seen. As I came home, for more than half a mile I saw hundreds of shoes and articles of every description which had been thrown away by the Yankees in their retreat. The road was filled with soldiers passing to and fro. Several dead negroes in blue uniforms were lying in the road. When I saw these things I knew that Forrest had gained a great and complete victory, but my heart sank within me at the prospect of our own losses. I found females of the family all on the back piazza. They were laughing and talking but under their mirth I could see a sadness concealed. They told me that the Yankees had taken every grain of corn and every ounce of wheat, leaving us nothing to eat; that they had not taken a bite to eat since the previous morning and that the house had been plundered. I walked through the rooms and found everything turned upside down and many things had been taken from us. Bullets had penetrated the walls of the house at various places. Negroes and white men had both plundered our dwelling. Nothing could move their pity, but with vandal hands they rifled trunks and bureaus. They entered every room. Destruction seemed to be their aim. They even entered the negro cabins and robbed them of their clothing. As they went down they cut the rope and let the bucket down into the well. As they went back, panting with heat and suffering with exhaustion and thirst, they were glad to drink such slop as they could find. . . .

"The final stand was made at my father's house. When

the fight began, my mother, wife, and sisters closed all the shutters, went into an inner room and lying flat on the floor awaited the issue of the conflict."

On the same Saturday on which young Agnew returned to his father's house with the horses and mules, to find there no corn or other feed for animals or food for humankind, Orlando Davis was making this entry in his diary:

"57. *Saturday, June 11.* At 4 A.M. Gen. Sturgis' army reached Ripley on their retreat from Brice's Cross Roads. They were the worst demoralized set ever seen in these parts. They rested here until after breakfast, when at 7 A.M. they were attacked by Forrest's pursuing army and the fight raged in and around the town for two hours. The Yanks were again defeated and left, scattering in every direction through the woods. They abandoned a portion of their artillery train in the northwest part of town, in Miller's field, to wit: one cannon, three caissons, two ambulances. Over 20 dead Yankees killed in the fight were buried here, besides about 100 wounded that were left behind. Every wagon, ambulance, and cannon was captured; 21 in all."

This fifty-seventh Federal visit to Ripley was not, however, to be the last. In less than a month there was a fifty-eighth, when Major General A. J. Smith marched that way with his column sent out to destroy Forrest—the fourth such expedition which had made its way from Memphis into Mississippi in pursuit of that object since February, 1864. Mr. Davis' diary entry for this 58th visit reads as follows:

"58. *July 8, 1864.* At 7 A.M. the Federal army under Gen. A. J. Smith commenced arriving on the Lagrange road, and were until 3 P.M. passing through the town. The scenes of this visitation were the most terrible of any we have ever experienced in Ripley. The Yankees were infuriated because of their former defeat here and came in swearing vengeance on the town. A total of 35 stores, dwellings and churches, including the courthouse were burned. The south side of the square was fired by the cavalry in the morning, the rest by the negroes in the evening. Mrs. Prince's, Col. Falkner's, and Mr. Ford's dwellings were burned. The courthouse, Cumberland Presbyterian Church, Methodist Episcopal Church, and Female Academy shared the same fate. My own dwelling was saved by the exertions of a guard left by Col. McMillan."[2]

General Smith marched on to receive and repulse the charges of the Confederate forces, commanded by Lieutenant General Stephen D. Lee, at the Battle of Harrisburg, or Tupelo, on July 14, before retreating to Memphis with his mission of destroying Forrest uncompleted. The return march, however, was not by way of Ripley, perhaps because of the lack of supplies along that thoroughly devastated route.

---

2. Andrew Brown, who has made the most thorough study of the burning of Ripley, thinks that the dwelling houses were probably destroyed by accident. Col. Falkner's home was immediately in the rear of the Methodist Church and that of Mrs. Prince was just across a narrow street. Mr. Ford's home was across a narrow street from the Cumberland Presbyterian Church. The local legend is that the wind was high.

CHAPTER SEVEN

An August Sunday Morning In Memphis

James Dinkins of Canton, Mississippi, self-described as "The Little Confederate," was the youngest and smallest of the 192 boys at the North Carolina Military Institute who followed Daniel Harvey Hill into the army in 1861. After First Manassas he was transferred into a Mississippi regiment, with which he served in Virginia during the first two years of the war.

Commissioned a Lieutenant while still under nineteen years of age, he was ordered back to Mississippi in the spring of 1863, to report to Brigadier General James R. Chalmers, who put him in command of a section of artillery and subsequently added him to his personal staff.

In January, 1864, General Chalmers' command became part of Forrest's Cavalry. From that time until the surrender at Gainesville, Alabama, in May, 1865, young Dinkins had opportunity to observe the leader of what he described as "the most remarkable command in the army." Of the men who composed that command, he wrote, "A man who can show that he was with Forrest the last year and a half of the war is no ordinary man, you can depend on that."

Toward the close of a long and successful career in the passenger department of the old Queen & Crescent Route at

New Orleans, Captain Dinkins published his delightful memoirs.[1] *In this volume he refers to himself as "Lieutenant Bleecker," presumably to enable him to write in the third person. At any rate, "Lieutenant Bleecker" is a genial and kindly observer of men and events.*

Not all his descriptions and comments are the result of direct eye-witness observation, since the needs of the service frequently required Chalmers and his staff to operate separately from the main body of Forrest's command. Thus, when Major General A. J. Smith led his heavy column of invasion from Memphis into Mississippi in August, 1864, Chalmers was left to delay his advance, while Forrest swung out and around Smith's right and rode hard for his base at Memphis.

What happened when he reached there on Sunday, the 21st, is told by Captain Dinkins as vividly and with as much zest as if he had been there himself, rather than in and around Oxford, Mississippi. It is not hard to imagine the eagerness with which he garnered the details of the many-sided story from the lips of those who rode into Memphis, not only immediately after their return but also through the years after the war, when he was a frequent visitor to Memphis. The same eagerness and exultation shine through his lively narrative, which follows:

GENERAL FORREST MAKES A DASH INTO MEMPHIS

The enemy under General Smith, ignorant of General Forrest's movement, advanced his entire force to Oxford, and after burning the town and resorting to the most cruel and inhuman acts toward the defenseless citizens, was preparing to

---

1. Dinkins, Captain James, *Personal Recollections and Experiences in the Confederate Army, 1861 to 1865,* by An Old Johnnie. The Robert Clarke Company, Cincinnati, 1897.

move further south and destroy that section. About an hour before night, however, they hurriedly began a retreat toward Holly Springs, marching all night. General Chalmers was quickly advised of this, and knew Smith had received information of Forrest's movement, and notwithstanding muddy roads, moved forward with great rapidity, sending Buford ahead with McCulloch's and the Kentucky brigade, while he in person led Mabry's brigade. Colonel Bill Wade was in command of McCulloch's brigade. He was an old infantry colonel, and had seen service in the Mexican War. Colonel Wade in advance struck the enemy's rear guard, just in the northern suburbs of Oxford. He rode at the head of the Fifth Mississippi, and when he reached the enemy, he formed the men in columns of eight, and with his saber cutting right and left, dashed through the Federal columns. His men used their guns as clubs, and rode over and trampled down a whole regiment. It was a desperate charge, but the men of the Fifth Mississippi were accustomed to desperate work. Wade afterward said: "D—n them. They have been running us for two or three days. I want them to know we are not afraid of them." The enemy halted after arriving at Hurricane creek, and formed his line, expecting an attack. They were evidently getting nervous, and would have retreated in greater haste but for the delay in crossing the Tallahatchie river. We have said very little about the artillery, though much credit is due that branch of the service, for several of Forrest's successes. During the retreat of the enemy on the 23d, Captain Ed. S. Walton, with his battery, performed some wonderful feats. He kept his guns fully up to the front during the whole day, and poured grape and shell into their ranks, crushing and tearing them to pieces. The conduct of Walton and his men was grand. Whenever the enemy fell back, they took right hold of the guns and ran for better position. It was difficult for the cavalry to keep up with them. The constant engagements for several days had exhausted our ammunition, and the horses were worn out, and they had very little feed for two days. Further, General Smith destroyed the bridge over the Tallahatchie, which made it impossible for General Chalmers to pursue the enemy beyond the river.

We returned to Oxford, and found the people in a desperate condition. They had no food of any kind. General Chalmers sent word to hurry all the supplies to Oxford that could be found. Ladies and children were, in many cases, homeless and hungry. Those who were fortunate enough to have their houses left, had nothing to eat, and had to live on soldier's rough meat and bread for several days, and were glad to get that. When the enemy heard that Forrest was in Memphis, they feared he would get in their rear. Numbers of them knew what it was to have him on their trail, and therefore, sought all the news obtainable. A Captain Cannon seemed very anxious to learn something about Forrest, and inquired of Mr. Cook, a citizen of Oxford, what kind of a man he was. Mr. Cook gave him a description of the general, and asked the Yankee captain if he would be willing to pick one hundred men and meet Forrest with the same number. "No," he replied, "I do not care to fight Forrest alone, with my whole company. I hope I may never see him."

It is remembered that when General Forrest left Oxford, Memphis bound, it had been raining very hard, and continued two days afterward. The creeks were all greatly swollen, and the Tallahatchie river also. The roads were as muddy as rain could make them. It looked like an unwise and a forlorn effort, but with that indomitable and indefatigable man in the lead of such soldiers as followed him on that expedition, obstacles which other men could not have surmounted, gave way. It was necessary to go as far west as Panola, in order to cross the Tallahatchie. They rode all night in darkness and mud, swimming creeks and often getting down in the mud and water to pull the artillery over, but they never complained.

They reached Panola about sunrise the next morning, August 19th, where it was discovered that several of the artillery horses were almost dead on their feet, but after feed and a rest of three hours, they pushed on to Senatobia; arriving there, the men and horses were completely broken down. So Forrest remained all night, and moved early on the following morning. He learned that Hickahala creek was full with the banks, and it was necessary to bridge it in order to cross. But Forrest and his band of superhuman men were equal to any emergency. The writer several times heard General Forrest tell how he overcame the difficulty, and will give it in his own words as near as can be remembered. Said he: "I had no idea of giving up my visit to Memphis, nor did I intend to lay around the creek waiting for it to fall. So I told Neely, Logwood, and McCulloch (Red Rob) to send their men to all the gin-houses for ten miles and bring in the flooring on their shoulders. There was a little narrow flat-boat not over twenty feet long on the north bank of the creek. Two of the men swam over and brought it to our side. I then set the men to work cutting grapevines which we twisted together, lapping them until we had a long rope. I fastened one end to a tree, and sent some of the men over in the flat-boat to tie the other end. I used the flat-boat for my middle pontoon, and bundled together cedar telegraph poles I had cut down, which I used for the other pontoons. Before we got our pontoons in position, the boys began to arrive with the plank, which were put down as fast as could be, and by the time the last man was there with his plank, we were crossing the bridge. It did not require over three hours to build the bridge and cross, but I had to build a longer bridge over Coldwater river, where I again made use of the grapevines for a cable. I found a lot of dry cypress logs, which we used in the same way we did the telegraph poles at Hickahala, and with the ferryboat for the middle pontoon, we soon made a bridge over Coldwater river, which we crossed in safety, and reached Hernando before night. I had to continually caution the men to keep quiet. They were making a regular corn shucking out of it. Wet and muddy, but full of life and ready for anything, I never had greater confidence in them. Those were great soldiers."

When the command arrived at Hernando, General Forrest received information from his scouts, just returned from Memphis, that the city was quiet and without the slightest idea of the approach of a rebel force. He left Hernando, and rode all night (it was Saturday night) reaching near the vicinity of Memphis before daylight Sunday morning. The honest people and the thieves were all asleep, unmindful of the storm which hovered about them. The Federal soldiers had retired to their bunks without the least solicitude. They knew that General Smith was after Forrest, and if he did not capture him, he would keep him on the move. What had they to fear? They slept peacefully. No danger could possibly reach them. But how vain are all human ideas! Before reaching the pickets, Forrest halted his command, and gave the officers instructions. He explained comprehensively what each was expected to do. Captain W. H. Forrest, a younger brother of the general, was to take the advance and capture the pickets, after which he was to dash into the city and go directly to the Gayoso Hotel, where it was said General Hurlbut was quartered, as were also a number of other Federal officers. Colonel Neely, with the second Missouri, Fourteenth Tennessee, and Eighteenth Mississippi, was to charge the camp in the outskirts, while Colonel Logwood was ordered to follow Captain Bill Forrest to the Gayoso with the Twelfth and Fifteenth Tennessee. Colonel Jesse Forrest, with the Sixteenth Tennessee, was instructed to dash through De Soto Street to Union and capture General Washburn and his staff. Colonel Bell, with Newsum's regiment and the Second Tennessee under Colonel Morton, also two pieces of artillery, was to be left on the outskirts as a reserve.

Captain William Forrest of all the men in our service was probably best fitted for the daring and desperate work assigned to him. He was a powerful man, five feet eleven inches tall, broad shoulders, weighing about two hundred pounds, and like the general, a physical giant. He was brave to recklessness. He did not fear one man, nor did he fear a hundred men, and yet he was as sympathetic as a woman. He never provoked a quarrel, but when disturbed, would shoot a man of the slightest provocation, and he would give the last cent he had to a person in distress. The writer has known him to do both. It has been often said that General Forrest never feared but one man, and that man was his brother, William.

Every thing understood, Captain Forrest moved forward with ten picked men about fifty yards in advance of his company. He reached the picket about two miles out from the city, on what was known as the Hernando road, near where Trigg avenue crosses Mississippi avenue. As Captain Forrest rode along, the Yankee vidette heard the tramp of his horses and called out quickly: "Halt! Who comes there?" Captain Forrest answered: "A detachment with rebel prisoners." The vidette replied: "Advance one." Captain Forrest whispered to his men to follow closely behind him. They rode quietly up and found a guard sitting on his horse in the middle of the road. It was just before daylight. As soon as Captain Forrest got within reach he struck the picket a deadly blow over the forehead with his heavy six shooter, knocking him off his horse. One of the men dismounted quickly and disarmed him. The others rushed at the picket guards, and captured them without firing a gun. General Forrest had cautioned every one to keep perfectly quiet. There was no noise. General Forrest followed the advance closely, and about the time the pickets were made prisoners he rode up. Captain Forrest again moved forward and met the second guard, but unlike the vidette they fired at him and ran for their lives. This circumstance excited our men, and simultaneously, though without orders, they dashed after the retreating Federals, and raised a yell. General Forrest, with his escort company, was close on their heels. He saw that the silence was broken, and that he could no longer conceal his presence. He told "Gaus" to blow the charge. At the first note of Gaus' bugle the regimental bugles responded with the charge, and before the first note ceased to reverberate the whole command raised a yell and lifted their horses off the ground.

No artist's brush will ever paint such a scene as that, and no pen will ever trace in words, language which can adequately describe it. Men who had been in the saddle for two days and night, wet and hungry, their horses worn out, now rushed over the enemy's camp yelling and shouting like flying devils. The Federals had no intimation that Forrest was near. They could not realize the situation. They must have thought the devils dropped out of the clouds. The wildest excitement spread in all directions. Captain Forrest with his gallant band of about forty men, depending entirely upon themselves, pressed forward, and ran into an artillery camp of six guns, caissons, horses, etc. They dashed on to the guns, killing or wounding nearly every man who exposed himself. This was near where the Kansas City, Memphis and Birmingham Railroad crosses Mississippi avenue.

This little band pressed on to Beal street, crossed Main, and then to the Gayoso Hotel. Like avenging devils many of them rode their horses into the rotunda. The men rushed over the hotel, looking for General Hurlbut and other Federal officers. They created a panic equal to that at Pompeii when the city was destroyed by Vesuvius. Federal officers, suddenly aroused from sleep, ran from place to place en deshabille. Two of them, who did not realize the situation, began to curse the intruders, and made an effort to put them out. Those unfortunates were killed. Men and women screamed, the men were worse frightened than the women. The situation was inexplicable. It suggested the most awful and horrible thoughts that ever chased each other through the brain of man. People in the third and fourth story rooms heard the screams of those below, and the reports of two or three pistol shots. As they ran from place to place, they asked: "What is it?" Very soon Captain Forrest's men were breaking open the doors. Officers hid under their beds and in the closets, but were dragged out. They begged for their lives. Big rough looking men, coarsely appareled and covered with mud, a pistol in each hand, smashed in the doors and were in full possession of the hotel. It was an awful situation to realize on getting out of bed. Those mud covered men wanted General Hurlbut. He was not there, but he ought to have been there.

Many of the men who rode with Forrest into Memphis that August morning are living, and are good and loyal citizens of the government of the United States. They are, in some instances, men of great prominence in affairs today. They are men of cultivation, refinement, influence, and wealth. They can be seen on the streets of Memphis any day, but a passerby would never suppose that those business-looking gentlemen, modest and unobtrusive, were the same daredevils who rode their horses into the rotunda of the Gayoso, ready to kill any Federal soldier who offered resistance, and who surprised and captured pickets and charged batteries. But such is a fact.

Captain Forrest, being in advance, aroused all the Federal forces. As soon as he passed, and the officers caught their breath, they formed their men in line for defense. Colonel Logwood, who followed Captain Forrest, encountered a double line of infantry drawn up along the road not far from the artillery camp. Logwood was moving at a gallop. The first gray streaks of dawn were appearing, and the first intimation he had of their presence was a volley at the head of his column. Logwood was tempted to charge them, but he knew the importance of giving Captain Forrest support. Therefore, he pushed on without halting. The enemy, greatly excited, shot over the heads of his men. As he reached Georgia street, Logwood found another line of infantry blocking his way. They opened fire, but at the head of the gallant Twelfth Tennessee, he led the charge against them. The men raised a yell, and with guns in their right hands raised above their heads, rode pell-mell over and beyond the line, scattering those who opposed and creating a panic. The Yankees dodged like squirrels. As he reached the point where Wellington street runs into Mississippi avenue, he discovered a company of artillery, and the men were hurriedly loading the pieces. There was not a moment to lose. His whole force would be shot to death in a minute more. But Logwood was the man for that occasion. With great presence of mind and courage, he dashed on the guns, and captured or killed the gunners before they could fire. He then rushed on to Hernando street, and by the old markethouse; then out Beal to Main, and to the Gayoso. As the men went rushing and yelling through the streets, the enemy fired at them from behind fences, from windows, and from house corners. But our men were wild. They dashed on without the faintest idea of danger; nothing but death could stop them. Numbers of our men had lived in Memphis, and were proud to see the city again. Women and men stuck their heads out of windows and doors, waving sheets, dresses, and anything they found handy. They recognized the muddy old Rebs, and welcomed them with all the enthusiasm in their power. Numbers of females, overcome by excitement, rushed out into the streets in their night-robes, forgetful of everything except the present moment. They had, figuratively, left the earth and walked in the air. Logwood and his gallant followers, after arriving at the Gayoso, renewed the search for Federal officers. He, however, posted a squad of men in each direction, to give notice of any advance of the enemy. After remaining in the vicinity until ten o'clock, he retired along Front street to Beal, and out to De Soto street. His scouts reported that the enemy was concentrating his forces and would cut him off unless he moved quickly. Captain Forrest, with that recklessness and indifference to all opposition and danger which characterized him at all times, decided to pay all his friends a visit. He was notified that the enemy on several streets was moving toward the Gayoso, but that made no difference to him. He had probably forty or fifty men. They mounted their horses in front of the hotel, formed company, and with Captain Forrest at the head, boldly rode through Gayoso street to Main, and up Main to Union, as leisurely as if they had been south of the Tallahatchie. They turned into Union going east, and when about the middle of the block a column of Federal infantry turned column left out of Second street into Union. The Federal soldiers carried their guns at a trail arms, and moved at double-quick. The moment Forrest saw them, not over fifty yards away, he fired on them with his pistol, killing one of the men in the first set of fours. His men dashed on the column with such absolute recklessness they paralyzed them. As Captain Forrest rode toward them, he continued to shout: "Put down those guns!" The head of the Federal column wheeled to run without firing a gun, and coming in contact with those behind, caused great confusion. They knocked each other down. It might have been that those in the rear supposed that a large force of rebels was at hand. They ran with all their speed toward Gayoso street. Forrest's men continued to fire at them, killing and wounding several. Forrest did not follow them up, but continued his course out Union in a gallop, his men firing at every bluecoat they saw. The men hooted and yelled like Comanches. They reached De Soto street, and saw Colonel Logwood's column going south, and joined them.

Colonel Jesse Forrest, with his regiment, the Sixteenth Tennessee, had followed Colonel Logwood as far as Colonel Robert Looney's place, on Mississippi avenue, then ran through Lauderdale to Union and to General Washburne's headquarters. Unlike the other column, Colonel Forrest met with little resistance, but found to his great regret that General Washburne had escaped. He heard the firing on Logwood, and left the house, though General Forrest captured the members of the staff who waited to put on their clothes before following their general's example.

General Forrest remained with the reserve under Colonel Bell. He knew an emergency might arise, in which case he wanted to be in a position to meet it. Colonel Neely, who had been ordered to attack the large infantry camp just south of Elmwood cemetery, was met by a terrific volley. The enemy heard firing and formed line before he reached them. This was unexpected, and checked Colonel Neely's gallant band. They, however, recovered, dismounted, and drove the enemy pell-mell.

The enemy's force numbered over a thousand, while Colonel Neely mustered six hundred. General Forrest noticed the check Neely had received, and quick as thought, called out: "Forward!" He dashed off to the east and right of the enemy, followed closely by his staff and escort, and Bell leading his command. It was General Forrest's intention to strike the enemy in the flank, but he passed near a cavalry camp, from which he was fired on. At no time or place during the war did General Forrest show to better advantage. There were several yard and garden fences intervening, over which he rode like a scythe over a wheat field. The cavalry, supposing the end of the world near at hand, fled in great confusion. He was riding old "King Philip" before which no fence would stand. General Forrest rode several paces ahead, as usual. He held a long cavalry saber raised in his right hand, and looked more like a devil incarnate than anything those Yankees ever saw. He was physically a large man, but on that occasion must have looked forty feet high, as "King Philip" mounted the fences. He captured one hundred horses and about sixty men. Colonel Neely, as above stated, dispersed the infantry in his front, who were joined by the dismounted cavalry which General Forrest drove off, all of whom took refuge in the state female college buildings, in which there were numerous windows that were used as port holes. General Forrest called on Lieutenant T. S. Sale, who commanded the section of artillery, to throw a few shells in the building, which he did with great celerity. The enemy, after reaching cover, opened a hot fire and defended the place with credit. General Forrest advanced a skirmish line, but concluded it would be too great a sacrifice to send his men against them; therefore, contented himself with watching Sale make holes in the wall and roof. It was the first chance Sale had on the trip, and he was anxious to batter the buildings, but General Forrest needed him for other work, and withdrew. Forrest, ascertaining that the enemy was massing his forces, having recovered from the shock, sent men into the city to collect stragglers and hurry them out to rejoin their commands. The commands under Colonels Logwood and Jesse Forrest, returning through De Soto street, to what is now Mississippi avenue, found a strong line of infantry, supporting a six-gun battery, just to the south of the Kansas City, Memphis and Birmingham Railroad, and extending across the Provine place. The force, as well as the guns, had full possession of the road, and commanded the approach from the city. That was a serious situation. Colonel Logwood sent Company "I" of the Fifteenth Tennessee, commanded by Captain Peter Williams, to take the battery. He charged at once, but was driven back. He recharged, however, reinforced by Company "H" also of the Fifteenth, commanded by Lieutenant J. M. Witherspoon and captured the battery.

In the meantime, Colonel Jesse Forrest had moved to the flank of the infantry, which frightened them off, leaving no enemy in front. The column quickly joined General Forrest who, with Bell's and Neely's commands, was near the building where the enemy had sought shelter. It was now about noon, and General Forrest desired to retire and let the pot stop boiling long enough to allow General Washburne to telegraph the situation at Memphis to Smith. Many of the men were dismounted, arranging such articles as they had captured on their saddles, when suddenly a long column of Federal cavalry was seen riding at a rapid gait in pursuit of a lot of twenty or thirty men, who had lingered in the city. General Forrest, ever quick as powder, knew what to do. It made him furious to see his men chased by such a large body. He wheeled "King Philip" in the road and called on Colonel Chalmers with the Eighteenth Mississippi and Colonel McCulloch (Red Bob) with his Second

Missouri to follow. He rode at the head of the great Second Missouri with Colonel "Red Bob" by his side, to the right of the road, and sent Colonel Chalmers with his regiment to the left. They charged down on either side of the enemy's column, striking him right and left. It was a curious movement the enemy did not understand. It looked like spreading the wings of a partridge net to drive the birds through. They halted, and our stragglers galloped to their commands. The Federal officers acted with great courage, and tried to lead their men on, but could not do it. A Federal, Colonel Starr, seeing General Forrest, no doubt recognized him, and thinking to distinguish himself in a hand to hand fight, made a dash at the general. Colonel Starr did not live over ten minutes. He was no more in the hands of General Forrest than a butterfly would be in the claws of an eagle.

General Forrest, with some six hundred prisoners, and a large number of horses, then fell back, going in the direction whence he came. After going a short distance he had an opportunity to discover the character of his captives, and found that quite a number were unable to march on account of having no shoes, while others were sick. He therefore sent a member of his staff, Lieutenant C. W. Anderson, back to the city with a flag of truce. He sent with him an officer, who was a member of General Washburne's staff, a prisoner. His instructions were to say to General Washburne that the prisoners in his possession were in a wretched condition, many of them without shoes or clothing, that he did not desire to see them suffer, and as an act of humanity he would propose to exchange them for such of his men as might be held prisoners. Should General Washburne not have an equal number to exchange, he would parol the remainder. Should General Washburne reject the proposal, he would suggest then that he send clothing for his men. He would await General Washburne's pleasure at Nonconnah creek, about six miles from the city. Lieutenant Anderson saw General Washburne who said he had no authority to recognize the parol of the prisoners held by General Forrest, but would accept the proffered privilege of sending a supply of clothing. In a short time two Federal officers, Colonel W. P. Hepburne and Captain H. S. Lee, with a wagon-load of clothing, were sent out. They reached General Forrest about three p.m. and the clothing was immediately distributed under direction of Colonel Hepburne. General Forrest then directed his surgeons to examine the prisoners and such as were found to be sick and unfit to undergo the hardships of the march might be sent back with the wagon, but with the promise they would not bear arms against the Confederate cause, or in any way injure the cause unless properly exchanged. About two hundred were turned loose on those conditions. The remainder, about four hundred, were mounted on the extra horses, and the march taken up to Hernando. Including the prisoners, General Forrest had about two thousand men without rations. He knew it would be impossible to obtain anything before reaching Panola, therefore, with that promptness which always stood him in hand, he decided to make requisition on General Washburne. He wrote General Washburne stating his inability to feed his prisoners and suggested that inasmuch as he would not receive them on parol, that the least he could do would be to send them something that night. He stated he would encamp at Hernando. This communication was sent by Colonel Hepburne. About daylight the following morning, the same two officers reached the camp with two wagons well loaded with provisions. Rations were issued to the prisoners for two days, and there was ample left to feed our men also. General Forrest, desiring to impress General Washburne with the idea that he might renew his attack on Memphis, gave instructions to make the men as comfortable as possible for a few days. The Federal officers returned to Memphis and as soon as they were out of sight, General Forrest moved rapidly to Panola.

Persons who heard the sharp call of the buglers on the morning just before daylight say it was the most awful and ringing sound they ever heard. No one except the men themselves knew what the situation was. People were left to depend entirely on imagination. Could it be that Gabriel was sounding the last call? The thunderous yells, the rush of the horses in the mud, the clanking of sabres and the rattle of spurs added to the awful situation. It was dark. Nothing could be seen. It had been said that the end of the world would come when no man expected it, and in the darkness of the night. Men and women asked themselves and each other if that was judgment day. They knew that war was cruel and spread desolation, but something worse than war was upon them. It was late for some of them to do so, but they prayed for their souls. They wondered if they would ever see the sunshine and the shadows again. Their brains were sizzing.

The caravan which Forrest escorted out of Memphis, Sunday afternoon, August 21, 1864, was in deep distress. The children of Israel, whom Moses led across the Red Sea, dry shod, were no more downcast and discouraged before the passage than was that lot of Federal prisoners. Moses' crowd had probably sufficient clothing, but those poor fellows were in an exceedingly bad condition. Some of them had on nothing but their underclothes, while others had nothing but night-shirts. Great numbers of them had no hats, and very few of them had shoes. Officers who had pranced about the streets of Memphis in their gay uniforms, in some instances doing duty as staff officers, mounted on good horses with elegant saddles, were now in a sad and pitiable plight, as they trudged along in the mud, their gowns wet and draggling. There was no merriment or humor in that party, and the old "Johnnies" felt too much sympathy for them to indulge in any levity. Terrible stories were told after the raid into Memphis of how Forrest and his men acted. A number of people anxious to appear as heroes told ridiculous tales of what they passed through. One of the best stories told was by a negro soldier who claimed to have seen General Forrest as he rode up to the front of the Gayoso Hotel. He described to his companions how Forrest looked and the size of his horse. Said he: "I was er stanning right in dis alley when I seed him come up. He rid his hoss right up to de hotel, and I'm telling you the Gord's truf, he hitched his hoss right to the second story bannisters. I seed him. I seed him."

And there are today old negroes in Memphis who can show you where he hitched his horse. The negro's idea was that he was as big as "Colossus of Rhodes."

CHAPTER EIGHT

A Soldier Sums Up

John W. Morton, nineteen years old but already a gunner of combat experience and an exchanged prisoner of war, showed up at General Forrest's headquarters in November, 1862, bearing orders from General Bragg that he be put in charge of the horse artillery of the new brigade which was then being organized. The young Lieutenant was distinctly not welcome, partly because his assignment was regarded as an improper interference, partly because—as Forrest afterward wrote—"his appearance was so youthful and his form so frail that (wishing stout, active men for my service) I at first hesitated to receive him." He "concluded to try him," however, and so rapidly and completely did young Morton win the General's confidence and esteem that he soon had a battery, entirely equipped with captured materiel, and when Forrest's artillery was organized as a four-battery battalion, in May, 1864, he was put in command. During the last twelve months of the war Captain Morton served as Forrest's Chief of Artillery until the surrender at Gainesville, when he still was under twenty-one years of age.

In 1909 Captain Morton, then Secretary of State of Tennessee, published at Nashville his The Artillery of Nathan

Bedford Forrest's Cavalry, *a volume of 374 pages. In his intro-
ductory note, the author describes his work as "a simple recital
of those occurrences in which the writer, a young officer in his
teens, under this incomparable leader was himself engaged."
The book opens with the author's summing up of his estimate
of General Forrest—a summation which, except for its more
rhetorical passages, might stand as that of most other Forrest
veterans.*

1

For nearly three years preceding the close of the Civil
War, as a member of General Forrest's military family and an
officer of his staff, I had unlimited opportunities for observing
and studying him as a man and as a commander, and that too
under all the varying conditions of the camp, the march, and
the battlefield.

Every structure in nature and in art necessarily rests upon
a base, a foundation, and it has been said that man himself is
in no wise exempt from this primal necessity; that for him,
as a living temple, heredity lays the foundation, while
environment becomes the dominant factor in shaping and
developing the superstructure." If this be true, my association
with and daily observation of the man warrants the assertion
that a massive brain, an inflexible purpose, unflinching courage,
tireless energy, and a will that could brook no opposition were
the bed rocks of the foundation upon which General Forrest
built—truly a combination of characteristics and attributes
rarely found in any one man.

Early in life General Forrest fell upon hard lines. The
death of his father left him, when only sixteen years of age,
the sole dependence for support and protection of a widowed
mother and eight young brothers and sisters. It was then he

began building on the foundation upon which all his subsequent career rested.

Deprived at this early age of every advantage of fortune, save a resolute soul and a robust constitution, he faced his duties and responsibilities with all that force of character displayed by him twenty years later as a cavalry commander. With no one to look to or lean upon, and so many dependent upon him, he was forced to think and act for himself, and thus, amid toil, privations, and hardships, he began the development of that complete self-reliance which characterized his whole military career.

As a soldier, by his intelligence, energy and bravery, he carved his way unaided from obscurity to fame—from the ranks to a Lieutenant-Generalship.

General Forrest, as a commander was, in many respects, the negative of a West Pointer. He regarded evolution, maneuvers and exhaustive cavalry drill an unnecessary tax upon men and horses. He cared nothing for tactics further than the movement by twos or fours in column, and from column right or left into line, dismounting, charging, and fighting. As attested by his unparalleled successes, these simple movements proved sufficient.

Except for officers, as an insignia of rank, General Forrest banished the saber from his command. In the hands of troopers he regarded them as a dangling, clattering appendage—of no value as offensive weapons. He armed his men with a Sharp's rifle, or short carbine, and two navy sixes, better in every way for either attack or defense. By his captures the Federal Government supplied him with guns and artillery and more ordnance, commissary, and quartermaster's stores than he could use.

With vastly inferior numbers he met on different fields and defeated Generals Hatch, Grierson, William Sooy Smith, and

Sturgis, all of whom were veteran soldiers and graduates of West Point. The two last named were specially selected by Generals Grant and Sherman, and sent out with splendidly equipped commands for no other purpose than to whip or kill that "devil Forrest." In the light of such events General Forrest can be excused for holding in contempt the idea that only West Pointers were fitted to command, and also for saying on one occasion: "Whenever I met one of them fellers that fit by note, I generally whipped h—ll out of him before he got his tune pitched."

By nature General Forrest was aggressive, consequently he was always an offensive fighter. He believed the moral effect was with the attacking party, and never failed, when it was possible to do so, to take the initiative and deliver the first blow. He believed that one man advancing in attack was equal to two men standing in line of battle and awaiting attack. When charged by the enemy, no matter in what numbers, it was his invariable rule to meet a charge with countercharge.

His restless nature would not allow him to remain in camp any longer than was necessary to rest his men and shoe his horses. Unlike some generals, who seemed content with holding their ground and keeping from being whipped, General Forrest was ever on the move, and never content unless he was whipping somebody. He cared little for army regulations or tactics; disobeyed or went outside of them whenever the good of the service or surrounding circumstances demanded it. Nor was he free from inconsistences common to us all. While he could not tolerate insubordination in his own command, he was himself at times the most insubordinate of men. However contrary to his own judgment a movement might be, an order from his superior officer on the battlefield was always obeyed, except in matters affecting himself or his command unwisely or unjustly. An instance of this kind I well remember. When General Hood crossed his army over the Tennessee into Florence, Ala., General Forrest was in command of all the cavalry of his army. We had our headquarters at a church a few miles out in the country. An officer came out with an order reducing the number of mules in wagons and ordering all surplus mules to be turned over to the quartermaster of transportation. General Forrest happened to be out and the officer left after giving specific directions to have the mules sent in the next morning. It was read to the General when he came in, and he said very quietly: "None of my mules will be sent in on that order." The next evening Maj. A. L. Landis came out and asked the General if he had received the order, and wanted to know why the mules had not been sent in as ordered. If the good people accustomed to sit in the "amen corner" had dropped in just at that time, they would have concluded that the good Lord had been ousted and old Nick had taken full possession of the sanctuary. The atmosphere was blue for a while. Stripped of General Forrest's bad words, he said to Major Landis: "Go back to your quarters and don't you come here again or send anybody here about mules. The order will not be obeyed; and, moreover, if Major Ewing bothers me any further about this matter, I'll come down to his office, tie his long legs into a double bowknot around his neck, and choke him to death with his own shins. It's a fool order anyway. General Hood had better send his inspectors to overhaul your wagons, rid them of all surplus baggage, tents, adjutant desks, and everything that can be spared. Reduce the number of his wagons instead of reducing the strength of his teams. Besides, I know what is before me; and if he knew the road from here to Pulaski, this order would be countermanded. I whipped the enemy and captured every mule wagon and ambulance in my command; have not made a requisition on the government for anything of the kind for two years, and now that they are indispensable my teams will go as they are or not at all."

Insubordination may be justified, but it cannot be defended. General Forrest's insubordination, in this case, was a Godsend and a saving clause to General Hood's retreating army. From Richland Creek to the Tennessee River the road was strewn with his abandoned wagons, and but for the help afforded the pontoon train by General Forrest's fine six-mule teams, great delay and probable disaster to the army would have occurred before a passage of the river was effected.

Long after the gray-haired veterans of the Confederate armies shall have passed away, and when, as far as possible, all error shall have been expunged from the pages of history, which should be illuminated by truth alone, a glorious constellation will shine undimmed in the sky of the Confederate States of America. It will be an empyrean of exalted memories in which these fixed stars, differing from one another in their own peculiar glory, will beam in their appropriate places, an enduring revelation to the world of the virtues and genius of our greatest commanders. In the zenith of the grand constellation will be a trinity of stars. The greatest and central luminary will send forth earth-wide rays, sustained and brilliant beyond all others, but beaming everywhere with softened radiance. The other two, different of element, but alike calling forth our admiration, will shine with their own brightness and effulgence to the right and left of the noble central star; one, Sirius-like, with far-flashing radiance of a light divine, from a Christian warrior's armor; the other with a rich, dazzling splendor that seems to fling lightnings of defiance to the sun's fiercest rays from the burnished shield of a dauntless heart. These stars are

Robert E. Lee, T. J. (Stonewall) Jackson, and Nathan Bedford Forrest.

The first was preeminent by reason of a superlatively noble nature and exalted purity of character, combined with world-wide fame as the commander of incomparable armies that loved him with a love as near adoration as ever blessed a mortal; the other two startled the solitudes of space and made the chasms of time to ring with the echoes of their matchlessly adroit and marvelously swift achievements. General Jackson prayed and marched, and prayed and fought. General Forrest, like a ruthless besom of destruction, charged the air with electric energy as he hurled himself upon the foe. He was indeed the "Wizard of the Saddle," self-reliant and aggressive, with the consciousness of one who seemed to know intuitively when, where, and how to strike. Without military training he forced his way from the ranks of the company in which he enlisted to a commander's fame as complete and brilliant as ever reflected honor upon any school of arms. We can picture him one spring morning at reveille, taking his place with comrades who barely knew his name, and four years later a lieutenant general, the resplendent and fiery star of whose glory still sheds a light that makes his deeds and his genius the theme of eager discussion in every camp and school where military science and skill enlist a thought.

He had absolutely no knowledge or experience of war gleaned from the study of what others had wrought. General Forrest grasped intuitively and instantaneously the strategic possibilities of every situation which confronted him, and with inspired native genius and complete confidence put into practice the tactics of the most famous generals in all history. His knowledge of men was in most cases unerring; and his ability to inspire and bring out the greatest power and endurance of his men was unsurpassed even by the great Napoleon himself. His eye for position was almost infallible, and his knowledge of the effect of a given movement on the enemy was intuitive and seemed to come rather from an inner than an outer source of information. His plans of battle were not chalked out on blackboards nor drawn on charts; they were conceived on the instant and as instantaneously carried out. He struck as the lightning strikes, and his tactics were as incalculable as those of the electric fluid and as mysterious to the enemy, for his movements were so rapid and his endurance and daring so remarkable that they could not be computed by any known rules of warfare.

2

About the personal altercation in which Lieutenant A. Wills Gould seriously wounded General Forrest and was, in turn, fatally wounded by the General, there has been an air of reticence and a confusion of testimony.

As to the main facts, however, there is no conflict. Forrest, dissatisfied with the way in which the Lieutenant had handled his section of artillery, asked for his transfer to another command and subsequently refused to discuss the matter with him. Lieutenant Gould insisted upon an interview, at the conclusion of which he fired a pistol almost against Forrest's body. Forrest, seizing the Lieutenant's pistol hand with his left, held him while he opened a pen knife with his teeth and stabbed him in the abdomen. Before the Lieutenant's death he and the wounded General were reconciled.

In Forrest's earliest biography, and the only one which he himself saw, there is no mention of the affair. Dr. Wyeth tells the story but does not mention the name of the Lieutenant. In this and most other accounts, the cause of Forrest's dissatisfac-

tion is given as the loss of the two guns captured by Streight in his counter-attack at the Battle of Day's Gap on April 30, 1863. There is one account, however, and an early one, in which the source of dissatisfaction is given as the handling of the guns by Gould in a reconnaissance in force made against Franklin, Tennessee, on June 3.¹ The altercation took place at Columbia, Tennessee, on June 14.

The only recorded eye-witnesses were four little boys of Columbia who had followed their hero, Forrest, when he entered the hall of the Masonic Building for the meeting which was to prove fatal to the Lieutenant. One of the four, Frank A. Smith, long a teacher at the Columbia Athenaeum and Secretary of the Maury County Historical Society, wrote an account of the affair, published in the Nashville Banner *of April 29, 1911. As a boy, of course, he had no first hand knowledge of the causes leading up to the difficulty.*

The best single account of the affair is that of Captain Morton, friend and confidant of both the Lieutenant and the General.² For the light it throws upon two sides of the character of General Forrest, and also upon the rash and high-strung impetuosity of some of his soldiers, it is here reproduced.

THE LIEUTENANT AND THE GENERAL

The unfortunate difficulty between General Forrest and Lieutenant Gould is a very painful recollection, and equally painful to describe, but perhaps there is no one better qualified to describe it impartially than the author of this book, esteeming, as he did, both men as close personal friends, and being

1. "History of a War Battery" (Morton's) by "T. C.," published serially in the Nashville *Rural Sun,* May-July, 1879. The incident is described in the issue of May 22, 1879. The series was preserved by Captain Morton in his scrapbooks but in his own account of the Forrest-Gould affair he does not mention the Franklin incident.
2. Morton, John Watson, *The Artillery of Nathan Bedford Forrest's Cavalry,* Nashville, 1909, pp. 101-104.

under the immediate command of the one, while having the other under his own command. As has been said, there never was a braver spirit than Lieutenant Gould. Cool, daring, and resourceful, he had given signal example of his ability in a great many instances, yet his judgment was only fallible after all, and when, at Sand Mountain, when Edmondson and Captain Bill Forrest's scouts had fallen back on his guns and found they could not hold them, Gould thought it best to abandon them, as nearly all the horses had been shot and had become entangled in the gearing. To General Forrest this seemed an unforgivable offense, and he personally rallied the men in an effort to retake the battery, but it proved unsuccessful. On reaching Columbia, he was assigned to the command of the cavalry on General Bragg's flank, as General Van Dorn had been killed *at Springhill* in his absence. One of his first acts on taking command was a request to have Lieutenant Gould transferred to some other command, though there was no charge made against the Lieutenant in any way. The latter, quick of temper and remembering the statements made in the excitement of the loss *of his guns* on the battlefield, construed this as a reflection on his personal honor, and sought an interview with General Forrest. The General was at a friend's house when the request was made, but agreed to meet the Lieutenant at 3 o'clock at Headquarters in the Masonic Building.

Captain Morton heard the news of the appointment and made an effort to see General Forrest in the hope that he could explain the matter satisfactory to both parties; but he was unable to find the General, and when he returned to camp, Lieutenant Gould was gone.

Both kept the appointment promptly, and the Lieutenant immediately demanded in excited tones why the transfer had been made. At this point a flat contradiction must be made of the story which has been current in the press for some years concerning the reason given by General Forrest for his action. It has been asserted that he replied: "Because, sir, you have been reported repeatedly by your commanding officer for cowardice." No such reply was made, and it was impossible for it to have been made, for Captain Morton was Lieutenant Gould's commanding officer, and so far from reporting him for cowardice at any time or on any occasion, he had repeatedly commended him to General Forrest for courage and gallantry. As it was equally impossible for General Forrest to have claimed a false reason for his action, this should prove conclusively that such an answer was not and could not possibly have been given. General Forrest simply replied that his mind was made up and that he would not change the order. The now thoroughly incensed Lieutenant put his hand into his coat pocket and fired a pistol he had there. The ball, passing through his coat, struck General Forrest above the left hip. General Forrest had a small penknife which he was idly handling, and at this action on the part of the Lieutenant, he opened a blade and struck him in the chest, exerting very little conscious force, as he told Captain Morton afterwards. Lieutenant Gould ran through the hall and into the street, and General Forrest, passing through the hall also, entered the office of Dr. L. P. Yandell, a few doors down the street. Relating the occurrence, General Forrest asked the Doctor to examine the wound. After a hasty examination, Doctor Yandell pronounced it a dangerous wound and was advising the patient to go to the hospital for treatment when General Forrest broke from him crying: "No d—d man shall kill me and live!" He ran in the direction Lieutenant Gould had taken, snatching a pistol from the holster of a saddled horse which stood in front of the Doctor's office.

Lieutenant Gould had run into a tailor shop and was lying on a counter, bleeding profusely, when General Forrest was seen by some of the men who had gathered around the wounded man. At their warning, Lieutenant Gould sprang up and running toward the back part of the store, jumped from the door to the ground, a distance of four or five feet. As he was in the act of jumping, a bullet from his pursuer's pistol missed him. In his haste, Lieutenant Gould fell to the ground as he leaped out of the door, and this created the impression that the shot had taken effect. "You have killed him, General!" cried the onlookers, as General Forrest reached the spot. In great pain as he was, and excited at the thought that he himself might be mortally wounded, General Forrest expressed regret that he had been forced into the affair, and ordered that Lieutenant Gould be sent to the Nelson House. He then went to the house of Col. William Galloway, where Dr. Yandell dressed his wound.

Hearing of the dreadful encounter, Captain Morton came in from camp and immediately visited both principals in the sad affair. To him both expressed their deep regret and each condemned his own hastiness. After some days, during which the writer was a daily visitor to each of the injured men, it became apparent that, while the Chief would recover, the Lieutenant could not do so, and this cast a pall of deep sadness over the entire camp. One other interview took place between the two men. Knowing that he could not live, Lieutenant Gould sent for General Forrest who rose from his own bed to make the visit. An eyewitness to this meeting related it to Dr. Wyeth as well as to the writer. The officer took the General by the hand and held it in both of his saying: "General, I shall not be here long, and I was not willing to go away without seeing you in person and saying to you how thankful I am that I am the one who is to die and that you are spared to the country. What

I did I did in a moment of rashness, and I want your forgiveness."

As General Forrest leaned over the bed on which the young man was lying, he told him that he forgave him freely and that his own heart was full of regret that the wound he had inflicted was fatal.

CHAPTER NINE

"I Was Not Willing To Surrender"

Soldiers who "rode with Old Bedford" never forgot it but in their recollection they tended to emphasize the high spots—the tremendous marches, the quick surprises, the great days of victory—as is the human way and particularly the soldier's way with memories.

But there were humdrum days, and there were hardships, and there was tragedy, too, in following Forrest—as is shown by two groups of letters from Private Emmet Hughes of Company E, 7th Tennessee Cavalry. One group, addressed to his "Dear Little Sister" Mary Elizabeth Hughes (afterward Mrs. William F. Alexander) was transcribed and published in The Daughters of the Confederacy *in the early years of the present century. The originals of the second group, addressed to another sister, Mrs. John Boyd, were found in an old house in Jackson, Tennessee, torn down in recent years.*

From the two groups of letters there emerges a private soldier's private view of the campaign of November and December, 1864, into Middle Tennessee, the defeat and retreat of General Hood, the subsequent distress in the command, and the revival of morale before the final campaign of the war.

Two letters were written, one to each sister, from "Near Nashville," on December 4, 1864. One records the death of a "brave brother," the other, the death of a "brave, noble and beloved husband," who had fallen in the charge on Columbia on November 26. Both refer to constant fighting—"we have been fighting every day nearly since we crossed Tennessee river"—but it was not until December 19th, while on the retreat after the Battle of Nashville, that Private Hughes found opportunity to send details either of the death of his brother John Boyd or the course of the Tennessee campaign. On that day two letters were written from Columbia, from which the following quotations are taken:

"We charged the works here [Columbia] the 26th Nov. and in fifty yards of the fortifications our brave brother fell and died. We had to leave him on the field all night. As soon as we could get his body, Mrs. Jerome Pillow gave him a grave on her lawn and when this terrible war is over we will bring him home."

"After he was buried I went on with my command fighting all the time until we got to Franklin. Their we had a general engagement when we sustained a heavy loss both in men and Generals . . . . The Battle field of Franklin was a very bloodyest seen I have ever witnessed General Hood expected more of his men than any General ever did. The next day . . . we were on the march to Nashville and reached in three miles of the City We halted and were fighting their two weeks when on the 15th of Dec the enemy brought on then their was great slaughter among the enemy but being heavily reinforced the next day broke our lines and we were forsted to retreat to this place . . . . Mrs. Pillow wrote to you and sent some of Brother John's hair I hope you have got her letter. I must close as I have to return to the command. . ."

The loss in his family, personal privation and profound discouragement at the result of the Tennessee campaign and the state of the army color Hughes' next letter, written from Rienzi, Mississippi, on January 4, 1865. To his sister he says:

". . . I send you these few lines to let you know that I am unwell and barefooted and no chance to get anything. If Billie Myric don't start before you get this send me a pair of Boots if you can get them if not a pair of shoes. If you cant get any new ones send me some old ones . . . anything to keep my feet off the ground. Sister this has bin one of the hardest trips that is on record I am broke down my horse broke down sick & six men left our company last night Their is only ten men with the company and forty seven with the Regiment we ware expect to be sent home any day until this morning and we learn the Yankees are crossing Tenn river as we have to stay here to see what they are going to do if they advance we are going to fight them if not we will be furloughed for twenty days . . ."

It proving not to be necessary to fight, Forrest's forces were furloughed for twenty days to go to their homes—many of which were within the Union lines—for refitting and recruitment. The results show in one of Hughes' letters from Verona, Mississippi, on March 1, 1865.

"You spoke of the demoralizing situation of our troops That is the people thought they were demoralized if the people that believe this had bin down here on yesterday they would have thought quite different."

And in another letter from Verona, dated March 3, 1865, he adds:

"Our camp is now pitched near Verona and this is March, 1865. . . . Our regiment is filling ranks every day. The Tennessee boys are coming in and we number four hundred. We are drawing better rations now, peas, bacon, potatoes and meal. Our horses' fare is rough, damaged corn and no fodder. . . . We expect orders to go to Selma, Alabama. Barefooted as I was, I was not willing to surrender."

Perhaps that is as good a note as any on which to close these notes of the men who followed and fought with Forrest —and who, barefooted, or shod, were not ready to surrender until he said the word.

That word he said in his farewell address to his troops, issued at Gainesville, Alabama, on May 9, 1865:

"That we are beaten is a self-evident fact. . . . The government which we sought to establish and perpetuate is at an end. Reason dictates and humanity demands that no more blood be shed. . . . I have never on the field of battle sent you where I was unwilling to go myself, nor would I now advise you to a course which I felt myself unwilling to pursue. You have been good soldiers, you can be good citizens. Obey the laws, preserve your honor, and the government to which you have surrendered can afford to be and will be magnanimous."

N. B. FORREST, Lieutenant-General.

CHAPTER TEN

Forrest's Own Words

In recent years several letters of General Forrest have been reproduced in the press with accompanying stories which either referred to them with a certain degree of astonishment as evidencing that he could write or else called attention to his original spelling, from which the unwarrantable conclusion was drawn that he might have said "git thar fustest with the mostest."[1]

Considering the fact that autograph letters of the General have been reproduced in almost all of the several bio-

---

1. The topic is discussed in Henry, Robert S., *"First with the Most"* *FORREST* (Indianapolis, 1944) pp. 14, 18-21, 248, 471-473 (f.n.), 506 and 507 (f.n.).

Particular attention is called to the item headed "General Forrest's Orthography" appearing as an appendix to Captain J. Harvey Mathes, *General Forrest* (New York, 1902), pp. 382, 383. The note is by General James Grant Wilson, editor of The Great Commanders Series, of which the volume is part. General Wilson, also editor of Appleton's Cyclopædia of American Biography, explained how certain alleged dispatches sent by Forrest after Fort Pillow had been used in the first edition of that work but when doubt was cast upon their authenticity had been omitted from later editions. The spurious dispatches contained some weirdly contrived spelling, which led General James R. Chalmers to give to General Wilson the following example: "A soldier came to him a third time asking for a furlough. Twice it had been refused . . . and when the application appeared the third time, General Forrest in his own handwriting indorsed upon the back of it, 'I told you twist (twice) Goddammit know,' and the man knew that he meant no." But for an instance where Forrest spelled "know" as "no," see facsimile letter in Henry, cited above, facing p. 385.

286

graphies of him, it is odd that astonishment at the existence of
such letters should persist. It is almost equally odd that it
should be thought that such letters are new evidence of the fact
that he was not a man of classical education or even, indeed, of
much "book learning" of any sort. There has never been any
doubt that Forrest no more spelled than he fought "by the
book."

But in spelling and in the plain expression of his meaning,
just as in marching and fighting, he went directly to the point
—as is further evidenced by the Forrest autographed expressions
which are here first reproduced.

> Corinth Miss May 23 1862
> D. C. Trader
> Sir your note
> of 21 Ins is to hand I did not
> fully understand the contents
> and ask for Information the
> amount you ask for is it for
> a publick contrabution or is
> it for my dues due the lodge
> I wish you to give me the amt
> due the log (lodge) from me as you
> did not State it in your notice
> or the amount asked for I had a
> small brush with the Enamy
> on yesterday I Suceded in gaining
> thir rear and got in to thir
> entrenchments 8 miles from ham
> burg and 5 behind farmington and
> Burned a portion of thir camp at
> that place they wair not looking
> for me I taken them by Suprise

they run like Suns of Biches
I captured the Rev Dr Warin
from Ilanois and one fin Sorel
Stud this army is at this time
in front of our Entrenchments
I look for a fite soon and a big
one when it coms off Cant you
come up and take a hand this
fite wil do to hand down to your
childrens children I feel confident
of our sucess

your Respct
N. B. Forrest

To
D. C. Trader
Memphis Tenn

1

Further evidence of General Forrest's unorthodox orthography as well as his vigor of expression is given in this letter which has recently become available for reproduction. The letter was written from Corinth, Mississippi, to which point Forrest had returned for duty in May, 1862, after his severe wound suffered in the retreat from Shiloh. Mr. D. C. Trader, the addressee, was an officer of the lodge of the Independent Order of Odd Fellows of which Forrest was a member. The letter remained in the possession of descendants of Mr. Trader until it was acquired by the late Foreman M. Lebold of Chicago, through whose permission, and with the assistance of Ralph Newman, copies were made available. The letter is here reproduced with the permission of Mrs. Mary Forrest Bradley of Memphis, General Forrest's granddaughter.

Corinth Miss May 23 1862

D. C. Trader

Sir your note
of 21 Ins is to hand I did not
fully understand the contents
and ask for Information the
amount you ask for — is it for
a publick contrebution or is
it for my dues due the leg
I wish you to give me the amt
due the leg from me as you
did not state it in your notice
or the amount asked for I had a
small brush with the enmy
on yesterday I Su cceed in giving
this river and get in to thir
intrenchments 8 mils from hear
busy and 5 behind farmington and
Burned a pertion of thir camp at
that place they was not looking
for me I taken them by suprise
they was like Sons of Bichus
I captured the Reg Dr Warim
from flammis and one fine Sorel
Steed this army is at this time
in front of our Intrinch ments
I look for a fite Som and a big
one when it coms off cant you
come up and tok a hand this
fite nice is to hand down to your
childrens children I feel confident
of our sucess yours Respct
N B Forrest
To
D. C. Trader
Memphis T

2

Nathan Bedford Forrest's middle name, by which he is usually called, came from the fact of his birth in Chapel Hill, a village of Bedford County, Tennessee. Before the war, however, this section of Bedford County became part of the new county of Marshall—a fact of which the General duly took account when, on Sunday, December 11, 1864, he was invited to write a bit in the diary of Dr. Charles Todd Quintard, then rector of the Church of the Advent in Nashville and chaplain of the First Tennessee Infantry, but soon to become the second Protestant Episcopal Bishop of Tennessee and to re-establish the University of the South at Sewanee, which he served as its first Vice-Chancellor.

Doctor Quintard noted in his diary, here reproduced from the original by the courtesy of the University of the South, that "Tonight Genl. Forrest shares my bed. Haggerty says 'It is the lion and the lamb lying down together.' He is certainly an uncut diamond of remarkably fine personal appearance & great vigor of thought & expression."

Following this entry, at the top of the next page of the ruled account book in which the diary was kept, appears the following in the General's autograph:

"I was borned in Marshal Co Tenn on 13th day of July 1821

N B FORREST
Maj Genl"

Courtesy University of the South, Sewanee, Tenn.

From the original diary of Bishop Quintard
Courtesy University of the South, Sewanee, Tenn.

"Sunday, December 11, 1864, Third Sunday in Advent.

"Tonight Gen'l Forrest shares my bed. Haggerty says, 'It is the Lion and the Lamb lying down together!' He is certainly an uncut diamond of remarkably fine personal appearance and great native vigor of thought and expression."

3

A revealing glimpse of Forrest's last years and of the closing scene of his life is to be had from this letter of the General to Lieut.-Colonel Minor Meriwether and the note signed "M. M.", here for the first time reproduced through the courtesy of Dr. Marshall Wingfield, President of the West Tennessee Historical Society.

Colonel Meriwether and General Forrest had been associated in the unsuccesful attempt to connect Memphis and Selma by rail. They had had deep differences but had been reconciled, as is testified in the General's note of May 26, 1875, as follows:[1]

> "Maj Miner Meriwether
>   Yours of yesterday by your son is to hand I am glad
> that all diferances between us air satisfactory setled and
> I asure you that thair is no unkind feling towards you from
> me I have all wase cherished a high reguard for your Self
> and good lady and never felt unkindly to wards your Self
> only when I felt you was using your influance against my
> Intrest hoping we may live and be as here to fore good
> friends
>   Yours Truly
>   N. B. Forrest"

Colonel Meriwether's endorsement upon the note shows for how short a time its closing wish was to be fulfilled:

> General Forrest, the writer of the letter below, died
> 7:15 pm 29 October 1877 at the house of his brother
> Jesse A Forrest 399 Union Street Memphis Tennessee.
> I closed his eyes in death. The last coherent words he
> spoke, uttered about 15 min before death, were "Call
> my wife"—M. M.

---

1. An account of their difference and reconciliation is given by Lee Meriwether, son of Colonel Meriwether, in his *My Yesteryears* (St. Louis, 1942) pp. 59-64. The son referred to in the Forrest letter was probably Avery, an older brother.

General Forrest, the writer of the letter below died 7.15 pm 29 october 1877 at the house of his brother Jesse A Forrest 399 union Street Memphis Tennessee. I closed his eyes in death. The last Cohe[rent] words he spoke, uttered about 15 minutes before death, were " call my wife " —— M.M

Memphis Tenn
May 26 1875

My Minor Meriwether

yours of yesterday by your son. is to hand & am glad that all differences between us are satisfactory settled and I am going that their is no unkind feeling to wards you from me I hope all ever cherished a high Regard for your self and good lady and have felt unkindly to wards your self only when I felt you was using your Influence against my Intrest hoping we may live and be as heretofore good friends

yours Truly
N B Forrest

ADDRESS

OF

MAJOR GEN'L .N. B. FORREST

TO

HIS TROOPS,

OLDIERS!
           The old campaign is ended, and your commanding general deems this an appropriate occasion to speak of the steadiness, self-denial and patriotism, with which you have borne the hardships of the past year. The marches and labors you have performed during that period will find no parallel in the history of this war.

On the 24th day of December, there were three thousand of you, unorganized and undisciplined, at Jackson, Tenn., only four hundred of whom were armed. You were surrounded by fifteen thousand of the enemy, who were congratulating themselves on your certain capture. You started out with your artillery, wagon trains, and a large number of cattle, which you succeeded in bringing through; since which time you have fought and won the following battles—battles which will ensbrine your names in the hearts of your countrymen, and live in history, an imperishable monument to your prowess:—Jack's Creek, Estinaula. Sommerville, Okolona, Union City, Paducah, Fort Pillow, Bolivar. Tishomingo Creek, Harrisburg, Hurricane Creek, Memphis, Athens. Sulpher Springs, Pulaski Carter's Creek, Columbia and Johnsonville, are the fields upon which you have won fadeless immortality. In the recent campaign in Middle Tennessee you sustained the reputation so nobly won. For twenty-six days from the time you left Florence, on the 21st of November to the 26th of December, you were constantly engaged with the enemy, and endured the hunger, cold and labor, incident to that arduous campaign, without murmur. To sum up, in brief, your triumphs during the past year: You have fought fifty battles; killed and captured sixteen thousand of the enemy; captured two thousand horses and mules, sixty-seven pieces of artillery, four gunboats, fourteen transports, twenty barges, three hundred wagons, fifty ambulances, ten thousand stand of small arms, forty block-houses; destroyed thirty-six railroad bridges, two hundred miles of railroad, six engines, one hundred cars, and $15,000,000 worth of property.

In the accomplishment of this great work, you were occasionally sustained by other troops, who joined you in the fight, but your regular number never exceeded five thousand—two thousand of whom have been killed or wounded—while in prisoners you have lost about two hundred.

If your course has been marked by the graves of patriotic heroes, who have fallen by your side, it has, at the same time, been more plainly marked by the blood of the invader. While you sympathize with the friends of the fallen, your sorrows should be appeased by the knowledge that they fell as brave men, battling for all that makes life worth living for.

Soldiers! you now rest for a short time from your labors. During the respite, prepare for future action. Your commanding general is ready to lead you again to the defense of the common cause, and he appeals to you by a remembrance of the glories of your past career, your desolated homes, your insulted women and suffering children, and, above all, by the memory of your dead comrades, to yield a ready obedience to discipline and to buckle on your armor anew for the fight. Bring with you the soldier's safest armor—a determination to fight while the enemy pollutes your soil—to fight as long as he denies your rights—to fight until independance shall have been achieved—to fight for home, children, liberty, and all you hold dear. Show to the world the superhuman and sublime spirit with which a people may be inspired when fighting for the inestimable boon of liberty. Be not allured by the syren song of peace, for there can be no peace save upon your separate independent nationalty. You can never again unite with those who have murdered your sons, outraged your helpless families, and, with demoniac malice, wantonly destroyed your property, and now seek to make slaves of you. A proposition of reunion with a people who have avowed their purpose to appropriate the property, and to subjugate or annihilate the freemen of the South, would stamp with infamy the names of your gallant dead and the living heros of this war. Be patient, obedient and earnest, and the day is not far distant when you can return to your homes and live in the full fruition of freemen around the old family altar.

N. B. FORREST,

Major Gen'l Com'd'g Dist. Miss. & E. La.

Courtesy Curtis Bray, Jackson, Tenn.

Forrest's address to his troops upon the occasion of granting a general furlough after the return from Hood's Tennessee Campaign, issued January 1, 1865, at Corinth, Mississippi. Note the contrast in tone and feeling of this address to his farewell address to his troops made five months later.

GEN. FORREST TO HIS TROOPS.

HEADQRS. FORREST'S CAVALRY CORPS,
GAINESVILLE, ALA., May 9, 1865.

SOLDIERS:

By an agreement made between Lieut.-Gen. TAYLOR, commanding the Department of Alabama, Mississippi and East Louisiana, and Major Gen. CANBY, commanding United States forces, the troops of this Department have been surrendered.

I do not think it proper or necessary, at this time, to refer to the causes which have reduced us to this extremity; nor is it now a matter of material consequence to us how such results were brought about. That we are BEATEN, is a self-evident fact, and any further resistance on our part would be justly regarded as the very height of folly and rashness.

The armies of Generals LEE and JOHNSTON having surrendered, you are the last of all the troops of the Confederate States Army, East of the Mississippi River, to lay down your arms.

The Cause for which you have so long and so manfully struggled, and for which you have braved dangers, endured privations and sufferings, and made so many sacrifices, is to-day hopeless. The Government which we sought to establish and perpetuate, is at an end. Reason dictates and humanity demands that no more blood be shed. Fully realizing and feeling that such is the case, it is your duty and mine to lay down our arms—submit to the "powers that be"—and to aid in restoring peace and establishing law and order throughout the land.

The terms upon which you were surrendered are favorable, and should be satisfactory and acceptable to all. They manifest a spirit of magnanimity and liberality, on the part of the Federal authorities, which should be met, on our part, by a faithful compliance with all the stipulations and conditions therein expressed. As your Commander, I sincerely hope that every officer and soldier of my command will cheerfully obey the orders given, and carry out in good faith all the terms of the cartel.

Those who neglect the terms, and refuse to be paroled, may assuredly expect, when arrested, to be sent North and imprisoned.

Let those who are absent from their commands, from whatever cause, report at once to this place, or to Jackson, Miss.; or, if too remote from either, to the nearest United States post or garrison, for parole.

Civil war, such as you have just passed through, naturally engenders feelings of animosity, hatred and revenge. It is our duty to divest ourselves of all such feelings; and, as far as in our power to do so, to cultivate friendly feelings towards those with whom we have so long contended, and heretofore so widely, but honestly, differed. Neighborhood feuds, personal animosities, and private differences, should be blotted out; and, when you return home, a manly, straightforward course of conduct will secure the respect even of your enemies. Whatever your responsibilities may be to Government, to society, or to individuals, meet them like men.

The attempt made to establish a separate and independent Confederation has failed; but the consciousness of having done your duty faithfully, and to the end, will, in some measure, repay for the hardships you have undergone.

In bidding you farewell, rest assured that you carry with you my best wishes for your future welfare and happiness. Without, in any way, referring to the merits of the Cause in which we have been engaged, your courage and determination, as exhibited on many hard-fought fields, has elicited the respect and admiration of friend and foe. And I now, cheerfully and gratefully, acknowledge my indebtedness to the officers and men of my command, whose zeal, fidelity and unflinching bravery have been the great source of my past success in arms.

I have never, on the field of battle, sent you where I was unwilling to go myself; nor would I now advise you to a course which I felt myself unwilling to pursue. You *have been good* soldiers; you *can be good* citizens. Obey the laws, preserve your honor, and the Government to which you have surrendered can afford to be, and will be, magnanimous.

N. B. FORREST, Lieut. General.

FORREST'S FAREWELL ADDRESS.

Fitted to the occasion and apt in expression, the reading of this address falls upon the ear like that of a classic, which does not suffer by comparison with more polished compositions of its kind. It comes from an unlettered man but at an eventful period, as did Lincoln's Gettysburg address, or Chief Logan's speech. Though written in small compass, it leaves, like them, little else to be said. In sentiment, it is lofty and full of patriotic fire. In literary form, though somewhat rugged, like the character of its author, it exhibits qualities of a trained writer, especially in that it teems with cogent expressions in proper connection, which are fully explanatory of the situation. It is a heart-word of a great commander to his soldiers, an appeal to their better instincts, a piece of sound advice upon which they were quick to act. To be its author brings more renown than can equestrian statues or tablets in bronze.

HEADQUARTERS FORREST'S CAVALRY CORPS
Gainesville, Ala., May 9, 1865.

Soldiers:—By an agreement between Lieutenant-General Taylor, commanding the Department of Alabama, Mississippi and East Louisiana, and Major-General Canby, commanding United States forces, the troops of this Department have been surrendered.

I do not think it proper or necessary, at this time, to refer to the causes which have reduced us to this extremity; nor is it now a matter of material consequence to us how such results were brought about. That we are beaten is a self-evident fact, and any further resistance on our part would be justly regarded as the very height of folly and rashness.

The armies of General Lee and General Johnston having

surrendered, you are the last of all the troops of the Confederate States Army, east of the Mississippi river, to lay down your arms.

The cause for which you have so long and so manfully struggled, and for which you have braved dangers, endured privations and sufferings, and made so many sacrifices, is today hopeless. The government which we sought to establish and perpetuate is at an end. Reason dictates and humanity demands that no more blood be shed. Fully realizing and feeling that such is the case, it is your duty and mine to lay down our arms, submit to the powers that be, and aid in restoring peace and establishing law and order throughout the land.

The terms upon which you were surrendered are favorable, and should be satisfactory and acceptable to all. They manifest a spirit of magnanimity and liberality on the part of the Federal authorities, which should be met, on our part, by a faithful compliance with all the stipulations and conditions therein expressed. As your Commander, I sincerely hope that every officer and soldier of my command will cheerfully obey the orders given, and carry out in good faith all the terms of the cartel.

Those who neglect the terms and refuse to be paroled may assuredly expect, when arrested, to be sent North and imprisoned.

Let those who are absent from their commands, from whatever cause, report at once to this place, or to Jackson, Mississippi; or, if too remote from either, to the nearest United States post or garrison, for parole.

Civil war, such as you have passed through naturally engenders feelings of animosity, hatred and revenge. It is our duty to divest ourselves of all such feelings; and, as far as in our power to do so, to cultivate friendly feelings toward those with whom we have so long contended, and heretofore so widely, but honestly, differed. Neighborhood feuds, personal animosities, and private differences should be blotted out; and when you return home, a manly, straightforward course of conduct will secure the respect even of your enemies. Whatever your responsibilities may be to government, to society, or to individuals, meet them like men.

The attempt made to establish a separate and independent Confederation has failed; but the consciousness of having done your duty faithfully and to the end will, in some measure, repay you for the hardships you have undergone.

In bidding you farewell, rest assured that you carry with you my best wishes for your future welfare and happiness. Without, in any way, referring to the merits of the cause in which we have been engaged, your courage and determination, as exhibited on many hard-fought fields, have elicited the respect and admiration of friend and foe. And I now cheerfully and gratefully acknowledge my indebtedness to the officers and men of my command, whose zeal, fidelity and unflinching bravery have been the great source of my success in arms.

I have never, on the field of battle, sent you where I was unwilling to go myself; nor would I now advise you to a course which I felt myself unwilling to pursue. You *have been* good soldiers; you *can be* good citizens. Obey the laws, preserve your honor, and the Government to which you have surrendered can afford to be, and will be, magnanimous.

N. B. FORREST, Lieutenant-General.

INDEX

Strange, J. P., 55, 56, 65, 156, 194
Street, Major Sol, 156
Streight, Colonel, 224, 225, 226, 227, 228, 229, 231, 235, 277
Streight Raid, 236
Stewart's Regiment, 190
Stricklins, 246
Stubb's Plantation, 237, 241, 247
Sturgis, Gen., 46, 113, 118, 123, 125, 135, 236, 238, 239, 240, 241, 242, 243, 246, 249, 272
Sulphur Branch Trestle, 199, 200
Sumter County, Alabama, 219
Sumterville, 216

Tallahatchie River, 159, 181, 183, 253, 254, 255, 261
Tanner, 112, 130, 131, 135
Tate, Dr. Hugh, 156
Tate, Captain William J., 141, 167, 169, 170, 177, 206
Taylor, Capt. James, 71
Taylor, Lieut. Col. W. F., 119, 120, 121, 129, 171, 193, 204
Taylor, Lieut. Gen. Dick, 218
Tennessee Cavalry, 2nd, 257
Tennessee Cavalry, 7th, Confederate, 67, 70, 71, 96, 97, 100, 101, 102, 103, 107, 109, 112, 117, 126, 138, 150, 159, 163, 167
Tennessee Cavalry, 7th, Federal, 67, 107, 109, 112, 129, 154
Tennessee Cavalry, Co. D, 103, 106, 146, 204
Tennessee Cavalry, Co. E, 141, 146, 147, 148, 149, 151, 154, 155, 156, 158, 163, 167, 168, 169, 175, 177, 178, 189, 198, 204, 209, 210, 219, 220, 221, 282
Tennessee Cavalry, Co. F, 90
Tennessee Cavalry, Co. H, 147
Tennessee Cavalry, Co. L, 90, 91, 92, 93, 96, 97, 100, 168
Tennessee Cavalry, 12th, 257, 260
Tennessee Cavalry, 14th, 181, 182, 185, 186, 193, 256
Tennessee Cavalry, 15th, 257
Tennessee Cavalry, 15th, Co. I, 264
Tennessee Cavalry, 16th, 262
"Tennessee Mounted Rifles", 26, 29
Tennessee River, 201, 208, 209, 273, 274, 284
Tennessee Street, 196
Tennessee Yankees, 101, 106
Thompson, Jacob, 188
Thompson, Gen. M. Jeff, 143
Thompson, Mrs., 188
Thompson's Men, 144
Tishomingo Creek, 66, 111, 136, 164, 167, 171, 208, 237, 240
Toones, 87
Trace Creek, 205
Trader, D. C., 287, 288, 289
Transou, Parmenia, 84

Trenton, 153
Trigg Avenue, 185, 257
Trimble, Charlie, 194
Tullahoma, 199
Tupelo, 162, 172, 173, 193
Tuscumbia, 194
Tuskaloosa, 211, 212, 214
Tyler, Capt. H. A., 171

Union City, 43, 67, 101, 102, 153, 186
Union Street, Memphis, 261, 262, 292
United Service Magazine of London, 18
University of the South, Sewanee, 290, 291
Vance, Judge, 148
VanDorn, General, 146, 184, 201, 278
Verona, Mississippi, 157, 171, 193, 209, 284
Vicksburg, 150, 174

Wade, Colonel Bill, 253
Walton, Capt. Ed. S., 253
Waring's Brigade, 237
Washburn, General, 262, 264, 265, 266
Waterloo Road, 204
Watkins, General, 144
Wayne, hills of, 206, 207
Wayne County, 205
Weir, Miss Bettie Rodgers, 68
Wellington Street, 260
West Point, Mississippi, 112, 151, 191
West Point Military Academy, 18, 20
West Pointer, 271
West Tennessee, 94
Wheeler, Gen. Joseph, 19, 55
White, Lieut. Col. Raleigh, 181, 182, 183, 186, 193, 198
White's Company, 143
Whiteville, 142
Whitlow, Dr., 246
Wilderness, 190
Wilkin, 240
Williams, Captain Peter, 264
Wilson, Gen. James H., 211
Wilson, Gen. James Grant, 286
Wilson Regiment, 97
Wingfield, Dr. Marshall, 292, 293
Winslow's Brigade, 240, 241, 242
Winslow, Col. Edw. F., 236, 237, 239
Witherspoon, Hewitt, 67
Witherspoon, John, 136
Witherspoon, Lieut. J. M., 264
Witherspoon, Capt. William "Billy", 67, 68, 71, 78, 136
Wizard of the Saddle, 95, 100, 113, 275
Wolf River, 148
Wolseley, Gen. Viscount Garnet, 17, 18
Wood, James E., 170, 206, 220
Wood, William H., 160, 177
Wyeth, Dr., 116, 117, 122, 123, 276, 280

Yandell, Dr. L. P., 279
Yokona, 181, 188, 189